CW00456094

Michael Abbensetts

FOUR PLAYS

SWEET TALK
ALTERATIONS
IN THE MOOD
EL DORADO

OBERON BOOKS
LONDON

Sweet Talk first published 1974 by Eyre Methuen Ltd.

First published in this collection 2001 by Oberon Books Ltd.
(incorporating Absolute Classics)
521 Caledonian Road, London N7 9RH
Tel: 020 7607 3637 / Fax: 020 7607 3629
e-mail: oberon.books@btinternet.com

Copyright © Michael Abbensetts 2001.

Sweet Talk copyright © Michael Abbensetts 1974

Michael Abbensetts is hereby identified as author of these plays
in accordance with section 77 of the Copyright, Designs and
Patents Act 1988. All rights reserved.

All rights whatsoever in these plays are strictly reserved and
application for performance etc. should be made before rehearsal
to Micheline Steinberg Ltd., 409 Triumph House, 187–191
Regent Street, London, W1R 7WF. No performance may be
given unless a licence has been obtained, and no alterations may
be made in the title or the text of the play without the author's
prior written consent.

This book is sold subject to the condition that it shall not by way
of trade or otherwise be circulated without the publisher's
consent in any form of binding or cover other than that in which
it is published and without a similar condition including this
condition being imposed on any subsequent purchaser.

A catalogue record for this book is available from the British Library.

ISBN: 1 84002 179 9

Cover design: Andrzej Klimowski

Typography: Jeff Willis

Printed in Great Britain by Antony Rowe Ltd, Reading.

Contents

5

Introduction

Roland Rees

El Dorado, set in Michael's home country of Guyana, is, by his admission, the most personal of his plays, based as it is on memories of his family, but not, he affirms, the most auto-biographical.

The opening page of the play sets the scene: a spacious drawing and dining room fill the interior of a once grand mansion, dating back to the 1700s. This dilapidated, wooden structure, resting on stilts the height of a person, protection against tidal erosion, is known locally as the 'Van der Bergh building'.

Grandmother Jessica, a white West Indian, whose accent is 'neither English or Caribbean', rules the roost now that the Grandfather, a leading black lawyer in his time, is dead. 'Mad' Aunt Judith has been banished upstairs and is locked in her room. Gregory, the grandson, has returned from London, where he has trained as a doctor.

Interestingly, *El Dorado* is the last piece Michael wrote of those in this collection of four plays, the first three being accounts of black experience in London.

From Queen's College, Georgetown, Michael was sent to boarding school in Canada, where he remembers being the solitary black face. The other strong memory was of a production of *Look Back in Anger*. It changed the direction of his life. Moving to London in 1963, he spent time at an actor's workshop in order, he says, to 'learn the art of writing dialogue'. He sent his first play, about being black in Canada, to Peggy Ramsay, whose response was, 'Write a play about being black in London, darling!'

Sweet Talk, the earliest of his plays, is also based on family experience, this time that of his married cousin. It opened in 1973, the same week that his TV film *Museum Attendant* was screened, the latter based on his own uniformed experience at the Tower of London. He took the job, he remembers, because it gave him the leeway to write. Clive Goodwin, by now his agent, engineered this double whammy and Michael insists this client/agent relationship was seminal to his development as a writer, lasting until Clive's tragic death in California some years later.

Sweet Talk is the most widely performed of Michael's plays; first at the Royal Court, subsequently at Joe Papp's Public Theatre in New York, and later in Canada, Nigeria, Guyana and Jamaica.

Like many of his plays, *Sweet Talk* is set in a single room, the walls of which define Rita and Tony's life. It is their small plot of freedom and also their prison. Tony often strikes his head, exclaiming, 'This room…this room!' as if it epitomises their failure to germinate life. This, in spite of Binkie, their five-year old, ever present in conversation but never apparent on stage, who spends the duration of the play being baby-sat by friends and relatives. A reminder that in many of Michael's plays, work and its influence play a dominant role.

Rita expects a second child despite being warned by doctors it will be her death. She loses it and is hospitalised. Binkie is sent home to Trinidad. On his own, Tony wobbles. He succumbs to his itch for gambling, placing all his money on the horses, including Rita's savings for his training as an accountant. Out of hospital, Rita wants a holiday, 'It'll do me good, Tony…a holiday, goin' home…seein' Binkie again…' Tony is unable to tell Rita it will be her last act.

Two enduring images emerge from the play. One is Tony's work-bench where he can play the part of the wizard he is at mending radios and creating sound systems. This is his place of escape, the place of his dreams. The second is Tony's memory of this 'Nice, nice chick,' he sees each morning at the tube station, who 'Screams and screeches…in some strange, mad tongue.' 'She's gone in here,' Tony says, tapping his head.

In 1977, Michael was walking down Carnaby Street with his script editor girlfriend in search of a tailor. Up three stair flights, they found a company with the name 'Alterations.' In one small room with two sewing machines and an ironing board, two black tailors had set up business. 'There's your play,' said the script editor, struck by the vision of black entrepreneurs off Regent Street in the Seventies.

Alterations, first performed the following year at The New End Theatre and subsequently in New Jersey and California, traces the desperate bid by Walker Holt to be his own boss. Mr Nat, a Jewish retailer of clothes, has a load of work on offer: vast quantities of trousers need their legs shortening, immediately overnight, for his Japanese clients.

The front row of the audience viscerally share the experience of frenzied sewing and ironing as Courtney, Buster and Horace go through their paces. Walker forfeits child, wife and friends in his race to put down the final payment to buy 65B Carnaby Street. This order clinches it for him. 'Welcome,' says Mr Nat, popping a cigar into Walker's mouth, 'to the club!' 'Now you can offer work to your friends!' Little by little black advancement in the world moves on.

Michael reflects that he rates the consistent achievements of Bill Morris, General Secretary of the TGWU, within the Labour Movement more than the luminary but transitory rhetoric of black militancy.

The germ for *In The Mood* (Hampstead Theatre, 1981) came from a meeting with West Indian Second World War veterans. Two of the characters, Orrin and T.D., emerge as friends who go back that far, each year attending Remembrance Day at the Cenotaph. Their contribution at least is not conveniently forgotten. Afterwards they have a Sunday lunch to mark the occasion.

Orrin and Sonia Harris – Sonia does not approve of 'noise and loudness' – and T.D. and his white teacher partner, Kate, daughter of a vicar, share an ascendant middle class world. Self-made men (Orrin has a successful plumbing business, T.D., a conservative at heart, is standing as a Labour Councillor), they, along with Sonia and Kate, are immersed in the Britain of the Forties and Fifties. Hence the title of the play, borrowed from Glenn Miller.

Orrin has asked an old acquaintance to the lunch: Trevor, actor, teacher, singer and con-man, erupts upon the scene. It emerges that he needs a place to stay and above all a loan, or he faces a jail sentence. His zest, consumption of alcohol and life-style have never endeared him to T.D. and Sonia.

When he leaves, with Orrin's loan in his pocket, the quartet are dancing to 'In the Mood'. He is compelled to remind them of his memories of the Forties and Fifties. 'For a start it's not about this country, it's about the West Indies, Guyana, home. Schooldays… Remember how we used to stand up in assembly …all clean, an' smiling, an' black… an' we used to sing "Rule Britannia"… We believed it all…! Now years later here we are in Britain…an' most of them jus' wish we hadn't come.'

Guyana and its memories are also central to the last play of this collection, the first mentioned, *El Dorado* (Theatre Royal, Stratford East, 1984), Michael finally turns to home matters. A middle class family seem interred in a formerly grand, now run-down house. The grandson, Gregory, home on a visit, wants to lay some ghosts. Confronting Grandmother Jessica with 'They used to keep slaves under the house here – ages ago, from about the 1700s. Slaves. Did you know that?' Like Aunt Judith, also interred upstairs in her room, nobody mentions these things.

Gregory, like Trevor, is a potential incendiary, but both leave what they find unchanged, immersed in memories, and return to the hurly-burly of their own lives. Gregory observes, 'The most guilty of all are middle class blacks…torn in two.' This would not have been Trevor's means of expression but it would accurately reflect his opinion of the *In The Mood* quartet.

Michael Abbensetts is one of the diminishing band of Caribbean-born dramatists living in the UK. Some, like Trevor Rhone, have chosen to remain in the Caribbean, others, like Roy Williams, were born in this country. Few straddle the two worlds. Long may Michael remain a dramatic curator of such a rich and valuable cultural interface.

Roland Rees
London
September 2001

SWEET TALK

Characters

TONY FLETCHER

RITA FLETCHER

DENNIS

SANDRA

YVONNE

OSCAR

Sweet Talk was first performed by the Theatre Upstairs at the Royal Court Theatre on 31 July 1973 with the following cast:

TONY, Allister Bain

RITA, Mona Hammond

DENNIS, Don Warrington

SANDRA, Sally Watts

YVONNE, Joan-Ann Maynard

OSCAR, Lee Davis

Director, Stephen Frears

Designer, William Dudley

ACT ONE

Scene 1

House in Shepherd's Bush. The FLETCHERS' room. Spring. Evening.
RITA FLETCHER is changing her dress; she is in her petticoat. She
puts on her dressing-gown. She seems very tired; she is dropping on
her feet. RITA is West Indian, about twenty-five, pretty enough,
takes a pride in her appearance. She crosses to bed, pumps up the
pillows. The radiogram is on: an Isaac Hayes LP.

RITA gets on top of the bed, adopting a sitting-up position with the
help of the pillows. She stifles a yawn. Her head sinks lower and
lower.

The room is not quite the size of a double room. It is an attractive
enough place. However, it is not large enough for the FLETCHERS
and all their possessions. All three FLETCHERS live in this room,
RITA, her husband, TONY, and BINKIE, their five year old son.
TONY also has his work-bench in this room. Here at nights he builds
and repairs radios and record- players and television sets. BINKIE's
bed is a foldaway affair; presently it is closed up in the interests of
space. A number of photographs around the room. A settee; a glass-
top table (their dining table); a TV set; a radiogram and also a tape
recorder. A defective paraffin heater. A few toys. What else? A child's
xylophone, not a toy it plays.

On TONY's work-bench: the guts or motor of a record-player (he has
just begun building a new stereo set); an old radio; voltmeter, soldering
iron, transistors, etc.

TONY FLETCHER lets himself into the room. He is twenty-eight.
West Indian; a very raffish looking young man. He is wearing a dark
suit and an overcoat but no tie. Plus a Russian styled fur hat. He has
been over in England longer than his wife has, so he has less of a
West Indian accent than she has.

TONY contemplates his wife for a moment or two, none too pleased.
He sucks his teeth. He crosses to radiogram.

TONY: You want this on, woman?

(*RITA wakes, slight start.*)

RITA: I din' even hear you come in.

(*TONY turns off radiogram.*)

TONY: (*A bit satirical, but not unkindly.*) You din' hear me come in, oh, Loopy Loo, eh? I mighta been a rapist, Loopy Loo. (*Sly.*) A *white* rapist. (*Boyishly.*) A sex-maniac from the Home Off-iss. Keepin' an eye on immigrants! An' not jus' an eye, neither.

(*Pause.*)

RITA: You finish?

TONY: (*Grinning.*) I've only just come in. You ain' heard nothin' yet.

RITA: (*Dismissing him with a wave of her hand.*) It's so cold. They call this Spring.

TONY: It's no wonder I always rush home. I like the way you leap outuh bed as soon as I get in. (*He takes off his overcoat, moves to hang it up behind the door. He still has his hat on.*)

RITA: (*Coolly.*) I'm tired. You know how hard I gotta work. You know that. So what're you playin' at? (*Pause.*) You think I jus' lie here 'cos I'm under contract to keep this bed company?

(*Pause.*)

TONY: Where's Binkie? (*Moving over to her.*) Give us a kiss, Loops.

RITA: I done kiss no man wit' a hat on.

(*Pause.*)

TONY: (*Stung.*) Everytime I come home, you in bed!

RITA: (*Mischievously.*) Correction: I'm lying on topuh the bed. They got some law that says I can't lie on topuh the bed…! Since when?

(*Pause.*)

TONY: All women mad as hell. White or black. (*He turns away. He hangs his hat up behind the door as well. He remains in his jacket for warmth.*)

RITA: I hope you realise the Tee Vee still not workin'. You mend other people's sets but not y'own. (*Pause.*) What I

got to stay awake for? To watch the radiogram? (*Pause.*)
You listenin' to me, boy?
(*TONY gets out another pair of shoes. Pause.*)
When you goin' to fix is. Tony?
(*TONY sits on edge of bed. changing his shoes, his back to her.*)

TONY: When you get outuh bed.
(*Pause. She gets off the bed. Steps loftily over to settee. Sits
herself down. Pause. TONY massages his foot.*)

RITA: Well...?
(*Pause.*)

TONY: Done bother me.

RITA: What's wrong wit' y'foot? (*Mischievously.*) I thought it
was y'mouth you never gave a rest I never knew it was
y'foot as well.
(*Pause.*)

TONY: (*His sarcasm is more playful than anything.*) Ow. Loopy
Loo, you too sweet. Sittin' there in y'dressin'-gown. Nice.
Too nice. You look – beau-ti-ful. Especially as it's not
even seven o'clock yet. (*Pause.*) You goin' out. Loopy
Loo? Is that why you dress up in y'Sunday best. Eh?
Answer me, Loopy. Where you off to? Buckingham Pal-
iss? They givin' a party? A-come-as-you-are-party. A
pyjama party?
(*RITA looks heavenwards, sucking her teeth.*)
(*Moving towards her.*) Loopy Loo, you done wanna know,
right? Eh? Eh? (*Pause. Giving her a playful dig.*) I'm talkin'
to you, Loopy Loo.
(*She fends him off.*)

RITA: (*Patiently, as if she were dealing with an overgrown
child.*) Tony Fletcher, stop being such an ass.
(*Pause. TONY moves away. He can be quite vulnerable,
sometimes.*)

TONY: (*Not looking at her.*) The manager called me in her
office today. I got another raise. Jus' five poun's. It's
better than nothing, but she always gotta act like she's
givin' me the keys to Fort Knox. (*Pause.*) Still she likes
me. (*Pause.*) She tole me, 'I knew you'd make a good
chargehan', Tony'. (*Pause.*) Anyway, I asked her what

made her say that. (*Sad smile.*) An' you know what she said, Loopy Loo? 'Cos I know you, Tony!' (*Pause. Wan.*) Pretty funny, eh, Loops? She feel she know me. (*Pause.*) Yeah. Pretty funny.

(*Pause. He sits at work-bench. Pause.*)

RITA: (*Gentle for her.*) You want y'dinner?

(*Pause.*)

TONY: This room...this room. (*Not loudly.*) Chrise, man... Christ. (*Pause.*) We never had it so good. Right? (*A grimace.*) Right, Loopy Loo? (*Pause. Then about paraffin heater.*) It's no wonder this room always chilly, chilly. That thing's useless. (*Sudden laugh.*) One day that heater boun' to freeze to death. Catch pneumonia! As a heater it would make a better fridge. (*He laughs some more. Stops. Then laughs to himself, boyishly.*) It'll catch a cold an' die one day. (*Pause.*) Well, let's get some work done aroun' here. (*He picks up the old radio. Sucks his teeth.*) Look at this. Just look at this...! Frank call this a radio, I call it crap. (*Pause.*) Even Marconi would call it crap! (*Pause.*) He should take this somewhere else. (*Laughter.*) Like a junkyard! Or the neares' ocean. (*He finally runs down. Pause.*) Yeah. Very funny. Black people always laughin'. It's better than havin' an ace up y'sleeve, I suppose. (*Pause.*) Yeah. (*Pause. Facing RITA.*) You know there's this girl...an African...she works under me... today she got fired. Not becauseuh me. I di'nt tell them to get riduh the girl. Anyway, anyway, she got her cards. (*Pause.*) An' you know what she do? You know what that African girl do? She got down on her knees in the manager office...her knees...an' she beg fo' her job back. Boy, how that girl beg them an' beg them.

(*Pause.*)

RITA: She get her job back?

TONY: Get what job back? You think it's a fairy story I'm tellin' you?! A Hans Christian Andersen story. Where everything always ends happy ever after...! Wake up, Loopy Loo.

(*Pause.*)

RITA: Poor girl.

TONY: Yeah. (*Almost to himself.*) We never had it so good. (*Pause. He puts the old radio aside. Lifts guts of record-player in front of him.*) This is goin' to be the best thing I ever built, Rita.

RITA: (*Sleepily.*) Good, that's good, Tony.

TONY: I should be able to sell it fo' about a hundred quid. At least. When I finish wit' it you couldn't buy one like it in any shop fo' under two hundred. I guarantee that! (*Pause.*) You think I'm boastin', Sweet Pea?

RITA: Eh? Oh. No. You're good at y'job. I only wish I could make you see jut' how good. Maybe then you wouldn't feel so frustrated.

(*She has got up intending to put on another record. She has to stop; dizziness, something.*)

TONY: (*Irritated.*) What's the matter wit' you?

RITA: I feel a bit...outuh sorts, that's all.

TONY: Done look at me. I only repair record-players.

(*Pause.*)

RITA: (*Quietly.*) It's never much use turnin' to you fo' help, right?

(*Pause.*)

TONY: (*Loss, something.*) It was supposed to be a joke. (*Pause.*) You've not been well at all recently. You better see the doctor.

RITA: (*Grimacing.*) I'll be okay.

(*Pause.*)

TONY: If you're in some kinduh pain fo' Godsakes jus' say so!

(*Pause.*)

RITA: Done shout at me, Tony.

(*Pause.*)

TONY: (*Quietly.*) Nobody likes being married to a martyr. (*Pause.*) Where's Binkie?

RITA: He's over at Joyce. It's Michael's birt'day. Frank said he'll bring him back after. I tole you alluh this las' night. Y'memory got more holes than a mosquito net.

TONY: You made sure the chile wrap up warm?

RITA: It's jus' over the road, Tony, it's not the Antarctic. Anyway he's five years old. He'll soon be old enough to vote.

TONY: Loopy Loo makin' jokes, eh? You swallowed a joke book, Loopy Loo. (*Pause. Loudly.*) This is Shepherd's Bush, not Port o' Spain, Trinidad. That's not sunshine out there, woman… (*Then.*) Only the English would call a night like this Spring. They do it in memory of their fondest hour. Dunkirk.
(*Pause.*)

RITA: Look, you want y'dinner or not?
(*Pause.*)

TONY: Done bother me. (*He stretches. Slumps. Pause. Pushes his work aside. Quiet whining.*) I shouldn't have to. After I come home from that factory I shouldn't have to frig aroun' all night with this. (*Suddenly sweeps a number of transistors and screwdrivers on the floor.*) Christ, man, all I do is work!

RITA: (*Crying out.*) An' you think I'm not tired too? You complain about me being sleepy, but you done think I got cause? All day long I'm on m'feet, I'm not any chargehan' you know, sittin' on m'ass all day. I got to be up an' down, up an' down, then when I come home I got to stand in frontuh the hot stove out there, cookin' his lordship's dinner! An then as you come in you start complainin'. What you take me for, some sortuh machine? Wondawoman? You think I done feel tired like everybody else? You think so?! (*Pause.*) You think so?!
(*Pause.*)

TONY: Okay, okay, so this is no life for a woman. But I buy you things, done I? What more you want? A holiday in Las Vegas?!

RITA: Things! Things!

TONY: You think all this drop from heaven. Radiogram – Tee Vee – tape recorder – you think they drop from heaven'?

RITA: Fo' me? A tape recorder! You buy that tape recorder fo' me? What would I do wit' a tape recorder, boy? Tape you when you asleep – snorin'?! (*Pause.*) Anyway, you din' buy it in the firse place, you made it.

TONY: I done want no more rudeness from you – put
y'dress back on. Before I lose m'temper, woman.
(*Pause.*)

RITA: It won't be the firse time you lost y'temper.
(*Pause. TONY rises. Crosses lazily over to her, smiling dangerously.
Pause.*)

TONY: I'm jus' the kinduh guy to make a masochist happy,
done forget that.
(*Pause.*)

RITA: (*Unflinching.*) Mr Big Man. Big Shot. Mr Big Shot.
(*Pause.*)

TONY: (*Shame, something.*) Look, jus' put on y'dress. Okay?
Okay? (*Then.*) Jus' done fight me all the time. Okay?
Please, okay?
(*Pause. RITA retrieves her dress. Discards dressing-gown. She
and TONY look at each other. TONY goes to her, strokes her
arm.*)
After six years I still can't keep m'han's off you.
(*Pause.*)

RITA: You in a bad way then, ain' you?
(*And then she moves out of reach. TONY not amused. RITA
puts on her dress.*)

TONY: (*Involuntary.*) Why you so perverse, woman...!
(*Pause.*)

RITA: You done own me.
(*Pause.*)

TONY: (*Surprisingly humble for him.*) I marry you, Rita; I'm
y'husban', woman.

RITA: That means a lotuh things to me, an I play fair by
you. But it done give you a right to own me.
(*Pause.*)

TONY: No woman ever baffle me like you.

RITA: (*Mocking.*) That's why you marry me. Right?
(*Pause.*)

TONY: They do away with the death penalty in England
now, done forget that, woman. (*Pause.*) You read me,
whore?

RITA: Whore? Yeah? An' who are all these men who had
me? Give me their names 'cos they never even bothered

21

to introduce themselves. (*Pause.*) You must be mixin' me up with oneuh them English girls you see at weekends.

TONY: Weekends? English girls? What's this, Loopy Loo? You mean I been walkin' in m'sleep again?

(*Pause.*)

RITA: Las' Saturday night you din' come home till Sunday afternoon.

(*Pause.*)

TONY: (*Truculent.*) You always tell me to go out more, so I follow y'advice.

RITA: I din' mean fo' the whole weekend!

(*Pause. TONY sucks his teeth, returns to work-bench. Picks up stuff he knocked on the floor.*)

Anyway las' Saturday was nothing special. You been out the week before that, an' the week before that, an' the week before that, an' the week...!

TONY: Okay! (*Pause.*) So occasionally I stay out a bit late-ish.

RITA: Late-ish!

TONY: Anyway, Sunday! Not till Sunday! You lucky I ever come back at all.

(*Pause.*)

RITA: Things are that bad fo' you, eh, boy? (*Sucks her teeth. Pause.*) When you want me, do I often turn away?

TONY: Many times you only put up with me!

RITA: You always hungry; I only hungry someuh the time. That's the root of all our troubles. (*She yawns.*)

TONY: The root of our troubles is that you're always tired. (*Pause.*) You're not takin' those iron tablets the doctor gave you. If y'sufferin' from anaemia then take the proper medicine.

RITA: Maybe I got an extra reason fo' being so tired these days. I'm pregnant.

(*Pause.*)

TONY: Come again?

RITA: Pregnant. Never heard of it? It's a habit wit' women. Never caught on wit' men, though. Done ask me why.

(*Pause.*)

TONY: Are you crazy! (*Pause.*) You forgot a'ready! (*Pause.*)
You nearly died las' time!

RITA: (*Simply.*) I want another chile, Tony… I won't stop
tryin' till I have one.

TONY: Or till you qualify for a free ride in a hearse. (*Pause.
Then.*) Well, one thing's certain: you can't have it. An'
that's that.

RITA: What y'mean 'I can't have it!' You think it's the same
as buyin' a new dress? You think I can sen' it back to the
manufacturers?

TONY: (*A cry.*) Rita, it's no joke! (*Pause.*) Havin' another
chile could kill you: the doctor spelled it out fo' you.

RITA: (*Gently.*) Hush. Done be afraid. (*Pause.*) I'll outlive
you. I promise.
(*Pause.*)

TONY: Maybe you should at lease stop work from now.

RITA: You forget you got y'heart set on studyin'
accountancy…!

TONY: Sure, but I can go at night. I've done it before.

RITA: Tony, done talk rot. It's not easy workin' in the day
an' goin' to class at night.

TONY: I did it las' term.

RITA: That was diff'rent. You had to get y'G.C.E.s. But if
you want to atten' full-time college now that means you
got to go in the day. You got no choice: from this
October you gotta stop work. An' that means I have to
keep on workin' as long as I can. Right? (*Pause.*) We could
never manage, if I done put by some money from now.

TONY: No man should make his wife work herself sick, so
he can stop work.

RITA: Boy, you too ole-fashioned.
(*Pause.*)

TONY: (*Quietly, almost rueful.*) I dunno how you do it, girl.
Any time I need money fo' anything it's always you who
save it up.

RITA: (*Simply.*) Tony, anything you want you must have.
Once it's in my power to help you get it…you're
m'husban'.

23

(*Pause.*)

TONY: I never met a woman like you.

RITA: You lucky.

(*Pause.*)

TONY: Even the radiogram. I talk a lotuh nonsense about it, but we're only able to afford it causeuh you. (*Pause. Almost sadly.*) I could never save a penny if I din' have you.

RITA: Yes, well. Anyway once you go through wit' it this time, I done mine. Workin' an' savin', I mean. If you sure that's what you want to be, an accountant, well fine.

TONY: (*Crying out.*) I done want to handle record-players all my life…!

RITA: But you got a talent fo' buildin' them. That's why all y'frien's want one. Each time you build another set I feel prouduh you, Tony. Proud, proud.

TONY: That done cut no ice wit' the Midlan' Bank! When anybody ask what's my occupation? I want to be able to say 'accountant an' done you forget it'. Not 'I'm a chargehan' who builds record-players'. When you're an accountant people call you sir, when you handle record-players all they do is call you names. Right? Am I right? (*Pause.*) Makin' tape recorders, record-players, that's a boy's game, accountancy makes you a man.

RITA: (*Sad about it.*) Whatever pleases you, Tony, it's up to you. I'll help as much as I can.

(*Pause.*)

TONY: (*A cry.*) It's not a dream, Loopy Loo…! (*Pause.*) As an accountant I could make fifteen, maybe twenty thousan' a year. Twenty thousan', Loopy Loo! Wit' that kind of money we could buy a little house, 'invest in a property'. A place where we could have room to invite frien's. Not like this – storeroom. (*Pause.*) You couldn't even invite the Thin Man here. Even if he went on a diet. (*Pause.*) Girl, we could really start to live, if only we had our own place. No more goin' out in a cold, cold passage jus' to do toilet. We'll have a toilet nex' to the bedroom. A centrally heated toilet! Gorgeous! The whole place could be centrally heated. Ow, Loops…! Happiness is a house with central heatin' – from top to bottom! (*Pause.*) Think of it, once we could afford it, we need never freeze in Englan' again. This country would be a different place all-together! Imagine it – imagine bein' so warm you gotta turn down the heat. BEAU-TI-FUL! (*Pause.*) Twenty thousan'. It's not like wantin' a million. There are guys who pay that much in TAX! (*Pause.*) Some women spend more than that on a neck-liss. One neck-liss. Then they leave it lying aroun' so any and everybody could steal it! (*Pause. Bitter laugh.*) You gotta laugh. The whole pattern is so unfair, it's almost funny. Man. (*Pause.*) Ole God, eh, Sweet Pea. He really got it in fo' black people. No doubt about it. He rather see all of us freezin' in a room in Shepherd's Bush – wrap up in a overcoat like a cocoon – than see us wrap up in central heatin', warm as a butterfly. (*Pause.*) No lie, Rita. There just gotta be a God. (*Another private laugh.*) I mean the black man been put down fo' so long – that can't be jus' coincidence. (*His jaundiced laughter trails away. Pause.*) They even talk to you diff'rent when you makin' that kinduh money. White people. You done have to take as much crap from them. If only 'cos they know with that money you can afford a good lawyer! An' in any white court havin' a good lawyer is better than being innocent! (*He laughs, boyishly. Pause.*) Four, five years. That's all it'll take to be a Certified Accountant. Four, maybe five years. (*Dismissing even the thought of failure with a wave of his hand.*) I should do that easy. Easy, easy. It's simply a matteruh retaining the right facts. Anybody could do it. Once they apply themselves. (*Pause.*) Then after I get m'degree I'm in business, Loopy Loo! I'm laughin'! (*Pause.*) I'll only work fo' Jews. An' they got to be rich Jews or I'll practise anti-semitism. (*Laughs a he-he-he laugh. Pause. Then.*) Jews an' nobody else! I got respect fo' Jews. Jews know. An' what they know is how to survive. Copy the Jews. That's all I gotta say to West Indians. (*Pause.*) Strictly fo' Jews. No Wasps. You got to draw the line somewhere, Loopy. (*He gives another soft, jaundiced laugh. Pause.*) Twenty thousan'.

Nothin' fantastic. (*Pause.*) A little house with nice central heatin'... Binkie could have his own room...you could buy y'self some good clothes, Rita. (*Pause.*) Twenty thousan'. Compared to what some people want from life that's sweet F.A. It would do me, though. (*Snickering.*) I'd make do with twenty thousan' a year any day.

(*Pause. RITA goes to dressing table. Brings out a cigar.*)

RITA: Here, make do with this, Mr Onassis. I got it fo' you today.

TONY: Loopy Loo, you're a queen! (*He unwraps cigar. She produces a box of matches. Gives him a light for his cigar.*) You spoil me, Rita. (*He puffs away, happy as a Captain of Industry.*)

RITA: (*Almost sadly.*) Jus' persevere, If you want a thing bad enough who knows...? You might be unlucky enough to get it.

(*TONY blows a smoke ring. Pause.*)

TONY: You needn't work so hard though, girl. I done like to see it. (*Pause.*) It's so asinine! Okay, so we need to put by the money. But I could get it easy, easy – without you killin' y'self out.

RITA: (*Testy.*) So what you sugges'?

TONY: (*Beaming.*) The horses, girl! What else?

(*Pause.*)

RITA: (*Moving away.*) I'll get y'dinner. I hope you choke on it.

TONY: Rita!

(*She stops. Pause.*)

What's a fifty pence bet between frien's?

RITA: You never stop at a fifty pence bet!

(*Pause.*)

TONY: When I start messin' about with the rent an' the food money, that's when you gotta worry.

(*Pause. She puts her hand on the door-knob.*)

Loops, how often have I nearly won big, big money? How often?

RITA: Nearly! A horse that nearly win a race is a horse that lost.

TONY: (*Boisterously.*) Done be so technical, Loopy Loo! (*Pause.*) Come'ere. (*He crosses to her.*) Sit down, come on.

(*Puts his arm across her shoulder, leads her back to armchair, the last of the great charm boys.*) Comfortable? (*Pause.*) Loopy Loo, have I ever lied to you?

RITA: Yes.

TONY: You being technical again, woman.

(*Pause.*)

RITA: Boy, I'm not amused.

(*Pause. But her defences are weak.*)

TONY: Kiss me, Queen Victoria.

(*Pause. She kisses him softly.*)

RITA: No other man ever touch me, Tony, you do believe that…done you?

TONY: Listen, Rita, Little Prince run today. At nine to one!

(*RITA sucks her teeth, turns her head away. TONY oblivious.*) Nine to one. What've I always tole you about a nine-to-one horse?

(*She faces him again.*)

RITA: You mean you had a bet today! Despite all you said!

TONY: Talk sense. You forget I done get paid until tomorrow. Which bookie you know would allow me to place a bet without money? You know any bookie that mad?!

RITA: Good, I'm glad. You mighta throw away y'money.

TONY: (*As if he is trying to keep calm because he knows he's dealing with someone who's mentally subnormal, and it's not her fault.*) How do I throw 'way money on a horse that starts at nine-to-one? How many times have you heard me say that a nine-to-one horse is lucky fo' me? You might laugh but it's a dead cert as far as I'm concerned. A dead, dead cert! It's bound to win, Bound to. Once it starts at that price I done care who's the fav' rite – that horse at nine-to-one odds bound to win!

RITA: Superstition.

(*Pause.*)

TONY: (*Not taking the bait.*) You think so? Yeah? Superstition? (*Sucks his teeth.*) Okay, if you feel facts is superstition, that's your problem. It works fo' me, that's all I know. I'll tell you this, woman, I'd bet all m'clothes on a horse that starts at nine-to-one odds.

RITA: In this country they lock you up if they ketch you runnin' aroun' nakkid. Bear that in mine before you go about makin' all kinduh stupid bet.

TONY: (*Wearily.*) I'm talkin' to you about something serious to me, an' all you got fo' me is jokes. (*He turns away. Brings out his son's xylophone. Picks out a tune.*)

RITA: Waituh minute...! You sure you din' have a bet, boy? You say you had no money but did you borrow any? (*Pause.*)

TONY: (*Singing: tapping out some kind of tune on xylophone.*) I'm dreamin' of a BLACK Chris'mus! (*Pause.*) That oughtuh sell a million copies in Harlem – what you think, Loopy Loo? (*Pause. Loudly.*) It's my money, my money. I done have to answer to you to' nothing! (*Pause.*)

RITA: (*Mildly.*) Okay, Tony. (*Pause.*)

TONY: Okay, I borrow a poun' from Frank – one poun'! Report me to the C.I.A. (*Pause. He can't keep a straight face.*) All this fuss. Done you prefer to see me in the arms of a horse than in the arms of an English girl? (*Pause.*)

RITA: (*Giving nothing.*) It's a free country. Do what you want. (*Pause.*)

TONY: Bitch. It was jus' a joke.

RITA: Grow up, Tony, f'Godsakes.

TONY: (*Stung.*) Bitch – you hate to see me happy!

RITA: (*Infuriatingly.*) Oh yes?

TONY: You only have to see a smile on m'face an' you're sure to throw a bucketuh cold water all over me. Bitch.

RITA: That the only word you know? Bitch!

TONY: Women drain a man. They never satisfy until they got a man wit' his throat cut an' his blood drainin' away. They oughtuh employ women in them places where they slaughter cattle. They'd teach the men a thing or two.

RITA: (*Untouched, almost amused by him.*) Boy, you fulluh shit.

TONY: Yes, I know. Everybody but you. (*Pause.*) All these years an' I still dunno where I stan' wit' you. I'm not

stone! I'm not a pieceuh wood. I gottuh right to know
how m'own wife feel about me. (*Pause.*) If I said to you I
was goin' to leave you to shack up wit' a dozen women
all you'd do is han' me m'hat an' m'coat.

RITA: What you expect me to do – beg you to stay?

TONY: (*Crying out.*) An' why not...! You're m'wife!
(*Pause.*)

RITA: I never betray you yet, you betray me countless
times a'ready. Countless!
(*Pause.*)

TONY: I still tell you I love you, I feed you the words over
an' over again.

RITA: Yes – words, words!

TONY: (*Shouting.*) An' what's wrong wit' words!

RITA: They breed lies like germs!
(*Pause.*)

TONY: (*Quietly, deadly.*) I'll make you say it, bitch, one day
I'll make you say you love me. I'll break you in yet,
bitch!
(*Pause.*)

RITA: An' you say you love me.
(*TONY pounds the xylophone with the sticks, his frustration
boiling over.*)

TONY: Break you! Break you! Break – you! I – swear – it!
(*He stops. Worn down. Pause.*)

RITA: Boy, if you ain' mad, well I dunno.
(*Pause.*)

TONY: (*Vulnerable.*) I'm alone in this country, Rita, if
I can't be sureuh you I might as well let them sen'
m'back home.

RITA: (*Sad smile.*) Leave me the radiogram before you go.
(*TONY slaps her; the side of her face. Nothing vicious, it is
just a warning blow. She does not even raise her hand to her
face. Pause. He tries to embrace her. She holds him off.*)
Leave me be. I'll get y'dinner.
(*RITA goes out to kitchen (off). TONY goes to his overcoat
behind the door. He produces an evening paper from one of the
pockets. He turns to Racing Pages. Begins to write out a bet.*)

TONY: Kempton…two forty-five…My Girl. Eleven to –
(*He hears RITA returning. Hides paper under the bed. RITA opens the door. Stands in doorway holding her stomach.*)
RITA: Tony.
(*She is evidently in some pain.*)
TONY: Girl, what's wrong?
(*He hurries to her. Helps her sit down.*)
RITA: Something's gone wrong. Get Dr Thomas. Quick!
(*Quick blackout.*)

Scene 2

House in Shepherd's Bush. The FLETCHERS' room. Summer. Day. Room looks rather neglected. Bed unmade etc. TONY has not progressed very far with the record-player. He has attached a turn-table to the motor now but that's all. TONY lets himself in. He is in a great hurry. He is carrying a large Coke. Deposits it. He rushes around the room tidying up. He removes all obvious traces of RITA as well. He stuffs their wedding photographs into wardrobe. DENNIS knocks at his door. TONY lets him in. DENNIS is a West Indian student of Sociology. He wears glasses. If he's not careful he will have a nervous breakdown.

DENNIS: Man, Tony, what're you doin'? If you've changed y'mind, it's okay, I'll understand.
TONY: Jus' keep quiet an' help me clean up.
(*DENNIS picks up some of TONY's clothes which are on the floor. Holds them up.*)
DENNIS: Really missin' Rita, aren't you?
(*Pause.*)
TONY: So?
DENNIS: Well, it's up to you, y'know, I done mind. I mean about the girls.
TONY: Jus' because I invite another woman up here that done mean I love m'wife less. Anyway it's not my fault Rita had to go into hospital. I mean she might be in there fo' ages, Dennis, what happens to me in the meantime…!
(*Pause.*) I mean I'm too old fo' cold showers, Dennis.
(*Pause.*)

DENNIS: I'll go an' get the chicks. They must be dying in the car. Sandra fancies you, I'm sure of it.

TONY: She's got good taste.

(*DENNIS laughs, goes. TONY crosses over to the bed, stands over it for a moment, thinking of RITA. He sucks his teeth, sighs, something. Makes up the bed. DENNIS returns with the two girls. One English, one West Indian. The English girl enters first. SANDRA: blonde, buxom, attractive in a rather obvious way. About twenty-two. Traces of a Yorkshire accent; hip vernacular. Too much make-up is inclined to make her look a bit tarted-up. She is fleshy, and her mini-dress is sleeveless, low-cut. She is well aware that English men prefer their women to be more slender, so she knows who her admirers are. Nothing hard or brassy about her, she is even-tempered, optimistic. She is a not very successful go-go dancer. Has a rather empty, self-conscious laugh. YVONNE: light-skinned, pretty West Indian girl of about twenty-one. She has no time for any kind of black past. She will marry an English-man some day. Colourful blouse, decorative belt, peach-coloured trousers.*)

SANDRA: What's up, man?

TONY: Come in, come in.

SANDRA: We're already in or haven't you noticed?
(*Gives her laugh.*)

TONY: Comic. Sit anywhere you want.
(*The girls sit on the settee. DENNIS remains standing. As does TONY. He hangs his jacket behind the door.*)

YVONNE: A bit cramped, this room.

TONY: Why, you thinkin'uh buyin' it?

YVONNE: No thanks. I already got a cupboard.
(*Pause.*)

SANDRA: (*Abruptly, jolly, to TONY.*) So what happened to you? One minute you were with us, the next minute you'd split. Haven't got a wife, have you? Where'd you hide her, under the bed?

TONY: (*An arrogant stare, faint smile.*) You like the sounduh yuh own voice, right?

SANDRA: I've had it a long time, maybe that's why.

(*Pause. They are looking at each other.*)

TONY: Siddown, Dennis. I'm not playing 'God Save the Queen'.

DENNIS: Man, let's have some soul.

(*TONY sits on the bed.*)

TONY: Put on the tape recorder, huh. What, you're a cripple?

(*DENNIS crosses to tape recorder. Puts it on. The music: 'By The Time I Get To Phoenix' by Isaac Hayes (without the long spoken introduction) from his LP 'Hot Buttered Soul'. Other numbers include: 'If There Is A Hell Down Below We're All Gonna Go' by Curtis Mayfield, or any other comparable number by Mayfield. Numbers by Otis Reading, The Temptations, and Smokey Robinson and the Miracles.*)

SANDRA: (*About Isaac Hayes number.*) Yeah, great, turn it up. Really moves me, that number.

(*DENNIS sits in armchair.*)

TONY: (*Looking at SANDRA.*) We got a real soul-sister here, Dennis.

SANDRA: (*Her laugh.*) Get thee behind me, you.

(*Pause.*)

DENNIS: (*Not to anyone in particular.*) Man, it's hot, eh.

SANDRA: Personally I like it when it's hot. I can sit out in the sun and get all nice 'n' brown. I can't stand to look like sliced white bread.

TONY: I know jus' what you mean.

SANDRA: (*Pleased.*) Shut up, you!

(*TONY laughs, rubbing his hands up and down his thighs with almost boyish glee. DENNIS sits hunched in his chair, moving his body back and forth in time to the music.*)

TONY: You like rum, Sandra?

SANDRA: In a glass, yeah.

TONY: You chicks better had like rum, that's all I got!

(*He laughs alone. Pause.*)

YVONNE: (*To SANDRA.*) The last of the big spenders.

(*The two girls laugh with each other.*)

SANDRA: Golden Boy entertains.

(*TONY sucks his teeth. Rises.*)

TONY: (*Almost to himself, but loud enough.*) Women, boy. Jesus. (*He has got up to go to the sideboard. But first stops off at tape recorder. He turns volume down. Continues on to sideboard.*) All your fault, Dennis.

DENNIS: (*You'd think he was being accused of the Great Train Robbery.*) What you mean, man? No, man.

TONY: (*From sideboard he gets out rum, glasses.*) I could be in the bettin' shop right now. (*With the Coke he has bought he starts mixing rum'n'coke for four.*)

YVONNE: Done let us keep you.

SANDRA: A real charmer, isn't he?

TONY: (*Still to DENNIS.*) Do me a favour. Nex' time you see me near a bettin' shop, ignore me. Even if you got Miss Englan' waitin' outside in y'car. Okay? Cut me dead.

YVONNE: (*On her feet.*) Look, I know when I'm not wanted.

TONY: Since when're you Miss Englan'?
(*Pause. No love lost between them.*)

DENNIS: Relax, Yvonne. The guy's underuh bit of a strain at the moment, dig? That's all.

TONY: Sit down, done mine me, I talk too much. Here.
(*Gives YVONNE a drink. She sits down.*)

YVONNE: (*Grudgingly.*) Thanks.
(*TONY hands SANDRA and DENNIS their drinks. Sits on the bed.*)

DENNIS: Rita's goin' to be all right, man. Trust Uncle Dennis, right? These things are sent to try us, man. I firmly believe that. Not by God – anyuh that rubbish – I done believe in God anymore. I mean once I was a good Catholic boy an' alluh that, but that was before I experience life in this country. You try to believe in God in this country, you jus' try. (*Pause.*) By nature. Not God, nature. To test us, man. To make sure we find it harder to survive. We, as a people.
(*Pause.*)

SANDRA: What's he on about?

YVONNE: You askin' me...! I done even work here.

TONY: (*Sucking his teeth, almost to himself.*) An' I coulduh been in the bettin' shop. Mindin' m'own business. (*Sucks his teeth again.*) God give me strength.

SANDRA: What're you mumbling about, man?

TONY: I said so you're a go-go dancer, eh? I wouldn't mind go-go-going to bed wish you.

SANDRA: Is he always like this? (*Then.*) I dance at Beanos. It's not much of a club but it's home.

TONY: Beanos! Christ! The las' time I went to that club the bouncer asked me for a dance.

SANDRA: Liar! You liar!

TONY: Maybe he wasn't gay, but everytime he had to chuck anybody out he went home wit' them in a taxi.

SANDRA: Oh, you liar!

(*They laugh together. Then continue to look at each other. Pause.*)

YVONNE: Who's Rita?

(*Pause.*)

DENNIS: His sister!

TONY: M'sister, yeah, yeah.

(*Pause.*)

SANDRA: What's wrong with her?

TONY: She's in hospital. (*Pause.*) In all she's been gone about three months now.

SANDRA: God, how terrible for her.

TONY: Yeah, well. (*Pause.*) I see her every evening, y'know. (*Pause. He moves over to BINKIE's photograph.*) That's the boy. Her son. I was lookin' after him, y'know, while she's been away. I couldn't manage, though. (*Pause.*) I had to send him to his gran'mother in Trinidad. (*Pause.*) Like a package. (*Pause.*) You feel you prepared fo' everything. Then something like this happen. (*Sucks his teeth.*) Shoot. (*Pause. More to himself than any of them.*) Man, I can hardly remember a time when there wasn't something goin' wrong…or when I wasn't out there hustlin' fo' bread by fair means or foul. (*Pause.*) Hustle, hustle, hustle, that's all it's ever been. (*Pause.*) Tryin' to win bread, tryin' not to lose bread. One endless hustle. (*Pause.*) I never had time to learn to trust others, or to think of those worse off than me. I never had time to be anything but hard. (*Pause.*) You gotta be rich to afford them kinduh luxuries. (*Sucks his teeth again. Quietly.*) This room...this room. (*Pause. He sits down on bed again. SANDRA offers him her cigarettes.*)

SANDRA: Here, help y'self. They're menthol. You shouldn't let things get you down.

TONY: (*Quick cover-up.*) Get me down...! Me! Not this boy. I done let things get me down. I might be a ass, but I'm not a madass. (*Pause.*) Once you let life get you by the neck, you might as well take up Hari-Kari. As a hobby. (*Pause.*)

DENNIS: (*Abruptly, creating enthusiasm.*) So how're things, man, Tony? How's the studies goin' eh? You should be startin' full-time college soon, right? September's jus' about a month away.

TONY: Maybe nex' year September. But not this year, that's fo' sure. Everything's changed, how many times I got to tell you that?

DENNIS: But man, you still could've done your studies, even with Rita in hospital.

TONY: (*Guilty outburst.*) I had to take careuh the chile, you forget.

DENNIS: Yeah, sorry.
(*Pause.*)

TONY: I jus' got to accept the fact this wasn't my year, that's all. Anyway when you consider the numberuh people takin' accountancy these days maybe it's best I put it off fo' a year or two. (*Pause. The others embarrassed.*) Maybe nex' year. Who knows?
(*Pause.*)

DENNIS: So what'uve you been doin' with y'self all this time?

TONY: Lotsuh things, man. Lots. Lots. (*Pause.*) There's a lotuh things a man wit' all my money can do in London. Join the Playboy Club, f'example. Or the Conservative Party.
(*SANDRA finds the thought of that funny indeed.*)

(*Wryly.*) You like the thoughtuh that, do you? Eh? (*Pause.*) Yeah. (*Pause. Wearily.*) Oh he can always gamble. No man is that poor that a spotuh gamblin' couldn't make him poorer.

DENNIS: I thought as much! You've gone back to heavy gamblin'.

TONY: (*Made angry.*) What you mean 'heavy gamblin'? Even if every Friday I was to put m whole week's salary on one horse, not even a pauper would call that heavy gamblin'.

DENNIS: Heavy gamblin' means bettin' more than you can afford.

TONY: That ain't 'heavy gamblin'! That's bein' a coon. (*Only he and SANDRA find that funny. Pause.*)

DENNIS: What about all that money you had put by to help pay the fees at that college an' everything? You haven't thrown is all away on the horses, I hope?

TONY: (*Harsh.*) What gives you that idea?

DENNIS: Be cool, man. No reason to get all hot an' bothered about anything I say.

TONY: Bothered! Me! Get away. Nothing bothers Tony. (*Pause. Abrupt infuriating laugh.*) Yesterday I lost ten quid on a horse. Not even that can bother me!

DENNIS: Ten pounds? An' you reckon that's not heavy gamblin'? (*Pause.*)

TONY: (*Bitter-sweet amusement.*) I was so sure about that horse, sure, sure. When I tell you sure I mean dead sure. Dead, dead sure! An' what happen? The flickin' horse end up in a photo-finish. Six to one, is was. Six to one! I could've won sixty poun's, plus m'ten poun's back. Seventy quid less tax. (*Pause.*) I coulda done wit' that money. (*Pause.*) Seventy quid. An' that horse had to get caught up in a photo-finish. (*Pause.*) Ole God done like Tony. In fact He must hate me. (*Pause.*) I still can't believe it. I got beat by a photograph. A photograph. (*Abrupt, self-mocking laugh.*) It's enough to put me off cameras fo' life! (*Pause.*) I coulduh cried, boy.

DENNIS: Cried! Fo' ten pounds I'd 'ave cut m'throat.
(*TONY sticks out his throat.*)
TONY: Looky here!
(*The others all laugh. But there is some disapproval in DENNIS's laugh.*)
DENNIS: You always were a very happy guy, Tony. Happy, happy. Too happy.
(*Pause. TONY gets up.*)
TONY: (*Getting some kind of jaundiced amusement out of it.*) I jus' seem to have gone crazy. I mean you won't believe it. (*Pause.*) There's jus' been no stoppin' me these las' three months. The bookies should get together an' send me a turkey fo' Christmas.
(*Pause. The others aren't laughing.*)
One turkey! I reckon they owe me a whole farmyard. (*Pause.*) Not that I always lose, mind you. (*Snickers.*) I jus' done win often enough, that's all...!
(*And laughs all by himself. Pause.*)
DENNIS: Ten poun's. Christ, man. Where do you get the bread? An' you're the guy who's always tellin' me about being in control.
TONY: Ach, I'm still in control. (*Sits.*) Complete control. Some guys put their house an' their car in hock to back horses, But not me, Mainly because I got no house nor car!
(*YVONNE waits until he's quiet again.*)
YVONNE: You make me sick.
TONY: (*Snickering again.*) That makes two of us.
YVONNE: (*Loudly.*) You think it's funny! It's a sickness.
(*Pause.*) You're playin' into white people's hands!
TONY: (*Quietly.*) This might come as a surprise to you, girl. I done think it's very funny. But I done think it's a crime neither. (*Pause. To DENNIS.*) Guess who I saw las' week – Oscar. (*He gets up again. Gathers up their glasses.*)
DENNIS: That ass!
(*TONY crosses to sideboard. Starts mixing them fresh drinks.*)
TONY: I was in the bettin' shop roun' the corner, tryin' to decide whether I should make a Yankee bet or not. When

in walks Oscar, large as life an' twice as loud. Right away he asks me to lend him a poun'. Months I ain' see the guy. Months. An' the first words he hits me with is – 'len' me a poun', Tony'! After that I knew I might as well jus' forget that Yankee.

DENNIS: That guy's a blight.

TONY: A blight! He's a one-man epidemic. He ought to be put in a isolation ward – fo' life! (*Pause.*) Len' him a poun'...! (*Sucking his teeth.*) He gets me so vex, that boy. Vex, vex. (*Pause.*) I mean when I win I'm prepared to len' a guy five poun's. Right? But before a race done bother me. If it's one thing I've had to learn from bitter experience it's that once you len' somebody money durin' gamblin' you sure to lose. He takes your luck away.

YVONNE: They ought to take you away. To a padded cell.

TONY: I suppose you call that superstition, right?

YVONNE: Wrong, I call it madness.

TONY: (*A sigh, he's dealing with another of the uninitiated.*) You wouldn't understan', you're a non-believer. You got to believe in gamblin' to understan' gamblin'. You gotta believe in all the rules, All gamblers got their own beliefs, their own signs: some gamblers done like to hear or watch the race they bettin' on, others think it's bad luck to drop anything when they're in the bettin' shop, even if it's jus' a pieceuh paper. You can dismiss such things as superstition but to a gambler it's the difference between good luck an' bad luck.
(*Pause.*)

YVONNE: I never heard such drivel in m'whole life.

TONY: (*Above it all.*) Per'aps. Per'aps.
(*Pause.*)

SANDRA: Racing, that's not my scene, man.

TONY: What's your scene, Minnie Mouse?
(*Pause.*)

SANDRA: That depends on what you're selling?
(*Pause. They are looking at each other.*)

YVONNE: (*Looking away, under her breath.*) West Indian men.

TONY: Pardon?

(*Pause. Some hostility between him and YVONNE.*)

YVONNE: (*Turning in DENNIS's direction.*) I could do with a turn-on. You still have that joint on you?

TONY: (*Flatly.*) I done want you smokin' here, please.

YVONNE: (*A great sigh as she faces him.*) What's this now?

TONY: I done hold with drugs. Sorry an' all that. What you do outside is your business, but I live here. Okay?

(*Pause.*)

YVONNE: (*Quiet dislike.*) You ever try getting a oh with the Vice Squad?

TONY: You want m'work number? It's nine, nine, nine.

YVONNE: I'll call you the next time I need a headache.

TONY: Fo' you I'd even arrange a head transplant.

(*Pause. YVONNE gets up.*)

YVONNE: Dennis, I'm going!

(*TONY's laugh is infuriatingly mocking.*)

DENNIS: (*He does not move from bed.*) Oh, f'Chrisesake, woman.

YVONNE: You coming or not?

(*Pause. DENNIS rises, sucking his teeth.*)

DENNIS: I see you, brother, Stay cool, okay?

TONY: Man, look, sit down.

(*YVONNE has gone to the door. SANDRA has not moved.*)

YVONNE: You coming, Dennis Tait?

DENNIS: Yeah, yeah.

(*YVONNE opens the door.*)

YVONNE: (*To TONY.*) At least I don't spend my life in a British bettin' shop. I have some pride.

TONY: (*Touching an imaginary forelock.*) God bless you.

(*YVONNE storms out. Disappears down the passage.*)

DENNIS: How about you, Sandra?

SANDRA: I'll stay. I'll be okay. Go and comfort her.

(*Pause.*)

DENNIS: Right, please y'self.

(*TONY rises. Goes to window.*)

You okay, man?

(*Pause.*)

TONY: (*At window.*) There's this chick, y'know…every morning when I'm goin' to work I see her at the tube station. She's always by herself. A nice, nice chick. A well-dressed black chick, I mean really well-dressed. Gorgeous, boy. Like a model, y'know. Only…only she always screams and screeches at everybody. Screeches anthem in some strange, mad tongue. (*Pause. Sucks his teeth.*) Jesus, boy. (*Pause.*) You should see how those English people pretend they can't see her…her distress. (*Pause.*) Lord only knows how long she's been in this country. (*Pause. Tapping his forehead.*) In here. She's gone in here. (*Pause. Hard, disgruntled.*) People talk about how we can't get proper jobs in this country, decent accommodation. But what nobody as yet really knows about is the price we're payin' up here. We're not even aware of someuh the pressures. But it's all takin' it's toll; right here. (*Pause.*) The way I see it, what's important, as far as we're concerned, is not that the English see us as the challenger. But that we see them as the champ. An' you can deny that all y'want, but it's that fact that our mines have gotta absorb daily. Like a kick in the crotch. It's no wonder that up here we sometimes short circuit under the strain. It's no joke to know you gotta be able to knock out the other guy, before the ref will even call the fight a draw. (*Pause. Almost to himself.*) Look about London. Look as the numberuh black people babblin' away to themselves, it's a cryin' shame. (*Pause. Then.*) An' since a lotuh English people aren't too sane neither, then God help us. (*And gives a laugh of sorts.*) Jus' think what that means eh? Our safe-conduc' depen's on one helluv an assumption, that they'll never go completely mad. (*Quietly.*) There's so few of us an' so manyuh them. (*Pause.*) Okay, sure they'd say such a thing could never happen. What with their well-known stiff upper lip an' everything. But how do I know that? (*Quiet cry.*) It's my life that's being laid on the line here! (*Pause. He can't keep a straight face.*) An' if my safety depen's on nothing more than somebody else's upper lip, then that's hardly guarantee to do my sanity much good. Right? Right!

(*He and DENNIS laugh together; whether they are very amused or not is another matter.*)

I mean, buddy, you ever see someuh them football crowds when they descend on London fo' a match. Eh?! You'd have to look pretty far to find even one stiff upper lip among that lot.

(*Their laughter renews itself. Dies away. Pause. Then hard, cold again.*)

So you tell her this fo' me, that girl down there, tell her it helps me manage. That's why I do it. Gamble. It helps me survive. Gamblin' helps keep me on an...even keel... (*Taps his forehead again.*) ...up here. (*Pause.*) Once you got a passion, the odds are in your favour. (*Pause.*) They're not goin' to make a eunuch outa me. Not this boy. Not if I can help it.

(*Pause.*)

DENNIS: (*At door.*) Take it easy, man, Tony. Okay? (*Then.*) See you, Sandra.

(*DENNIS waves, goes. Pause.*)

SANDRA: Cigarette?

(*TONY has not moved from his vigil by the window.*)

TONY: What? Oh, no, no thanks. (*Moves from window over to sideboard. Pours a little rum in his glass.*) Want some moreuh this? (*And not waiting for a reply crosses to her and adds some rum to her glass.*)

SANDRA: Thanks.

(*TONY sits in armchair.*)

You're an interesting sort of bloke, aren't you?

TONY: (*Quite mocking.*) Reckon so, do you?

(*SANDRA looks at the drink in her hand. She watches it swirling around in her glass as she speaks.*)

SANDRA: Pretty potent stuff, isn't it? (*Pause.*) All this black anger. (*Only then does she look at him. Pause. Then a nod in the direction of his workbench.*) What are you building?

TONY: Who? Oh, that. A record-player. (*More to himself than to her.*) Haven't even finished it yet. (*Pause.*) I can usually build oneuh those things in about a month. Just workin' at nights, after work, y'know. But I jus' haven't had the time recently. (*A sigh.*) What with havin' to go to that hospital an' everything. (*Pause.*) It jus' done pay to plan ahead. (*Pause.*) I gotta get holduh some bread. No two ways about it. A quick killin' that's the tonic I need. The right money on the right horse.

(*Pause.*)

SANDRA: Horses, horses, horses. I can hardly credit it. (*Pause.*) When do I start to fight for my white virtue, that's what I want to know? (*Pause. Impish.*) You call y'self a black man?

(*Pause.*)

TONY: Sixty poun's I could've had now. That horse coulda won easy, easy. That jockey play the ass, that's why.

SANDRA: No racialist worth his salt would believe this.

TONY: (*Rubbing his hands together, suddenly acknowledging her presence.*) Well, how're you, eh, Minnie Mouse! (*He gets up.*)

SANDRA: I'm okay. How're you?

TONY: You got nice thighs.

(*Sinks down beside her. He's on the prowl now.*)

SANDRA: I thought you'd never notice.

(*He plays with her hand, then works his way up her arm, massaging, caressing.*)

Do you mind!

(*But doesn't remove his hand.*)

TONY: Gorgeous.

(*The buzzer in his room sounds.*)

Aww, Chrise, Dennis musta come back, You want to go?

(*Pause. He still has his hand on her arm.*)

SANDRA: Do you want me to go?

(*Pause.*)

TONY: Course not.

(*Pause.*)

SANDRA: Then I didn't hear any bell. Did you?

TONY: Bell? What bell?

(*Pause.*)

SANDRA: So how come you've been actin' like some English gent ever since we've been alone?

(*Pause. TONY's hand freezes on her arm.*)

TONY: Me? An English gent? You gotta be jokin'. (*Pause. He removes his hand.*) I got m'reasons. Maybe I done wanna do anything in this room.

SANDRA: You don't think my thighs are too fat?

TONY: Woman, done talk rubbish. I like to see a woman wit' nice, heavy thighs. Or else where's the diff'rence between women and men?

SANDRA: English men like their women skinny.

TONY: (*A little laugh.*) Good, I glad. That leaves all the more women fo' me.

(*He hears someone putting a key in the lock.*)

Who's that!

(*RITA enters, TONY jumps up.*)

Girl, what you doin' here!

(*Pause. Somehow RITA looks less pregnant than one would expect her to be.*)

RITA: I discharge m'self. I wanted to come home. Where there wasn't no white people about!

(*Pause.*)

Scene 3

The FLETCHERS' room. Summer. Evening. The room is tidy again. RITA alone in the room polishing glass-top table. She has to stop; she still does not seem very well. She crosses to wardrobe, brings out BINKIE's xylophone. Pause. She places it on the bed. Plays it softly. Stops. Pause. She traces her hand over is sadly. Kneels, burying her face in the bed. Pause. She hears TONY returning and quickly gets to her feet. TONY enters. They look as each other. Pause. TONY is as usual tie-less.

RITA: (*Quietly.*) Soon be his birt'day.

TONY: Who?

RITA: His birt'day. Binkie. We'll get 'im something nice... Okay? An' a card wit' a lion on is.

(*Pause. TONY hangs up his jacket.*)

TONY: Put that thing away it'll only make you feel worse.

RITA: Remember when you bought it fo' 'im? Remember how I nagged you when you tole me how much you paid fo' it?

(*He has crossed to bed to change his shoes.*)

TONY: Where's m'shoes?

(*Pause. RITA sighs, puts xylophone away. TONY concerns himself with his shoes. Finally.*)

You been feelin' okay, Loopy Loo?

RITA: Yeah. Sure.

(*She sits in armchair. Sucks her teeth softly. Pause.*)

TONY: Had y'medicine?

RITA: (*Rising; preoccupied.*) Boy, stop bothenin' me, y'hear me. I'll get y'dinner. (*She opens the door. Pause. Faces him.*) You'll never know how I feel not havin' that boy here. I miss Binkie so much. Especially now. (*Pause.*) I dunno what I'll do if I lose this baby.

(*Pause.*)

TONY: (*Loud guilt.*) Wasn't my fault we had to sen' Binkie to y'mother, jus' done forget that!

RITA: I wasn't away a lifetime…!

TONY: You blame me?!

(*Pause.*)

RITA: I want m'boy chile near me, that's all I'm sayin'.

TONY: (*Crying out.*) You have me, Rita…! I'm here.

(*Pause. She goes off to kitchen. Pause. TONY turns on the tape recorder. RITA returns with his dinner, deposits it on glass-top table. She has brought in a beer with his meal; she pours it out for him. He turns tape recorder off. He comes over to sit down. RITA moves away. Pause. He picks at his food.*)

I suppose now fo' the restuh the night we'll jus' sit an' watch Tee Vee. (*Pause. Then a snicker.*) It's no wonder so many young white people envy black people, it's the full, vital life we lead.

(*RITA ignores him. Pause.*)

I done feel like eatin'. (*Pause.*) They hire a new guy at work today. I dunno where they find the guy. He dunno a thing about amplifiers. To tell you the honest truth the guy dunno a thing about nothing! Naturally he's a student. (*Pause.*) I hate Tuesdays. Everybody else hate Mondays, but I got to be diff'rent. (*Pause.*) Friday is payday; Monday is the day you wonder what happen to

the weekend. But what's a Tuesday? (*Pause. Snickering.*)
Tuesday is not a day it's a punishment. (*Pause.*) Come to
thinkuh it, I done much care fo' Thursdays, neither.
(*And guffaws boyishly. Then.*) You like that, Loops? You
like m'lecture on the daysuh the week? Eh?
(*She ignores him. His genial mood dies out.*)
I'm talkin' to you, woman. (*Pause.*) Rita! (*Pause.*) Only
white women punish their men by not talkin' to them!
(*Pause. Worn down.*) Bitch. (*Pause.*) (*Almost a plea.*) Talk to
me, Rita. Done turn away. (*Pause. Sad, wistful.*) No cigars
fo' me today? Done you have no cigars hidden away like
a squirrel? (*Pause. Almost to himself.*) I never was easy to
live with. (*Pause. Loudly.*) I din' touch that English girl,
how many times I gotta tell you that! (*Pause.*) I shoulda
really given you something to complain about. (*Shouting.*)
I shoulda had her stripped naked, her legs wide open, her
blonde pie exposed like it was SUPPERTIME! Then you
woulda had something to complain about! (*Pause. He gets
up, glass in hand. A bit patronising in his wooing.*) Come on, be
nice. Look I even left you some beer, Loops.
(*She moves away, he follows her, crazy as a fox.*)
Come on, you know you can't hate y'daddy. Eh, Loopy
Loo? Not a finger. I wouldn't lay a finger on a white girl.
M'whole han', yes. But one finger, never.
(*He has managed to jump in front of her. Pause.*)

RITA: (*Quietly.*) Tony, done depress me. Enough is enough.
(*Pause.*) It's that money, that's what makes me sick not
some white girl.
(*Pause.*)

TONY: Money? What money?
(*But moves out of her reach just in case. Pause.*)

RITA: You take me fo' a real fool, right? (*Pause.*) The money
I save up like some ass that's what money. Din' you
think I'd fine out? (*Pause.*) You throw is away on the
horses, right?

TONY: Horses! How y'think Binkie got to Trinidad? On an
envelope! You think he store away on a postage stamp!
I had to pay more than halfuh that money on his passage
– you forget!

(*RITA sits down on settee.*)

RITA: (*Mildly.*) Sure, I know that, but where's the restuh it?

TONY: Rest! What rest! Restuh what? Rest!

(*Pause.*)

RITA: Ninety-five poun's.

TONY: You've got at least fifteen poun's left – what ninety-five poun's you talkin' about?

RITA: Okay, eighty poun's. (*Pause.*) What have you done with it? You seem to have gone insane since I been away. (*Pause.*)

TONY: I must be hearin' things. I thought I was in my own room, my own home, but apparently this is some police station. New Scotland Yard! (*Pause.*) You want me to empty m'pockets? Done you have any pot you want to plant on me?! (*Pause.*)

RITA: Eighty poun's. (*Shaking her head over him.*) Honest to God, Tony. (*Pause.*)

TONY: (*A cry.*) You baffle me...! You done even lose y'temper. (*Pause.*) You done even care enough about me to shout at me! You done give a damn about me! (*Pause.*)

RITA: Maybe I've had to put up wit' so much from you, I jus' can't be bothered anymore. You're not worth me losin' m'temper. (*Pause.*)

TONY: (*Guiltily.*) I never spent it on horses, fool! I had to pay off back rent! I owed rent! Rent, stupid, not gamblin'...! Rent, rent. (*Pause.*)

RITA: You should see y'self. You look like an advertisement fo' some all-night horror film. (*Pause.*) Anyway how come you owe all this rent? Eh? Cosuh y'gamblin', right? (*Pause.*) So what's the diff'rence? Either way it's the bookie who's laughin'. (*Pause.*)

TONY: (*A bit overbearing, not loudly.*) Ach, done bug me. One day you win, one day you lose. You never know y'luck.

RITA: (*Sudden dislike.*) I'm sick to my stomach hearin' about your luck.
(*Pause.*)

TONY: (*Vulnerable little laugh.*) You should neveruh married me then, right?
(*Pause.*)

RITA: (*Not particularly loud.*) Sometimes I wish to Jesus I hadn't.
(*Pause. TONY backs away from her like an old man, he feels behind him for something solid to hold onto, a chair, a bed, a wheelchair. He lowers himself on the bed. Pause.*)
Boy, is that suppose to impress me? That little act you jus' perform there? (*Pause.*) Can't take it, can you? You can dish is out, but y'can't take is. Right?

TONY: (*He still can't focus.*) I'm not easy to live with…
I know. But I never set out to cripple others…that's not my game.
(*Pause.*)

RITA: (*Quietly.*) Boy, you're too weak, tha's your trouble.
(*Pause.*)

TONY: (*Not loudly at first.*) This room…this room. (*Getting to his feet.*) I never been anything but lonely in this country. (*Prowling the room.*) Lonely, lonely! Okay, so the money's better an' the education…! But the – price! (*He stumbles blindly into armchair. Gives it a shove out of his way.*) This room is too small for me!

RITA: Tony!

TONY: (*Unhearing.*) Sometimes I want to howl! I done have to be the big hustler everybody thinks I am. Howl! Jus' let is all out. But who'll hear me? Who wants to know? You go in oneuh their churches an' you lucky if they done have you on a cross before the collection plate even come aroun'! (*Pause.*) One visit to an English church an' you're an atheist fo' life. Life! (*Pause. To RITA. Quieter.*) As fo' you. How much comfort do I get from you? Eh? (*Quiet cry.*) I done even know where I stan' with you anymore. You got me on a string like a yo-yo! Christ, man, Christ!

RITA: (*Rising, her hands out to him.*) Be quiet. Come here.

TONY: (*Brushing her off like a fly.*) Han's off. (*Quietly deadly.*) I'll get you y'money. Every cent. I'll get you y'flickin' money! (*He grabs for his tie, swings is around his neck, starts tying it furiously.*) To listen to you anyone would think I was oneuh them West Indian jig-ahoos who divide their time between the pub an' the bettin' shop. I never been on the dole fo' one day in this country. Never, never.

RITA: (*Fearful.*) Tony, what you doin'?

TONY: I'm goin' to get y'money, bitch.

RITA: Is wasn't all my money.

TONY: Now you remember? Oh yes?

(*He is putting on his jacket. She holds on to his arm.*)

RITA: Please!

TONY: (*Quiet warning.*) Leggo, woman.

(*Pause. She lets go of him. Pause, He opens the door.*)

RITA: Tony.

(*He hears it in her voice. Turns.*)

TONY: Oh. Lord, what now?

RITA: Something's gone wrong again, do something, Tony.

(*TONY has to help her sit down on the bed. He returns to the door and closes is slowly. His eyes survey their room: he is not going anywhere.*)

ACT TWO

Scene 1

*House in Shepherd's Bush. Passage outside the FLETCHERS' room.
Summer. Day.*

*We see the back of OSCAR first. He is wearing tight red trousers
and red shirt. He knocks at TONY's door. Pause. He peers through
the keyhole. Knocks again. Again he peers through the keyhole. Unseen
by OSCAR, TONY comes up the stairs behind him.*

TONY: Oscar, I'm not at home.
  (*OSCAR straightens up, startled.*)
OSCAR: I dropped a shillin'.
TONY: An' it rolled through the keyhole, right?
OSCAR: You saw it happen, eh? Good, you owe me five
  pence.
  (*TONY doesn't even bother to reply; he unlocks his door.*)
TONY: I'm glad you could make it, Oscar, I need a favour.
  (*OSCAR turns and heads for home.*)
OSCAR: I got no money.
  (*TONY brings him back.*)
TONY: The day I ask you fo' money, Oscar, is the day I
  take up suicide.
  (*TONY leads OSCAR into the room and into a chair.*)
OSCAR: Got any straights?
  (*TONY sucks his teeth, offers his pack of cigarettes.*)
  How come you home on a Wednesday?
  (*OSCAR is helping himself to at least three cigarettes. TONY
  rescues them firmly.*)
TONY: You only got one mouth, Oscar.
OSCAR: Jus' testin' you.
  (*Pause.*)
TONY: How come *you're* not at work?
OSCAR: I workin' nights now. Nex' question.
TONY: (*Loudly.*) Jus' shut up, Oscar, Christ, man, Christ.
  (*Pause.*) Rita's sick again. She's downstairs with Mrs

Frazier. She couldn't sleep las' night, an' the doctor came this mornin'. He made me phone fo' an ambulance. She has to go back to hospital. But up to now no ambulance. Nearly two hours an' still no ambulance. It's got me so worried. (*Pause.*) Anyway, I can't leave her, that's why I need y'help.

OSCAR: Sure, sure, man, anything.

TONY: I want you to put on a bet fo' me.

(*Pause. OSCAR gets up.*)

OSCAR: (*Quietly.*) Boy, you're not an ordinary bastard.

(*Pause. He moves over to TONY's tape recorder. Turns it on.*)

TONY: Will you turn that flickin' thing off?

OSCAR: I mean, she's y'*wife*, man.

TONY: I know she's m'wife. I was at the weddin', remember! (*Pause.*) We need the money. Okay! We need the money. (*Pause.*) She had some money put by, but... I had a few bad horses, an', well, mostuh the money jus' went. (*Sad.*) You know how it is. (*Sits, pause. He looks surprisingly...alone.*) You can't win 'em all, as they say. (*Pause.*) You can't help tryin', tho'. Once you pick one or two winners there's no holdin' y'back. Only...you can't expect others to understan' that. (*Pause.*) I never was a easy person to live with. (*Pause.*) That woman is oneuh the few good things that ever happen to me. An' yet the way I treat that girl sometimes... (*Sucks his teeth.*) ...shit. (*Pause.*) I never was easy to live with. (*Pause.*) It's not jus' the money, neither. Not always. It's the winnin' itself. The *uplift*...y'know what I mean? (*Brightening.*) Seein' or listenin' to them horses *poundin'* away, knowin' that you back the winner, watchin' them chalk up the results afterwards on the board in the bettin' shop - beau-ti-ful! Too beau-ti-ful. At such times, boy, I feel on *top*. Top, top! Everybody needs something to keep their spirits up. I done care if they happen to he royalty! They need that something to keep their spirits up.

(*Pause.*)

OSCAR: Okay, man, okay, I'll do it.

TONY: (*Blessing him.*) The Lord bless y', Oscar.

OSCAR: Boy, you're a real hustler...! A real sweet-talkin' man.

TONY: Who, me? Nah. Not me. (*But laughs all the same. Then.*) Anyway, anyway, Oscar, here's what I want you to do. I got fifteen poun's, right?

OSCAR: Fifteen poun's!

TONY: Tha's the lastuh the money.

OSCAR: You mean you ain' satisfy to lose mostuh the girl's money, you want to lose *all!*

TONY: Oscar, that's my business, Oscar. Okay? (*Pause.*) You see that red shirt you got on, Oscar, an' them red trousers? If I report you to the American Embassy, they'd arrest you as a communist. Immediately, if not sooner! (*Pause.*) As fo' y'trousers being so godalmighty tight - they sure to throw the book at y'! Add that to the fact that you black as well – well Jesus, boy, they'd have you in the Electric Chair by nightfall!

OSCAR: Boy, you too fanciful.

TONY: (*A moment's exhaustion, something.*) Yeah...? Fanciful? Then all I gotta say is that you haven't looked at the Yanks recently.
(*Pause.*)

OSCAR: Okay, so you got fifteen poun's to throw away...

TONY: Right! So what I want you to do is put five on one horse an' ten on another – I got it all written –

OSCAR: (*On his feet.*) Hold it! You said one bet! Now you tellin' me about 'five on one horse, an' ten on another'. What you take me for, man? Ladbrokes!

TONY: Will you sit down, Oscar? Will you flickin' siddown... (*Pause.*) There's a fiver in this fo' you if I win.

OSCAR: Bribery?

TONY: Call it your commission.

OSCAR: Well, tha's diff'rent. (*Sits.*) I'm y'man.

TONY: Right! Now they're both fav'rites so they're pretty safe horses, but done play them as doubles or anyuh that, right, even fav'rites can lose, right?

OSCAR: Okay, Okay.

TONY: Good. (*Pause.*) Naturally they won't pay much being fav'rites. Accordin' to Mrs Frazier's paper – I ain' even had a chance to go out an' buy a mornin' *paper* – anyway accordin' to her Mirror they're givin' three to one odds on bothuh them. Which should bring about sixty poun's if they both come in.

OSCAR: Nice. How much you owe Rita?

TONY: I'm not finish yet. I got another horse fo' you.

OSCAR: Another horse! Jesus, I'll be in there all day. I'll have to carry san'wiches.

TONY: Done talk crap, man. (*Pause.*) A twenty-to-one horse; I want you to put the whole sixty on it.

OSCAR: The whole amount? A twenty-to-one horse! Tha's…six by two…tha's…that's…over a t'ousan' *poun's*. (*Pause.*) Plus y'sixty back. Lord, tha's *money*, boy.

TONY: One thousan', two hundred an' sixty poun's. Less tax of course.

OSCAR: I like it, I like it. (*Pause. Doubt.*) But a twenty-to-one horse?

TONY: This horse boun' an' oblige to win. When I say it boun' to win, I mean it *can't* lose! There ain' no way this horse can lose. No way, no way.

OSCAR: Who say so!

TONY: I say so! Me. (*Pause.*) Oscar I had m'eye on this filly since las' season! They breed is to run a mile, they breed this horse *special.* One *exact* mile. No more, no less. Right? An' that horse runnin' today in the four ten at Goodwood. An' guess what's the four ten at Goodwood today?

OSCAR: A mile?

TONY: You better believe it.

OSCAR: Money, I smell money!

TONY: Now you see why I want so put as much bread on that horse as I can get my han's on.
(*Pause.*)

OSCAR: An' what's the nameuh this horse?

TONY: Lady Laughter.

OSCAR: (*On his feet again.*) You *MAD!* Lady Laughter! You're an *ASS,* boy! That horse is so *lazy* my own daughter could run away from it!

TONY: That horse is a dead cert!

OSCAR: That horse is a dead duck! Sixty poun's on Lady Laughter! Fo' that kinduh money you done need to bet on it, you could *buy* it.
(*Pause.*)

TONY: (*His faith a bit shaken.*) You dunno what y'sayin', boy. My mind tell me to bet on this horse.
(*OSCAR's laughter says exactly what he thinks of TONY's 'mind'.*)
Okay – okay, tell me what you got against it. If you know something I dunno, tell me. Done jus' stan' there laughin'.

OSCAR: Well fo' one thing, I know no self-respectin' jockey would even take it fo' a *walk*, much less ride it.

TONY: A concrete fact, Oscar! Give me one concrete fact against that horse.

OSCAR: It can't win: what more concrete fact you want than that?
(*Pause.*)

TONY: Oscar you're a blight. They oughta take you up to Heathrow airport an' put you on the nex' plane *outuh* here.
(*Pause.*)

OSCAR: I'm tryin' to save you money an' all the thanks I get is insults. If tha's not ingratitude, well, I dunno.

TONY: Oscar, I'm foamin' at the mouth, but I'm tryin' not to lose m'temper...!

OSCAR: Okay, okay, buddy, if you won't take advice.
(*Pause. TONY produces three fivers and a betting slip.*)

TONY: Fifteen poun's, right? An' I got it all written out here. Right? The fav'rite in the two o'clock, the fav'rite in the three ten, an' then the full sixty poun's on Lady Laughter in the four ten. You got that?

OSCAR: Yeah, I got it. It's your funeral. Personally buddy, I wouldn't put a wreath on that horse much less sixty poun's.

TONY: (*A warning.*) Oscar, done mess me about. (*Pause. A cry.*) I got no choice, I owe it to Rita...!

OSCAR: Okay, Tony, you know bet'.

TONY: (*Moving towards the door.*) Well, look I gotta get back down there. (*At door.*) She's pretty sick really. (*He doesn't open the door.*)

OSCAR: Tell her I'm sorry to hear that.

TONY: (*Almost to himself.*) She seem to have real bad luck that girl. (*Pause.*) You reckon maybe I shouldn't do it... have this bet, I mean...when she's so sick, y'know? (*Pause.*)

OSCAR: (*Embarrassed.*) It's your wife, man, I couldn't answer that.
(*Pause.*)

TONY: We been waitin' an' waitin' fo' that ambulance. We could've walked there by now. (*Pause.*) If you ain' got money, not even the ambulance wants to know.
(*He opens the door. They leave the room. Disappear down the passage. Pause.*
Blackout.)

Scene 2

The FLETCHERS' room. Summer. Evening.

TONY comes bounding into the room, newspaper in hand. He has just learnt that all his horses have won. He switches on light in room.

TONY: Oh God, oh God, boy...! (*Throws paper up in the air.*) Oh God, boy!
(*OSCAR approaches his door. Knocks. TONY opens it with a flourish.*)
Oscar! If you were a flag, I'd salute yuh!

OSCAR: Flag? What flag?
(*TONY shuts the door. Rushes over to glass-top table.*)

TONY: Put is right there! Right on top here. (*Wipes it with his hand.*) There, it's clean enough fo' any amountuh money.

OSCAR: You done want to sit down?

TONY: Thanks all the same, Oscar, but I live here, remember? Jus' forget y'*eti-ket* fo' once an' let's jus' see

the colouruh the bread. Or maybe they give you a
cheque, right?

OSCAR: (*Not exactly happy.*) Cheque? No, no cheque.

TONY: Good, I'm not fussy. (*Pause.*) Well?
(*Pause. OSCAR brings out some money. Lays out a hundred
pounds in ten pound notes. Pause.*)

TONY: What's that, Oscar? *Bus fare?*
(*Pause.*)

OSCAR: That's how much they gimme.
(*Pause.*)

TONY: What you mean 'tha's how much they gimme'! Even
nurses make more money than that. Even *black* nurses.

OSCAR: Tha's a hundred poun's there, man. Good British
money.

TONY: Okay, so you're a patriotic black Englishman – now
cut the foolin', where's ma money?

OSCAR: Tha's it.

TONY: What crap is this, Oscar?!

OSCAR: Will you jus' siddown, man, Tony.

TONY: I live here, Oscar!
(*Pause.*)

OSCAR: Okay, so I'll siddown.
(*Does so. Pause.*)

TONY: Jesus Christ Almighty, if I had a dog, he'd be
maulin' you right now. *I swear it.*

OSCAR: Will you let me explain, man, Tony!

TONY: Okay, okay, I'm all ears.
(*Silence from OSCAR.*)
Speak up, Oscar, I can't hear you.

OSCAR: Okay, okay, I bet the firs' two horses, y'know, the
fav'rites…

TONY: An' what?

OSCAR: An' they won. Sixty poun's less tax, they pay me.

TONY: So then I tole you to put the full sixty on Lady
Laughter to win, so what's the problem?

OSCAR: (*Rising.*) I felt sure the horse had no chance.

TONY: I done believe it…

OSCAR: I only put two poun's fifty on the horse.
(*Pause.*)

TONY: (*He still can't believe it.*) You jokin'. You got to be jokin'. But I tole you...!

OSCAR: I know, I jus' din' think the horse could walk, never mind run. (*He doesn't like the way TONY is looking at him. He backs away.*) Man, I sorry bad.
(*TONY has to sit on the bed.*)

TONY: I coulda got a lunatic. I coulda stop by the nearest nuthouse an' got me a lunatic, an' everything woulda been fine. Instead I had to rely on a rass like you. All the mental hospitals in this country to choose from an' *look who I pick*...Judas. I pick Judas Escariot.

OSCAR: I did it fo' Rita. Fo' bothuh you.

TONY: I mean, that money woulda help to see me outuh here.

OSCAR: I wanted to make sure you at least had fifty poun's to pay back Rita.

TONY: (*A cry.*) That money woulda help see me outuh here...!

OSCAR: Tony, man, I'm sorry.

TONY: That money woulda help see me outuh here!
(*And he suddenly erupts. He throws himself at OSCAR, and pins OSCAR's head in a hammer-lock, snarling and murderous as something from the forest.*)
Murder yuh – I'll murder yuh!

OSCAR: Jesus – m'neck – Tony...
(*The rest of his words degenerate into a series of strangled sounds. TONY seems bent on choking him to death. No one is playing games here.*)

TONY: Shut it! Shut y'mouth!
(*And draws back his fist as if he means so damage OSCAR's brain. But checks himself at the last moment. Pause. He releases OSCAR. OSCAR can hardly straighten up, not at first anyway. Pause. TONY tries to calm himself down.*)
You lucky...! I made a pact wit' m'self never to hit a fellow black man. (*Pause. He sits; worn down.*) That money was to help see me outuh here. (*Pause.*) She lost the baby, Oscar. M'wife jus' lost 'er baby. The doctors give 'er about three months to live.
(*Pause.*)

OSCAR: (*Close to breaking point.*) I'd give m'right arm…
m'arm. If it would help, I'd give m'right arm…! (*Pause.*)
M'arm, Tony. I'd give m'right arm.
(*Pause. TONY rises, goes to door, holds it open.*)
Ow, Tony. I feel so bad. Done sen' me away like this,
Tony. (*Pause.*) Tony. (*Pause. Abruptly.*) Everybody treats
me like I'm garbage. White people – black people…! I'm
NOT GARBAGE…! (*Pause.*) I'm not garbage. (*Pause.*) I
feel so bad. (*Pause.*) I'd give m'right arm.
(*Pause. OSCAR shuffles out. Pause. TONY crosses over to the
money; he seems to have no will, no volition left of his own.
He brushes the money off the table with a disinterested flick
of his fingers. Pause. His eyes rake the room: they reflect the
weight of the room.*)

TONY: (*A mumble.*) This room…this room.
(*Pause. He throws himself down on top of the bed. Pause. A
knock at his door. DENNIS. TONY sits up on she bed.*)
Get lost! Or I swear, they'll give me a knighthood fo'
murdering you…!
(*DENNIS knocks again. TONY leaps at the door. Swings it
open.*)
Oh it's you, Dennis, sorry!

DENNIS: Peace.
(*Both laugh loudly. DENNIS enters.*)

TONY: I thought is was Oscar.

DENNIS: You thought I was Oscar…!
(*TONY suddenly realizes the money is still on the floor.
DENNIS can hardly help noticing it, as well. TONY gets
down on all fours to collect it.*)
My God, Tony. You rob Barclay's Bank?
(*Pause. No reply from TONY.*)
Tony…?
(*TONY slowly rises to one knee. Holds the money against his
chest. He seems to he staring at something just out of reach.
Then.*)

TONY: It was supposed to be my insurance against white
people. God had other ideas. (*Pause.*) Never misses a
trick, does 'e?

(Pause. He gets to his feet. Puts money away in RITA's dressing table. DENNIS has found himself some place to sit.)

DENNIS: I come to enquire about Rita? How is she?

TONY: She loss the baby.

DENNIS: Oh no. Poor Rita.

TONY: Yeah, well, you can get used to anything.

DENNIS: How come you so hard, boy?

TONY: *(Angry.)* You studying Sociology at that Poly-tec-nic. I work in a factory. Tha's how come.

(Pause. DENNIS takes off his glasses. Studies them. Pause.)

DENNIS: *(Gravely.)* You make me sound like one o' them rich students. Onassis son-in-law. I work weekends, done forget. I'm not even a distant cousin of the King of Ethiopia.

TONY: I'm sorry, Dennis. It's just m'nerves talkin', man.

DENNIS: That summer job I've just finished... You think that was a joke? Compared to that job your job is paradise. For a start there's no such thing as a union when you work at Morgan's Dress Hire shop. My job was to press the clothes after the customers brought them back; frock coats and dress suits and dinner-jackets smelling of wine and sweat. I mean most times that's all we did to them, iron the damn things. No nonsense about them being dry-cleaned first or anyuh that. Just a good pressing an' we pass them on to the next customer. You talk about the size of this room, that room was so small this room would swallow it. An' no windows. As God above me, no windows...! A door so the shop, that's all. I use to iron with me shirt off. They din' call me Man Friday for nothing. An' to top it all they had a boiler in that room. *(He laughs.)* A boiler. Honest to God. *(Pause.)* I used to think I was going crazy. Heat...! Jesus, boy. I never was that hot in Trinidad. Never. *(Pause.)* Yet, it's not the heat I remember most. It's the sweat. When that hot iron mixed with all that sweat something jus' had to give. Me, in the end.

(Blackout.)

Scene 3

House in Shepherd's Bush. The FLETCHERS' room.

RITA is sitting propped up on the settee. TONY has bought a number of flowers in honour of her return. He has only been able so locate one vase so he has had to resort to a number of milk bottles. He still has not completed the stereo set. He has however built the amplifier now. The television set he has been repairing is gone. DENNIS is having coffee with them. A bottle of Lucozade and a glass on glass-top table.

TONY: I never heard nothing so crazy in m'whole life!

RITA: (*Great sigh.*) Try not to shout, Tony. (*Pause.*) I need a holiday an' I want so see Binkie. An' that's that. How much those flowers coss you? An' why milk bottles, if you done mine me askin'? Why milk bottles?

TONY: Done knock them, they're genuine antiques. From United Dairies.

(*RITA turns away, bored by him. Pause.*)

You sure you won't prefer to be in bed, girl?

RITA: (*A sigh.*) What? What's this now? Bed? What for? I'm comfortable enough here.

(*Short pause.*)

TONY: (*Quiet, sad.*) Suit y'self. (*Pause. Abruptly.*) You mean to go even if it kill you!

RITA: You sure you're sane, boy?

(*Pause. TONY stalks over so the bed. Starts changing his shoes.*)

DENNIS: Am, I think what Tony means Rita, is that, well, you're not exactly in the bestuh health, girl, an' Trinidad is so far away.

RITA: Dennis, the doctor let me outuh hospital because I really need a holiday, Dennis.

(*Pause. Both men look down at the floor. Pause.*)

Well, ain' that true? (*Pause.*) I haven't seen Binkie in months, Dennis. (*Pause.*) A woman's chil'ren are important to her. Men done understan' jus' how important. (*Pause.*) I jus' lost a baby. I need to be wit' Binkie. Fo' *my* own good. (*Pause.*) No man can understan' what an

abortion or a miscarriage can do to a woman. The effect
it can have on 'er.

(*Pause.*)

TONY: I understan' all that – but you can still wait an' see
how things go. Insteaduh rushin' off like Speedy Gonzales.
(*A cry.*) I mean suppose something was to happen to you,
Rita! F'Godsakes Rita, done do this to me...!

(*Pause. DENNIS embarrassed.*)

DENNIS: I think I'd better split, leave you two to be alone.

RITA: Done talk rot, Dennis. Stay an' have some more
coffee.

DENNIS: No. Thanks. (*Yawning.*) Gotta be off. (*Then.*) Tell
you what, if you get y'ticket an' things fixed up in time
fo' Tuesday an' if you haven't changed y'mind by then,
I'll give you a lift to the airport. Gimme a ring, okay?

RITA: You're an angel, Dennis.

TONY: Boy, whose side're you on, eh?

(*DENNIS laughs ruefully.*)

DENNIS: See you, Rita. Take care.

RITA: Bye Dennis.

(*DENNIS leaves the room. Steps into passage. TONY follows.
Closes door behind him. RITA turns her head away. She falls
into an abstracted state.*)

DENNIS: You got to tell her, man!

TONY: Keep y'voice down, Chrise.

DENNIS: You got so tell her.

TONY: You tell 'er, nuh . Go ahead.

(*Pause.*)

DENNIS: I know it's hard man, Tony, but you got no choice.

TONY: (*Not looking at DENNIS.*) Boy, I dunno what to do...
I jus' dunno what to do. (*Pause.*) Chrise, man, Chrise.

(*Pause.*)

DENNIS: Maybe the doctor, y'know, maybe he made a
mistake. Half the time doctors dunno what they're doing.

TONY: A mistake...! Wit' her luck. God hates us both too
much fo' that.

(*Pause.*)

DENNIS: (*Blurting it out.*) You should at least go with her!

TONY: To Trinidad. You know how much it costs, there and back. Eh? It's not the same as a day trip to Sout'end, sport.

DENNIS: Okay, okay. Then tell her an' get it over with. I'm sure she wouldn't go anywhere if she knew.

TONY: (*Almost too disgruntled to laugh.*) Boy, you dunno Rita. My wife is so stubborn mules queue up fo' her autograph. The only reason she never won a prize fo' stubbornness is because she's too stubborn to compete wit' other people.

DENNIS: Boy, you're too much. Be seeing you, man, Tony.

TONY: See yuh.

(*DENNIS goes. TONY returns inside. RITA is still just sitting there looking abstracted.*)

TONY: (*A bit unsure of her reaction.*) You okay, honey?
(*No reaction. Pause.*)
Why take things out on me, Rita?
(*Pause.*)

RITA: You got this place in a state again. (*Pause.*) What'd you do when I'm not here? Entertain all those jockeys that never win a race fo' you? (*Pause.*) An' do they always have to bring their horses along as well?
(*Pause.*)

TONY: (*Loudly.*) You're not goin' on any trip an' that's final!
(*Pause.*)

RITA: (*Unperturbed.*) I got to go, Tony.

TONY: Over m'dead body.

RITA: Done tempt me, boy.
(*They look at each other. Pause.*)
Maybe you care to tell me this, how you expec' the chile to come back if I done go fo' him? You plan to hire a nanny, perhaps?

TONY: He can come back the same way he went.

RITA: Wit' Mrs Gomes. Y'jokin' or what? She won't be back till December. You think I could live wit'out m'son fo' that long. What kinduh parent are you?
(*Pause.*)

TONY: Why not write y'mother an' ask 'er to bring him 'ome. Write an' invite 'er fo' a holiday. (*Pause.*) I done mine 'er stayin' a day or so. (*Pause.*) We can always sen' 'er out to work if she stay longer. They always need traffic wardens so she won't have to worry. (*Pause.*) She could even bring y'father if she done mine walkin' wit' him. A his difficult findin' him a job, though. Not much work about these days fo' a pensioner who flatly refuses to leave his wheelchair. (*He laughs boyishly.*) Lead me to the Palladium, I'm wasted here.

RITA: Tell me when y'finish *ramblin'* on an' I'll lead you to the *cemetery.* You'd really *waste* away there.
(*Pause.*)

TONY: I done fine anyuh this amusin' *neither*, believe me. None of is need ever'uve happened if you hadn' disobeyed me in the firse place!

RITA: Disobeyed you! Since when yo' m'father?

TONY: I still can't comprehend it...! The way your mine works! Why'd you go through wit' it?! What sortuh loser are you, girl!

RITA: (*A yawn, then.*) I done even know what yuh talkin' about.

TONY: The chile. That's what! The chile! (*Pause.*) You knew the danger – Jesus, Jesus, the doctor spelled is out fo' you – *no more children* – yet you went right ahead an' got y'self pregnant.

RITA: I can't believe it...! My name is not the Virgin Mary. I had some help, done forget that.
(*For a moment or two TONY seems stuck for words. Then.*)

TONY: You were fitted wit' a coil. A coil. It's supposed to be *at least* as effective as a chastity belt.

RITA: The maternity hospital's fulluh women who put their trust in the coil.

TONY: (*Low.*) Then women must be more stupid than they look.

RITA: (*Dagger-sharp.*) I beg y'pardon?

TONY: Nothing. I never said a word. (*Pause.*) Anyway, the point is you wanted the chile, you were detemined to have it. That's the point. You wouldn't even *hear* about an abortion. Chrise man, Chrise. Wit' your medical history you coulda had an abortion as easy as fallin' down the stairs.

RITA: (*Loudly.*) *Shut up.*

(*Pause. She gets up. Pours herself some Lucozade. Sits down again.*)

TONY: (*Sad.*) It's y'mentality. I done mean to hurt you honey, God knows, but it's y'mentality, that's what bothers me. Ow, Rita, you coulda died. You coulda died. You knew that, yet there was no gettin' through to you. (*Pause.*) All these months all this expense, girl, it need nevera happened, Rita. *Do you comprehend what I'm sayin'?* All that's happened these las' months – Binkie havin' to go home, the hospital, everything – none of it need ever'uve happened! (*Pause. A cry.*) Rita, I've had to pay fo' *your* stubborness...!

(*Pause.*)

RITA: (*A stranger.*) Leave me then. Go on. Why done you leave me, eh? If that's the way you feel. Jus' go. Bye, bye.

TONY: (*Quietly.*) Done say that, Rita.

RITA: (*Losing control.*) Leave me be! I wish to Christ you would jus' clear outab m'sight! You're always underfoot, *Jesus.* (*Pause.*) All fo' nothing...after four ripe months... an' now you come telling me about my mentality. Who the hell you think you are? (*Ugly.*) You can't make up fo' what I lost: you want it any more plain than that? (*Pause. Sad, trying to be less unkind.*) You are not enough...not any more, daddy.

(*Pause. TONY leaves the room, blindly. Pause.*)

Scene 4

The FLETCHERS' room. Night. TONY and RITA in bed. Darkness.

TONY: Rita. (*Pause.*) Rita. (*Pause.*) Rita...!

RITA: Boy, I'm trying to sleep.

(*Pause.*)

TONY: Are you okay?

RITA: (*Not particularly positive about it.*) I'm okay.
(*Pause.*)

TONY: I'll get y'medicine if it'll help you feel better.

RITA: I said I'm okay, give it a rest.
(*Pause.*)

TONY: I almos' finished the set. The stereo. You want to see it?

RITA: At two o'clock in the morning...! (*Pause.*) Not even Lassie should be awake at this hour.

TONY: I know, you feelin' bad, but Christ...!

RITA: Now where you off to?
(*Pause. Apparently he has got out of bed. Pause. The room is still in complete darkness.*)

TONY: Rita, what's gone wrong wit' us? What 'ave I done wrong, girl?

RITA: Boy, we have to discuss this now? Eh?
(*Pause.*)

TONY: I can't get through to you. This is no time fo' a... wall between us. (*Pause.*) Done lock me out, Rita. (*Pause.*) Please, please. (*Pause.*) Please, Rita. (*Pause.*) What've I done wrong, girl? (*A cry.*) Rita, ah'm fightin' fo' m'life, Rita!
(*Pause.*)

RITA: I can't be consoled... I refuse to be consoled.
(*Pause.*)

Scene 5

The FLETCHERS' room. Day. TONY alone in the room. At his work-bench. Soldering iron in hand repairing a transistor radio, He is wearing a matching shirt and tie, grey trousers; he is dressed to go with RITA to the airport. He has finally finished building the stereo set. The complete set is laid out on the floor and covered over by a dust sheet. Two suitcases, one larger than the other, packed and ready for RITA's departure. The door opens: RITA. She remains in doorway. She does not seem very well. She has bought a pair of shoes.

TONY: (*Rising.*) Are you mad, girl? Eh? Dennis will soon be here, you forget. (*Pause. He goes to her.*) Girl, you look like hell!

RITA: I'm okay.

(*But she has to hold on to him. Pause.*)

TONY: It start again?

RITA: I'm okay, I said.

(*Pause.*)

TONY: (*A cry.*) Why'd you go out!

RITA: (*Wan smile.*) In a few hours I plan to cross a mighty ocean, I should at lease be able to cross the street by m'self.

(*Pause. TONY helps her towards the settee. She spies covered-up stereo set.*)

What's that, Tony – a shroud? Who y'got under there – Vincent Price?

(*She sits gingerly. TONY moves away trying to find her medicine.*)

TONY: Where's y'medicine?

RITA: You finally finish it, the set? What you hidin' it for?

(*He gives her two of her tablets. With some Lucozade to wash them down. Pause.*)

RITA: (*Looking down at the floor, more to herself than to him.*) I nearly died the las' time. (*Pause.*) (*Still not looking at him.*) Did they tell you that? (*Pause.*) One more time like that an' they can sen' fo' the hearse an' the flowers…an' the man in the black suit who keeps his han's behin' his back. (*Pause.*)

TONY: You pack everything?

RITA: What? Nat'rally. Excep' fo' those shoes. That's how come I went out, I needed new shoes. You want m'mother to think you can't afford to buy me a proper pairuh shoes. You want 'er to think I'm married to a black Scotsman.

(*TONY's reaction is to suck his teeth.*)

How about you, you ready?

TONY: Sure, I'm only goin' to the airport. I won't be gettin' on the plane, so you done have to worry about that.

RITA: What're you gettin' at now?

(*And looks away: it's all such a drag. Pause.*)

TONY: (*Crying out.*) You can't even bear my company any more…! It's obvious. I'm not a complete ass! (*Pause.*)

Firse you're away fo' three months, then fo' nearly two weeks, an' now when you're finally home, what d'you do? You jump on the first plane to Trinidad! Obvious! I'm not a complete ass. A holiday trip, you call it. I call it grounds fo' divorce! (*Pause. Plaintive.*) Other women put their men firse. The way you treat me anyone would think you married the Hunchback o' Notre Dame. (*Pause.*) You'd rather go in hospital than be wit' me. (*Pause. A cry.*) If I was to get on that plane wit' you, you'd pay them to hi-jack it.

(*Pause. He stands before her, worn down.*)

RITA: Boy, I'm feelin' drained...y'understan', drained...too drained to go through a vaudeville act wit' you. Okay? (*Pause.*)

TONY: (*Nakedly.*) These days you never have time fo' me, Rita...! (*Pause. Hardly a joke as far as he is concerned.*) You're never aroun' when I need you. Even Count Dracula stays home in the daytime (*Pause.*)

RITA: I've been sick, in case you haven't noticed. (*Pause.*)

TONY: Even before you got sick you never had much time fo' me.

RITA: Done talk rot, boy. (*Pause.*)

TONY: Many's the time I try to touch your skin, an' I watch you draw away...like I had leprosy or something.

RITA: Rubbish. (*Pause.*) Sheer rubbish. (*Pause.*) Anyway I done go wit' other men, that's all that matters.

TONY: (*A cry.*) That's not enough...! I need joy too, an', an' warmth, man. A woman who's faithful but cold jus' faithful alone, but without juice or – joy. Oh God, such a woman is like ah marble egg: perfec' outside, a perfec' shape, but you can't get no nourishment from it. (*Pause.*) Well, say something, Rita. (*Pause.*) Rita, I'm so sickuh m'own company you got no idea. (*Pause. Anything to get through to her.*) I know it's not nice to say, but I want a companion not a hospital patient! (*Pause.*)

RITA: Thanks. Thanks a lot.
(*Pause.*)

TONY: I haven't been happy fo' months – years. An' you done even know it! I AM A HUNDRED PERCENT DISSATISFIED WIT' OUR MARRIAGE! God, Rita. (*Pause.*) Things used to be so diff rent. Coulda been diff'rent. (*Pause.*) You done seem to be able to give me what I need any more. (*Pause.*) Either you're never there or when you're there you're ambulance material. (*Ugly.*) Either way you're useless to me. Useless, useless! (*Pause.*)

RITA: (*Leaving settee.*) Boy, you're a bastard an' a half. (*She helps herself to more Lucozade.*)

TONY: (*Wearily.*) I am a hundred percent dissatisfied wit' our marriage. (*Pause.*) This room…this room. (*Pause.*)

RITA: (*Sitting down again.*) Okay, let's talk about this room shall we? You always goin' on about this room, well let's talk about it Mr Smartass.

TONY: (*A threat.*) Watch y'step, woman
(*Pause.*)

RITA: Is this the bes' we can do? As a chargehan' you make enough, not a pile, not too much, but you done do too badly, so how come this one room? Can't we do better? Eh?

TONY: Our Lord started out in a manger…!

RITA: An' look where he ended up, on a cross. (*Pause.*) Come on, let's have it out.

TONY: (*Walking away, low growl.*) You can't be sick in truth.

RITA: Come back here. Hide is the one thing you can't do in here. (*Then.*) We're always talkin' about y'gamblin', right? But what we never get down to is how long you been gamblin'. Right? (*Pause.*) You been gamblin' fo' so long even the horses should club together an' buy you a gold watch.

TONY: Joke. Big joke. Ask y'self this question, would I spen' so much time in the bettin' shop if I was gettin' the right odds at home?
(*Pause.*)

RITA: All I know is how much money you lost. Y'thrown away at least a fiver every week – fo' years now.

TONY: (*Holding his head in his hands.*) I'm talkin' about our marriage – God knows any way you look at it we got about as much future as the Titanic – yet this girl got nothing else on her mine but money.
(*Pause.*)

RITA: Five poun's, sometimes ten poun's. Its madness!

TONY: What're yuh talkin' about? Every week who loses ten poun's…! You're talkin' to a professional. A professional. (*In spite of himself.*) Not Donald Duck.

RITA: You make me sick. (*Pause.*) I could throw up. Jus' throw up. (*Pause.*) Five, ten poun's, time after time. You're lucky you're married to me, damn lucky. Most other women woulda been off by now. They wouldn't even bother to wake yuh up to say goodbye.
(*Pause.*)

TONY: (*Almost to himself.*) Women, boy. They never try fo' a knockout. They jus' cut yuh up. Scientifically. (*Pause.*) After that the only hope you got is that the ref might take pity on you…an stop the fight in time.

RITA: What yuh mumblin' about? (*Then.*) You know how much you threw away las' year? I figured it out Mr Sportsman. Know how much? Eh? (*Pause.*) Something like three hundred poun's. Three hundred poun's, Tony. Oh Lord. (*Pause.*) To some white people three hundred poun's is nothing but to people like us its the diff'rence between a proper place to live an' being stuck here like Bostik! (*Pause.*) You never stop goin' on about the house we could buy if you were a big-shot accountant: try thinkin' about the nice flat we could be in right now if you weren't such a big-shot gambler. (*Pause.*) What sortuh man would dump his wife in one room like this… Call y'self a man? Call y'self a man?
(*Pause.*)

TONY: An' you're supposed to be sick. Boy, it's good a thing you're not alive an' well, or I'd be done for. (*Then.*) Who'm I tryin' to kid? I'm done for now. The nex' time

that guy comes by shoutin' fo' scrap-iron, I'll jus' throw
myself on 'is cart an' 'is mercy.
(*Pause.*)

RITA: (*She can afford a little mercy now.*) Jus' can't take it, can
you? (*Pause.*) You take me too seriously, Tony. (*Pause.*)
Come on. I got a bit angry, so what? (*Pause.*) Boy, you
take me so seriously. (*Pause.*) Comeon, show me that set
you got buried under that shroud. (*Pause. Neither moves.
Loss.*) These days I ain't exactly good value m'self, am I?
(*Pause.*) I talk about you, what kinduh wife am I? I can't
even let you make love to me.
(*Weary laugh. Pause.*)

TONY: Yeah, well, this ain' exactly the bet' time to worry
about that.
(*Pause.*)

RITA: (*Sagging, for the first time.*) No, I suppose not. (*Pause.
Her head down.*) When I come back...if that's what you
want...

TONY: I can't hear a word.
(*Pause.*)

RITA: Come 'ere. (*Pause. He goes to her. She touches his hand.*)
I said when I return you can divorce me...if that's what
you want.

TONY: (*Moving away.*) What y'talkin' about... (*A cry.*) Jus'
how sick do you have to be before you wake up to how
sick you really are...!
(*Pause.*)

RITA: That sounds like double dutch to me.
(*Pause.*)

TONY: Use y'head fo' once in y'life. Doctors done let their
patients out to visit their relatives without havin' some
good, good reason. They're not in the travel business,
woman!
(*Pause.*)

RITA: What you tryin' to say, boy?
(*Pause.*)

TONY: I'm no doctor. I got nothing to say.
(*Pause.*)

RITA: It'll do me good, Tony. A holiday, goin' home, walkin' down Henry Street, seein' Binkie again, seein' m'chile again, it'll do me good... Boun' to do me good.

TONY: Jesus, Jesus.

(*He has to sit down. He hides his head in his hands. Pause.*)

RITA: We gotta keep believin', Tony, or we'll never make it. (*Pause.*) What's the matter?

(*He straightens up.*)

TONY: Nothing.

(*Pause.*)

RITA: I'll be back in a month's time. One month.

TONY: Yeah, sure.

(*Pause.*)

RITA: Tell you what would be nice, if on m'way back I could perhaps visit Guyana.

(*Pause.*)

TONY: (*Trying to focus.*) Eh...? Eh...? Guyana?

RITA: Sure, why not? A wife should visit her husband's birt'place at lease once in 'er life. (*Pause.*) Tell me about the seawall.

(*She flinches.*)

TONY: You okay?

RITA: I'm okay. I feel a bit... (*Pause.*) I'll be okay. (*Pause.*) Tell me about the seawall.

TONY: The seawall?

RITA: The Georgetown seawall, silly. You use to tell me about it. Tell me again, daddy.

TONY: Why the seawall...! It keeps the sea out, like any other seawall. You see one, you seen 'em all. (*Pause.*) Funny, I done even think about it anymore. (*Pause.*) It use to be a great place to take a chick at night. I mean if a chick allowed you to take 'er out on the seawall after nine at night, it was a pretty safe bet she'd let you in by half pas' nine! (*Pause.*) But it was in the afternoon, that's when you'd fine the most people out on the seawall. Aroun' six o'clock, it use to be like a promenade out there. A parade. Everybody would turn up on their bicycles. The girls firse. They'd park their bikes an' sit out on the wall an' wait for the boys, they'd wear their prettiest frocks. You'd see them all the way along the wall, birds on a fence…black chicks, brown chicks, Chinese. Indian, even one or two white chicks, all waitin' to see an' be seen. An' then the guys would arrive, some wit' sunglasses on, an' some wit' han'kerchiefs tied roun' their necks. I mean those guys use to look pretty sharp, you know what I mean, Loopy Loo…! They were pretty sharp guys an' they'd ride up an' down, up an' down in frontuh the girls, tryin' to chat them up, tryin' to pull a chick fo' Saturday night. But the girls would stay cool. They'd stay cool an' laugh among themselves an' play hard to get, the way girls do the worl' over. (*Pause.*) Later aroun' seven o'clock we'd all get back on our bikes an' head fo' home, makin' plans to meet again the followin' night, same time, same place. (*Pause. Wearily.*) I use to be so young, Loopy Loo. (*Pause.*) I knew nex' to nothing about white people. (*Almost in spite of himself.*) That's the kinduh ignorance that's real bliss, Loopy Loo. (*Pause.*) I use to be so young, girl, now I back horses that boun' an' 'blige to win, only how come they never do? (*Pause.*) How many years you reckon we got to live in this country before they stop callin' us immigrants? (*Pause.*) Eh, Loopy Loo? How many years?

RITA: Tony, there's something I been meanin' to ask you fo' some time now…done be angry but, I wish you won't call me Loopy Loo no more, Tony.

TONY: (*Involuntary.*) God, oh God. (*He squats down beside her, hugging her awkwardly, fiercely.*) Done go, Rita…! Ow Rita.

RITA: Y'hurtin' me.

(*She holds him off. Pause. Struggles to her feet.*)

I gotta go. Be sensible, there's no two ways about it. (*Pause. She crosses to the covered-up set.*) Can I see y'set now? (*Pause.*) Come on. Or are you gettin' the queen to unveil it?

TONY: (*Almost in spite of himself.*) I was thinkin' of gettin' one of yuh relations. Y'half mad uncle, perhaps. The one who sleepwalks so much at night he's got to take a map to bed wit' 'im to help him fine his way back in the morning. (*Pause.*) I'll even provide a fancy ribbon fo' 'im to cut when the time comes. Wit' any luck he might get so carried away he might cut his own throat as well.

RITA: Boy, why you done appear on Tee Vee? We could turn y'off then. (*She unveils the set. Turntable, amplifier, two large loudspeakers.*) Oh Tony, it's beau-ti-ful. (*Pause.*) Boy, what you want wit' any bettin' shop when you can build something like this? Eh? (*Pause.*) Put a record on. (*Pause.*) Once you can build something like this the odds are in our favour, Tony.

(*He puts on a record. Pause.*)

TONY: Not a bad sound at all, even if I say so m'self.
(*DENNIS arrives in hallway. Knocks. TONY turns set off. Pause.*)

RITA: You make me feel proud, proud, Tony.
(*Pause.*)

TONY: (*Wry.*) Yeah, well, better late than never.
(*Pause. She takes his hands in hers. Touches her lips to them. DENNIS knocks again.*)

TONY: (*Not looking away from RITA.*) It's open, Dennis.
(*DENNIS enters.*)

DENNIS: What's up? Y'ready?

RITA: (*Not looking away from TONY.*) Come in, Dennis, I'm all ready. (*Then.*) Keep at it, Tony. The odds can only get better.
(*Pause. TONY puts on his jacket. RITA has kept her coat on throughout this scene. DENNIS takes larger suitcase. TONY takes smaller one. He moves to help RITA. She prefers to walk with as little help as possible. All three leave the room.*)

The End.

ALTERATIONS

Characters

BUSTER

COURTNEY

WALKER HOLT

MR NAT

HORACE MOORE

DARLENE HOLT

Alterations was first performed at the New End Theatre on 14 August 1978 with the following cast:

BUSTER, Trevor Butler

WALKER, Don Warrington

HORACE, Lloyd Anderson

DARLENE, Elizabeth Adare

It was subsequently revised, and the new version, as published here, was performed at Stratford East on 30 January 1986, with the following cast:

BUSTER, Allister Bain

COURTNEY, Gary Beadle

WALKER, Rudolph Walker

MR NAT, Peter Halliday

HORACE, Jim Findley

DARLENE, Marsha Millar

ACT ONE

Scene 1

The room has been turned into a tailor's shop. The shop is called 'Alterations.' It is one of those tailor shops around Carnaby street that the local boutiques use when they need alterations done in a hurry. It is up three flights of stairs.

What is essential: two sewing machines: two ironing boards and irons. There is a third ironing board standing folded up in a corner – an old, battle-scarred ironing board. A tailors dummy, pairs of scissors, etc. There is a certain amount of clothing about the shop, stuff to be collected, stuff to be altered, on hangers or in carrier bags. A rack of dresses on hangers. One or two dresses thrown over chairs. There is a small portable TV set: a good cassette recorder and a number of cassette tapes. A broom. Pictures of blues singers around the room – Son House, Bessie Smith, Charlie Patton etc. lots of rubbish on floor.

There is a small room at the back (off) where they make tea. It also leads to the toilet.

BUSTER and COURTNEY in shop. BUSTER on telephone. Back to audience. A burly forty year old West Indian. COURTNEY is sweeping up. Well, at least he has a broom in his hands. COURTNEY is a black youth.

BUSTER: (*On phone.*) Hello, maternity ward, please!…is dat de maternity ward? …My name is Buster, Buster Gibbs, she had it yet? …M'wife, m'wife, she had 'er baby yet?… (*COURTNEY stops sweeping to listen to BUSTER's conversation.*) Mrs Hortense Gibbs…well, what's the hold up about? …okay, okay, ah'll try again later, she might have better luck by den…thank yuh, nurse…sorry, ah mean, sister. (*BUSTER hangs up. He looks at COURTNEY. More a plea than a command.*) Courtney, we haven't got all day, man! (*COURTNEY gives him a look. But he returns to his sweeping. BUSTER picks up a pair of jeans that need to be taken in. He sits at his machine. His back is to COURTNEY. COURTNEY sneaks up behind BUSTER, sweeping.*)

77

COURTNEY: Move! Move!

(*BUSTER jumps up.*)

BUSTER: Boy, you too rude!

(*COURTNEY laughs. BUSTER rounds on COURTNEY.*)
What's so funny, Courtney? Walker will be here soon,
an' –

COURTNEY: (*Interrupting.*) Why you always stick up for
Walker? Anybody would think it was your shop.

BUSTER: Walker's my friend. We came over on the same
boat. (*Then.*) Get on wit' the sweepin'.

(*COURTNEY ignores BUSTER's command.*)

COURTNEY: So wha' happenin' Buster? Let's go for a
drink after work tonight. Dat pub near me.

BUSTER: Dat pub? Dese days, I don't go anywhere near
Limewood Estate, muchless dat pub.

COURTNEY: What's wrong with Limewood Estate?

BUSTER: You boys too hard fo' me.

COURTNEY: Boys?

BUSTER: Yout's. You too hard.

COURTNEY: Dese days you got to be hard to survive.

(*BUSTER sucks his teeth.*)

BUSTER: Boy, you too much fo' me.

(*WALKER comes bursting in. WALKER is West Indian,
fashionable suit, tie. A man with lots of energy. Same age as
BUSTER. He is carrying a number of pairs of trousers.*)

WALKER: Courtney – give me a hand, quick, quick. Go
down to Mr Nat's car – bring in all the trousers in the
car (*To BUSTER.*) Buster, I hold in my hand the answer
to all our problems.

BUSTER: A pair of trousers?

WALKER: Correction: a number of pairs of trousers.
(*Then.*) Courtney, you still here? Get on wit' it. I don't
want Mr Nat to come in here.

COURTNEY: Why? You ashamed of us?

WALKER: Courtney!

COURTNEY: Okay, Okay.

(*COURTNEY starts to leave the room. And runs into MR
NAT who is coming in.*)
Oops! Too late, Walker.

(*NAT enters. JEWISH. Though in his fifties he is a sporty,
athletic sort, or at least that is his image. He wears a sports
jacket with leather patches at the elbows and a cravat at his
throat. Has a loud, almost theatrical voice. An abrupt, insecure
laugh. MR NAT takes in the room. He also tries to catch his
breath, after three flights of stairs.*)

MR NAT: Walker! Those stairs. (*He pants, then.*) So this is it?
Not exactly Yves Saint Laurent is it? (*To COURTNEY.*)
You must be Buster.

COURTNEY: No, I must not be Buster. (*He points to
BUSTER.*) He's Buster, I'm Courtney.

MR NAT: Sorry. (*Abrupt laugh.*) So sorry.

WALKER: Courtney, the trousers!
(*COURTNEY glares at WALKER. Then he goes. WALKER
turns to BUSTER.*)
Um, Buster. We have Mr Nat to thank for all dese
trousers.

BUSTER: (*Not impressed.*) So…?

WALKER: (*To MR NAT.*) Buster here is a regular genius wit'
a sewin' machine.

BUSTER: (*Sotto voce, mimicking WALKER.*) Buster here is a
regular genius with a sewin' machine.

WALKER: (*Fixing BUSTER with a withering look.*) He's also
a flippin' echo.
(*MR NAT continues to look around the room. He is not very
impressed. COURTNEY had not finished sweeping, so there
is still a lot of junk on the floor.*)

MR NAT: A bit of a tip, isn't it, this place? I hope I'm
doing the right thing, Walker.

WALKER: (*A bit apprehensive.*) What d'you mean, Mr Nat?

MR NAT: Well, it's quite a large order, you know. All those
trousers. What makes you think you can handle this job?

WALKER: Mr Nat, all we're talkin' about is alterin' a few
trousers, not Open Heart Surgery.

MR NAT: Yes, but are you bitin' off more than you can chew?
Young Panos tells me, you're not very reliable, sometimes.

BUSTER: Panos is a friggin' crook. He loves to bad mouth
Walker!

WALKER: Okay, Buster, okay. (*To MR NAT.*) Young Panos
owes me money. So he'll say anything.

MR NAT: I don't know which of you to believe. You or Panos.

BUSTER: You callin' my spar a liar?

MR NAT: No, no, oh God, no.

(*COURTNEY comes back in, bearing a large stack of trousers. And MR NAT is in his way.*)

COURTNEY: Move! Move!

(*COURTNEY knocks into MR NAT. MR NAT goes flying.*)

WALKER: Courtney!

COURTNEY: Well, I warned him to move.

(*COURTNEY puts down the trousers. WALKER sighs. He helps MR NAT to his feet.*)

WALKER: You okay, Mr Nat?

(*MR NAT pulls free from WALKER.*)

MR NAT: Is this a place of business, or a gym?

WALKER: (*An apology of sorts.*) Sometimes, things get a bit hectic in here, Mr Nat.

(*MR NAT gives WALKER a look as if to say 'a bit hectic?' WALKER turns to COURTNEY.*)

Is dat all the trousers from Mr Nat's car?

COURTNEY: Yeah, that's it.

WALKER: Right. I got another job for you. I'll fix Panos. (*He indicates the rack of dresses.*) See dose dresses dere. Take dem over to dat Greek shop on the Kings Road.

COURTNEY: 'Lemnos'?

WALKER: Dat's the one. Ask for Mr Panos. He owes me money. Fifty dollars in all. Courtney, I don't care how you get it, jus' get me my money. We understan' each other?

COURTNEY: Licks! Licks! I'll put some discipline in 'im.

BUSTER: Walker!

WALKER: No, Buster. If Panos wants to play rough, I'll show him rough. Right, Courtney?

COURTNEY: Right!

(*COURTNEY goes with the rack of dresses. MR NAT looks at WALKER.*)

MR NAT: What a very cavalier way you have of doing business, Walker. (*Then.*) It reminds me, though…this whole place reminds me.

WALKER: What?

MR NAT: I started off in a place like this.

WALKER: Den you know how hard it is...

MR NAT: Yes. Yes. (*Almost to himself.*) Sometimes I forget...
(*A beat. Then.*) But I got out. I had what it takes. Do you
have what it takes, Walker? (*Pause.*) Gotta go now. I have
an eleven o'clock appointment, then a business lunch.

WALKER: A business lunch? I should be so lucky.

MR NAT: (*Waving his finger at WALKER, a warning.*) I'm
going to keep an eye on you, Walker. G'bye. (*MR NAT is
going.*)

WALKER: G'bye, Mr Nat.
(*BUSTER remains silent. WALKER pokes him. BUSTER
perks up.*)

BUSTER: Yeah, Goodbye.
(*MR NAT goes. BUSTER turns to WALKER.*)
I don't like dat man.

WALKER: Why? He's jus' a businessman. (*Then.*) Beggars
can't be choosers, Buster. If only we can handle enough
of dese trousers by tomorrow night, we'll be laughin'.
I could make dat downpayment on dis shop. Easy, easy.
An guess who we got to thank fo' our good fortune. A
Japanese importer. He turned up at Mr Nat's office dis
mornin' an' bought up de whole flickin' warehouse.
Every gaddamn pair uh trousers! Yuh like it? My friend,
if it's not de Arabs buyin' up Englan', it's de Japanese.
Anyway, de Tokyo gentleman wants the trousers ready
by five o'clock tomorrow. An' dat's the trouble. Mr Nat's
trousers are made for guys like dis. (*WALKER walks
around on tiptoe.*) Not guys like dis. (*WALKER gets down
on his knees and starts walking on his knees.*)

BUSTER: Rass, get up, Walker!
(*WALKER stands up.*)
Boy, you're what's known as a nut-case. A fruit 'n' nut
case.

WALKER: Anyway, dat's where we come in. Our job is to
alter all dese trousers. Fo' guys who walk like dis...! (*And
WALKER gets down, walking on his knees again.*)

BUSTER: Walker!
(*WALKER gets up. He shares out the trousers.*)

WALKER: Here, some fo' you. Some fo' me.

(*They start at their respective sewing machines.*)

BUSTER: How much 'e wants dem taken up? De bottoms?

WALKER: Six inches.

BUSTER: Six! God, boy, dem Japanese small.

WALKER: Dey might be small but dey're everywhere.

BUSTER: Is dese all de trousers?

WALKER: No, dey'll be more. But we're not the only ones he's got doin' dis. He got Panos as well. An' dem two pale, good lookin' white boys who like to touch everybody's bottom when dey pass by.

BUSTER: In odder words, we still in trouble.

WALKER: Dat's right. He's got a whole heap of trousers, but he's only givin' dem out to the ones who can do the job de quickes'.

BUSTER: So all we got to do is kill ourselves out.

WALKER: An' we can have all de trousers we want.

BUSTER: Nice guy dat Mr Nat. Big hearted.

WALKER: It's business, banner.

BUSTER: Yuh know how many trousers we'll have to alter to make de kind uh money yuh need. We'll be here all night. My wife will divorce me an name you as de odder woman.

WALKER: (*Lightly.*) Ah'm glad you can joke about it, Buster. (*Then.*) Banner, ah doan intend to go back to workin' in a factory. Not ever again, sport. I had enough of factories. Remember Old Street, eh?

BUSTER: Old Street, boy. Old Street.

WALKER: Buster, my own shop… Nice, nice. An' now jus' when I almos' got it in de palm of my han', ah find ah might not be able to hold on to it after all. Blasted estate agents! Findin' dat extra thousand pounds is goin' to kill me.

BUSTER: You'll do it, you'll be successful, you'll see.

WALKER: How's yuh wife? She had her baby yet?

BUSTER: My wife? Boy, my wife is an artist when it comes to being late. If she has dat baby before next Christmas, ah don't think ah'll ever get over the shock.

WALKER: Pass me dem scissors.

BUSTER: Walker...! Get somebody to 'elp us or we're gonna be signin' on fo' Social Security.

WALKER: Be calm.

BUSTER: Ah am calm.

(*Pause.*)

WALKER: Ah've already done something about our predicament. Ah've got somebody.

BUSTER: Who?

WALKER: Where's dat black t'read? We got a least a hundred spools uh black t'read yet everytime I want some black t'read ah can't find none.

BUSTER: It's right in front of you.

WALKER: Oh.

BUSTER: Who?

WALKER: Doan shout. Horace.

BUSTER: Horace? Horace Moore? But you hate the guy.

WALKER: Dat's not true. Ah admit ah can't stand de man but ah doan hate 'im.

BUSTER: Well he sure doan like you. He never has nothing good to say about you.

WALKER: Jealousy. Plain jealousy.

BUSTER: (*Relishing it a bit.*) He says since yuh got dis shop you act like youse part of de white establishment.

WALKER: If he thinks ah'm part of the white establishment now when all ah've done is rent dis place, what's 'e gonna say about me when ah buy it? (*Then.*) Anyway. How come they always attack me? Guys like Horace. How come nobody ever has anything bad to say about you? Why only me?

BUSTER: Maybe dey tryin' to tell you something. That youse a shit. (*He smiles.*) No offence of course.

WALKER: (*Pleased.*) Banner, flattery will get you nowhere. (*WALKER indicates the cassette recorder.*) Put on dat cassette recorder for me.

BUSTER: Why me? Ah'm not yuh slave.

WALKER: I doan think you're my slave, slave. (*WALKER is pleased with himself over that one.*)

BUSTER: The cassette is nearer to you.

WALKER: Jus' put on de friggin' cassette recorder.

BUSTER: (*Pointing to recorder.*) Dere it is. You put it on. Maybe if it was Rhythm 'n' Blues or Reggae. But dat mournful noise, no way.

WALKER: Blues is good fo' you.

BUSTER: Rhythm'n'Blues makes you want to get up an' dance. Blues makes you want to cut yuh throat. Blues is de sort uh sound a toothache might make if it could sing.

WALKER: Put on dat music for me, an' give yuh mout' a rest.

(*BUSTER just sucks his teeth. Pause. WALKER Crosses to recorder. WALKER switches on. Recorder: Black Snake Moan' by Blind Lemon Jefferson... WALKER returns to his sewing machine.*)

Listen to that man moan!

BUSTER: He's moanin' awright. Soun's like 'e got indigestion.

WALKER: It's called 'Black Snake Moan'. It's about a trouser snake.

BUSTER: Dirty beast!

(*They laugh. Phone rings. BUSTER answers.*)

BUSTER: 'Alterations'...oh, yeah, hold on... (*To WALKER.*) It's Liz.

(*WALKER switches off cassette. He takes phone.*)

WALKER: (*Into phone.*) Hello, Blondie...busy?...yeah, ah'm a bit busy, a whole lot busy...no, no, no you know ah love to hear yuh voice...how you feel today, after las' night...still feel sore?

(*He gives a little laugh. BUSTER overhearing the conversation, laughs as well.*)

...one thing yuh got to admit, baby, ah'm not the boy nex' door...what?... tonight?...well ah'm not too sure about tonight... Liz, doan start, please...ah have to work late, dat's why... Liz it's not true ah'm always busy when you want to see me, it's jus' today an tomorrow are important to me... Liz, look, I'll call you back later, okay?...yes, yes I do...because Buster is here an' he's listenin' to every gaddamn word ah say, so ah can't say ah love you, not wit' him listenin' in like a bloody spy.

BUSTER: (*Loudly.*) Dat's a lie! Ah haven't heard a word!

WALKER: G'bye, baby. I'll ring you later. (*He hangs up.*)

BUSTER: So tell me…how does yuh wife take all of this?

WALKER: Darlene is okay. We get along fine, as long as we doan live together.

BUSTER: Soun's like you an' yuh wife got a perfec' recipe fo' marriage.

WALKER: Ah'll never divorce 'er. We jus' can't live togedder, dat's all.

BUSTER: You doan help.

WALKER: What yuh mean?

BUSTER: Not what, who.

WALKER: Boy, Liz din have nothing to do wi' me an' my wife breakin' up. (*Crosses to cassette recorder.*) Ah know you doan like Liz, but fair's fair… Let's hear some more of dat blues. (*He puts recorder on again.*)

(*HORACE MOORE enters. HORACE is older than the other two men. Some people will tell you that HORACE is crazy. He certainly is an extrovert. He wears a gold earring in one ear. Smokes a fat, tycoon-sized cigar. He is liable to do anything. He whispers, shouts, makes faces. Braying laugh. Can be a buffoon or a tyrant. He wears a suit – a suit that has seen better days. He adopts a sort of W.C. Fields' voice.*)

HORACE: Damn, what is all dat bellyachin'! Sounds like de man's in agony. Operate immediately. (*HORACE turns off the cassette.*)

WALKER: Horace, who asked you to turn dat off?

HORACE: My dear sir, it sounded like somebody was rapin' a man. If dere's one thing in life ah can't stand it's to hear a grown man being raped.

WALKER: Ah'll have you know dat was Blind Lemon Jefferson.

HORACE: Oh, well, dat explains why 'e was cryin'. Blindness is no joke. (*He brays.*)

WALKER: The Black Man's answer to W.C. Fields.

HORACE: So, my good man, how're things?

BUSTER: (*To WALKER.*) See. What'd I tell you. A mental case.

HORACE: Well, here ah am. All ready to help you two out. Ah'm not only beautiful, ah've got a heart of gold as well.

WALKER: Take my advice . Gold being what it is dese days ah'd pawn it if ah were you.
(*A beat.*)
Den at lease yuh could buy yuhself a proper suit.

HORACE: (*To BUSTER.*) You're witness, he's de one started first.

BUSTER: Look, ah don't want you two getting' at each throats de minute yuh see each other.
(*A beat.*)
We'll never get done in time.

HORACE: Have no fear, Papa Horace is here.

WALKER: Horace, before yuh start, yuh understan' the conditions. It's fo' two days. An' tonight we work til ten o'clock. Until ten tonight. Okay. Ah an't pay you until the end uh de month. For de down payment on this shop, I need another thousan' pounds. So ah'm countin' on the money ah make on dese trousers. Yuh follow me? Ah will pay you. Dat's a prom'ise. But not immediately. What do yuh say?

HORACE: Goodbye! (*Pretends to walk out. Stops.*) Nah, ah'm only jokin'. Ah'll help. But I got a condition as well. If yuh can't pay me until de end uh de month yuh'll have to pay extra fo' my services. Fifty pounds extra. No, make it a hundred pounds.
(*A beat.*)

BUSTER: (*To WALKER.*) Did you hear dat?

WALKER: (*Not taking his eyes from HORACE.*) Doan worry, Horace. Ah'll pay yuh. Every gaddamn penny. (*Quietly.*) You son uva bitch.
(*A beat.*)

HORACE: Yuh want my help or not?
(*A beat.*)

WALKER: Banner, a promise, ah won't forget dis.

HORACE: (*To BUSTER, with a nod in WALKER's direction.*) Ungrateful, ain' 'e?
(*WALKER grabs up two or three pairs of trousers. He walks up to HORACE. Close. As if to hit him. Instead he bungs trousers in HORACE's hands.*)

WALKER: Here. Get to work.

(*HORACE sits at WALKER's sewing machine. Begins to work.*
Blackout.
In the darkness, a blues is heard.)

Scene 2

Lunchtime. HORACE and COURTNEY (he is back now) are watching horse racing on the portable TV. WALKER and BUSTER are both out.

Most of the first pile of trousers have been altered, WALKER has taken them away to get more pairs.

We hear the TV ANNOUNCER quoting the betting prices on the horses. Both BUSTER and HORACE have mugs of coffee at hand. HORACE eating a cheese roll.

ANNOUNCER: Tudor Mate nine to two now. Gone from four to one to nine to two. Belling seven to one. Tim's Delight also at seven to one.
(*The race will, of course, be a real television broadcast, but the following gives some idea of their reactions.*)
They're under orders, they're off, Tim's Delight is very fast away… Tim's Delight disputing it with Belling and Volume One.

HORACE: Ride, ride, ride Tim's Delight!

ANNOUNCER: Tudor Mate against the rails.

COURTNEY: Watch dat horse! Watch dat Tudor Mate!
(*BUSTER returns, with a long breadstick. He sees HORACE and COURTNEY.*)

BUSTER: (*To COURTNEY, displeased.*) So you're back? What took you so long?

ANNOUNCER: It's Tudor Mate on the rails, Belling in the centre, and Tim's Delight on the outside…

BUSTER: (*To COURTNEY.*) I see you've met Horace.

HORACE: Buster, ah can't hear gentleman! Horse racin' is de Sport Of Kings. A way of life to be savoured in silence.

ANNOUNCER: As they race towards the half way marker it's Ron Miller on Tudor Mate disputing it with Tim's

Delight. With the white face of Belling lying third. Volume One also trying to make headway behind the leaders.

HORACE: That damn Ron Miller – he's de only man I fear in this race.

ANNOUNCER: As they come inside the five furlong marker, it's Tim's Delight who hits the front now.

HORACE: Now yuh talkin'.

COURTNEY: Come on, Tudor Mate.

HORACE: (*To COURTNEY.*) Judas! Traitor!

ANNOUNCER: Tim's Delight and Tudor Mate dispute the lead. Now Tudor Mate has regained the lead. Tim's Delight second.

HORACE: Goddamn horses!

(*BUSTER, meanwhile, has cut his breadstick lengthwise, and is making a giant cheese'n'ham sandwich.*)

ANNOUNCER: Tudor Mate two lengths in front now, well inside the final furlong and it's Tudor Mate going further and further away from Tim's Delight and Belling. Tudor Mate going well clear! Tudor Mates wins easily. Belling second. Third comes Tim's Delight. Then Volume One. So a very, very comfortable win for Tudor Mate!

(*HORACE switches off the set.*)

HORACE: Fuck the sport of kings! (*Then.*) Never…

(*Produces a betting slip and tears it up.*)

Never again. My good man, ah'll never bet on another horse.

(*HORACE sees BUSTER's sandwich. He does a double take.*)

Mercy, mercy! What have you got there, my good man?

BUSTER: Dis is what yuh call a san'witch.

HORACE: A sandwich? Looks more a double decker bus if yuh ask me.

(*BUSTER takes a mighty bite out of his sandwich. Chews. Then reaches for the telephone. He dials. Then.*)

BUSTER: (*Into phone.*) Hello, de maternity ward, please…

HORACE: Buster, ah hear your wife is havin' a baby. Only one question I have for you. How come? (*Very funny to him.*) How Come!

(*COURTNEY laughs.*)

BUSTER: (*Into phone.*) ...Dis is Buster Gibbs, has m' wife had de baby yet? No?...okay, ah'll try again later.
(*BUSTER hangs up. HORACE lights a fresh cigar.*)

HORACE: (*Abruptly. Apropos of nothing.*) Jamaica! Las' year dis time ah was over in Jamaica.

BUSTER: We know. Every time I see yuh, yuh tell me about it.

HORACE: No matter, dat won't stop me tellin' you again. Ah went dere to set up a film.

COURTNEY: A film?

BUSTER: (*To HORACE.*) You?

HORACE: Why not? Why else you think I smoke dese fat cigars. Ah'm not jus' a tailor. Ah'm a film wheeler-dealer in my spare time.

BUSTER: In yuh spare time, eh? A wheeler-dealer?

HORACE: Ah think you're tryin' to say you doan believe me. Am ah right?

BUSTER: (*Sucking his teeth.*) Yuh rass. Films. You? Ab doan mind yuh lyin' a bit but dis is ridiculous.

HORACE: (*As if he is secretly laughing at BUSTER.*) Boy you doubt me? Am ah not known for my integrity? Doan answer that.

COURTNEY: What's dis film about?

HORACE: About a tailor.

BUSTER: A tailor? Who wants to see a film about a tailor?

HORACE: Other tailors!

COURTNEY: When is all dis gonna happen?

HORACE: Well, de deal isn' quite settled yet.

BUSTER: Over a year an' it's not settled yet? Oh Yes?

HORACE: My backers are trying to get Dousollini.

BUSTER: Douso-who?

HORACE: (*A bit pompous.*) Surely even you have heard of Dousollini? Famous Italian director.

BUSTER: Am. Yes, sure. Din 'e do dat...am, film.

HORACE: Dat's right. Dat Italian film. Dat's de sort of thing Italian directors have a tendency to do. Italian films.
(*BUSTER give HORACE a look. BUSTER returns to his sewing machine.*)

BUSTER: Yuh rass. De sooner dey lock you up, de better.
(*DARLENE HOLT enters. DARLENE is WALKER's wife she is not a bouncy, little girl but a woman who gives the impression of being rather irrepressible. Unstoppable. She is far more complicated than she seems. Having to bring up her child alone is no joke. Also she feels partly to blame for the failure of her marriage.*)

DARLENE: (*Appearing, unstoppable, almost as if she is looking for a fight.*) Where is he? Where is dat husban' of mine?

BUSTER: Darlene?

DARLENE: Why yuh soun' so surprised? 'Darlene?' Like Ah'm a ghost or something.

HORACE: Mercy, mercy. She's a fine piece of prime steak, ain' she?

DARLENE: Courtney. It's a good thing ah know Horace used to be a butcher before he became a tailor, or I might take offence. Anyway, what you doin' here, Horace?

HORACE: Slummin'. (*Funny to him.*) Slummin'.

DARLENE: Slummin', eh? (*Then.*) Is that a new shirt you have dere?

HORACE: You like it?

BUSTER: A new shirt? (*He crosses to HORACE. He opens HORACE's jacket to take a better look.*) You call this ole thing a new shirt? (*He tugs at HORACE's shirt like it's a rag.*)

HORACE: What the hell you doin?

BUSTER: Dat ain't no new shirt. If you want to talk about shirts look at Walkers shirts.

COURTNEY: (*To DARLENE.*) Notice how he always behaves like he's Walker's publicity agent.

BUSTER: (*Annoyed.*) At lease Walker knows how to dress which is more dan Horace does.

DARLENE: Walker dresses too much like a peacock.

HORACE: (*To BUSTER.*) Yuh hear dat. She means I'm the one who dresses more the way a man should.

BUSTER: She never said dat, yuh ass you.

DARLENE: Buster, how come you haven't even asked me how I am, or nothing?

BUSTER: Okay, how are you?
(*She smiles at him. A beat. Then she turns to COURTNEY.*)

DARLENE: There was a time when Buster quite fancied me. (*To BUSTER.*) Didn't you, Buster.

BUSTER: Well, you're not an ugly woman.

HORACE: (*Funny to him.*) But you're an ugly man!

BUSTER: Give yuh mout' a rest. Okay, boy?

(*A beat.*)

DARLENE: Come on, you two.

(*A beat.*)

HORACE: How is Janet?

DARLENE: Little terror. She's worse dan a boy.

HORACE: Funny, ah had a dream a couple of nights ago. She was in the dream.

BUSTER: Janet?

DARLENE: (*To HORACE, shutting him up.*) You had a dream, did you? Oh yes.

HORACE: Forget it, forget it.

DARLENE: (*Changing the subject.*) Where's my husban'? Don't he work here anymore?

BUSTER: (*To her.*) He's gone to see Mr Nat.

DARLENE: Mr Who?

BUSTER: Mr Nat. A gentleman of the Jewish faith.

(*WALKER returns. With many more trousers, practically hidden behind a hill of trousers.*)

DARLENE: Oh God. What is dis? My husban' has finally gone completely mad.

WALKER: Darlene? (*He deposits all the trousers on the floor.*)

DARLENE: Why is everybody so surprised to see me? Am I supposed to be dead? Cremated? What?

WALKER: No work today?

DARLENE: I lost my job.

(*WALKER starts sharing out the trousers for himself, HORACE and BUSTER.*)

WALKER: (*Working.*) Ah'm sorry, baby. But we're busy, okay? (*To COURTNEY.*) Courtney, where you been all dis time? What's the use of me employin' a van driver, if I got to do my own fetchin' an' carryin'?

COURTNEY: Dat man Panos kept me waitin'.

WALKER: Skip the excuses. Where's my money?

HORACE: (*To BUSTER, about WALKER.*) He's gettin' worse, ain' he?

(*COURTNEY hands over the money to WALKER. WALKER counts the money.*)

COURTNEY: (*To WALKER.*) You can trust me.

WALKER: (*Great innocence.*) Man, have I accused you of anything?

DARLENE: My husban'. (*To HORACE.*) Five years. Ask me what dey were like. Go on, ask me. Five years being married to Walker Kong. King Kong's brodder.
(*HORACE thinks that very funny. Even BUSTER is somewhat amused. WALKER waits for them to run down.*)

WALKER: (*Anger.*) You weary me out. All of you. Like children. Black people are so child-like. You really think dat's funny. Walker Kong. King Kong's brother. We laugh at anything. What do we have to be so happy about? (*Shouting.*) DEY THINK YOU'RE STUPID 'COS YOU ACT STUPID! (*Pause.*) Walker Kong. King Kong's brodder. Jesus Christ.
(*Pause.*)

HORACE: (*To DARLENE.*) Forgive me sayin' dis, my dear, but you were married to a madman.

DARLENE: Now he tells me.

WALKER: Horace. You wanna begin to work?
(*HORACE sighs, loudly. But he works.*)

DARLENE: (*To HORACE.*) Lord…ah was married to dis man fo' five years an' sometimes ah think all ah ever knew about 'im was 'is name.
(*A beat.*)

WALKER: Darlene, ah'm paying Horace to work, not to listen to you.
(*A beat.*)

DARLENE: Walker, I finish jokin' wit' you, okay. Now that I don't have a job, I'm goin' to have to get some money from you.

WALKER: Not now Darlene.

DARLENE: (*Firm not loud.*) Yes, now.
(*A beat.*)
Walker…ah'm still waitin' for the las' three months money. Even if yuh doan care about me, fo' godsakes, man, Janet is yuh daughter.

WALKER: Look, woman, ah doan wish to discuss our private life in front of any an' everybody.

DARLENE: Walker, you want to know why I lost the job? I always have to take time off because of Janet. If you were to help me take care of the child, I wouldn't need to take so much time off.

WALKER: You blame me fo' everything. Even fo' losin yuh job.

(*WALKER sucks his teeth, wishes she would disappear, die, go away.*)

DARLENE: Mos' men dey at lease care about dey chile.

WALKER: An what? Yuh think I doan care about Janet? Surely you must see how happy ah am when ah'm wit' de chile?

DARLENE: Dat's jus' selfish love.

WALKER: (*In BUSTER's direction.*) Boy, yuh can never win against a woman, canyuh? She's always got an answer fo' everything.

DARLENE: Sometimes you come to see her, sometimes you don't. The poor chile don't know if you're her father or not.

WALKER: Darlene, ah work here, ah don't want our private business laid out like a carpet fo' everybody to walk on. Now ah've tried to tell you a hundred times…ah'll pay you as soon as ah can. Ah can't give you maintenance money right now because every penny I have is tied up in buyin' dis place.

DARLENE: Man, you beat all. It's your chile we talkin' about, an' you radder put dis shop first. You're not ordinary, yuh know.

WALKER: Here we go. She g'un start getting all emotional now. Jesus.

DARLENE: (*Not loudly.*) She's yuh chile, she should come first.

WALKER: (*From gut level.*) Can't yuh see! Dis shop drives me on! It's to help me get over. If ah miss out now on dese four, flickin' walls, ah've had it. Ah'll never forgive myself.

DARLENE: An' what about yuh daughter? What about her?

WALKER: Wit'out dis shop ah can't help Janet. If I don't get dis place ah can't help anybody.

DARLENE: Fine. Dat's fine. But how do we live in the meantime? (*No histrionics, genuine feelings.*) Walker, ah can't afford to take care of Janet by m'self. Not proper care.

WALKER: Oh Christ. Christ.

DARLENE: A woman on 'er own, little or no money, yuh doan even have to be black to know dat's no joke. (*Pause. Sadness, not resentment.*) Ah can't forgive yuh, Walker... walkin' out on us.

WALKER: Hell. Oh hell!

DARLENE: I'll see you later, Walker. G'bye, Buster. Courtney. Bye Horace. Ah gone, Walker.
(*DARLENE leaves. Pause. WALKER gathers himself together. Then.*)

WALKER: Awright, awright! Let's be havin' you! Back to work! Work, work!

(*They work. Dark to blackout. In the darkness we hear the blues. 'One Room, Country Shack' by Buddy Guy.*)

Scene 3

The pressure is on. HORACE and WALKER at the two sewing machines working furiously. BUSTER ironing. They work. Eventually.

HORACE: (*Working.*) Mercy! Mercy! M'back, Walker. M'back! Buster, de man's worse dan a slave driver.

WALKER: (*Working.*) Jus' call me Simon Legree!

HORACE: (*Working.*) Worse dan purgatory, dis job. Worse dan friggin' purgatory. Enough! Bloody hell! Enough!
(*HORACE turns off his machine.*)

WALKER: (*To HORACE.*) What is it?

HORACE: I'm not doin' no more!

WALKER: It's not ten o'clock yet, Horace.
(*COURTNEY continues to wrap the trousers, but his attention is on WALKER and HORACE.*)

HORACE: Walker, my nervous system is cryin' out. 'Slow down', it's sayin'. Can yuh hear it? Listen.
(*A beat.*)

WALKER: Doan annoy me, man.

HORACE: You need a slave, my friend. (*He stands Up.*) Find yuhself a white man.

(*BUSTER laughs.*)

COURTNEY: Ah like it, ah like it.

HORACE: (*Bowing.*) Thank you.

WALKER: Horace. Ah'm in no mood fo' jokes.

HORACE: Jokes, my man? Ah've stopped wit de jokes. (*Genuine.*) Ah am fatigued. Fagged out. Exhausted.

WALKER: Ah'm tired too, Horace, but how can we stop now?

HORACE: Jus like dis, mate. Jus like dis. Goodbye. (*He disappears into the back room.*)

COURTNEY: (*To WALKER.*) Discipline! The man needs discipline. He's askin' for it!

HORACE: Any more coffee left, Buster?

BUSTER: Dare's always coffee, dummy, all yuh got to do is make it.

(*HORACE reappears, towel in hand.*)

HORACE: Coffee is not a drink for a gentleman like me. (*He stands drying his face.*)

BUSTER: Lazy bastard.

WALKER: Horace, ah'm payin' you to work until ten bloody o'clock!

HORACE: You want to be annodder Mr Nat. Dat's your trouble, Pops.

WALKER: Meanin' what?

HORACE: Yuh want to be a big, Jewish boss. King of de Garment Jungle. Everybody knows how you admire de Jews. Odder people when dey die dey hope to go to Heaven. When you die you hope to go to Tel Aviv. (*BUSTER and COURTNEY laugh. HORACE turns to them.*) You like dat one as well, eh? (*WALKER gets up. HORACE's coat is lying nearby. WALKER picks it up.*)

WALKER: You can't leave now, Horace. (*A beat.*)

HORACE: Give me back m'coat.

(*Pause – tension between them.*)

WALKER: Listen, ass-hole!

HORACE: (*To BUSTER.*) He's got a way wit' words, hasn't 'e?

WALKER: Okay, okay. Ah'm askin' you.

HORACE: An' ah'm turning yuh down.

(*A beat.*)

COURTNEY: Buster, I think we got a riot brewin' here.

(*COURTNEY is ignored.*)

HORACE: (*To WALKER.*) My coat, please.

(*A beat.*)

WALKER: (*Deadly.*) Ah'm payin' you to work, Horace.

HORACE: Ah'll see yuh tomorrow, man.

(*Pause.*)

WALKER: Yuh not gettin' dis damn coat till yuh help me do de damn work.

(*A beat. BUSTER rises.*)

BUSTER: Fight! Fight!

COURTNEY: Riot! Riot!

HORACE: (*A bit pompously.*) Doan be so stupid, Buster.

BUSTER: Yuh Rass, yuh tryin' to talk yuh way out of it, eh? Come on, ah want to see a clean fight.

HORACE: (*As before.*) Moron.

WALKER: Ah'm still waitin' , Horace.

HORACE: (*Quietly.*) My coat, boy.

WALKER: Ah'm payin' you a good basic wage.

HORACE: My coat.

WALKER: Plus a small bonus. Plus fifty poun's extra, for yuh cigars. What more do you want?

HORACE: Sleep! Blasted sleep!

BUSTER: What is all dis fockin' talk. Let's see a few punches being thrown.

HORACE: Hear dat. All 'e wants is a fight. Typical black man.

BUSTER: Dat's right! Dat's right! Dat's me. Mister Typical Black Man. Now cut de chat. Come out fightin'.

HORACE: No wonder de whites think we're all chil'ren. Blood-thirsty moron.

BUSTER: Ah want my money back. Dis is a fix, not a fight.

WALKER: Horace, ah'll try one more time. Try to see things my way. Ah doan want to fight you. Here. Here's yuh coat. (*He hands back HORACE's coat.*)

BUSTER: What sortuh fight yuh call dis? (*He sits down again.*)

WALKER: Horace, ah need dis shop. My life won't begin till ah own dis shop.

HORACE: Not tonight, Walker. Ah have a previous engagement, you see.

WALKER: What're you talkin' about? You never said nothing about no previous engagement.

HORACE: (*Overbearingly.*) Can't stop now. Ah'm off to the theatre. Sorry an' all that.

BUSTER: De theatre?

WALKER: What de hell yuh playin' at, Horace?

HORACE: Ah'm not playin' at nothing. But de Royal Shakespeare Company, dey're playin' at de Barbican.

WALKER: Very funny, Horace!

HORACE: (*A lit pompously.*) You see my lates' venture is actin'. Actin' in plays.

COURTNEY: Actin'?!

WALKER: (*To BUSTER.*) What's 'e talkin' about?

BUSTER: (*To HORACE.*) Actin' in plays?

HORACE: Why not? Dese days it looks like every odder black man in London thinks he can act. Why not me?

WALKER: (*Boiling now.*) Horace!

(*HORACE stops.*)

Have you listened to yuhself lately? Ah remember when ah firse knew you, yuh was full uh fantasy even then. But, man, you were fun in dose days. We'd all jus' arrived in dis country, an' we were runnin' over wit' hope. How many years ago was dat, eh? Christ. A lifetime. Now listen to you. You're all fantasy now. From start to finish. Sometimes ah wonder if yuh even know what day it is. One week you're a tailor, de nex' yuh talkin' about producin' films fo' chrisake. Now yuh come tellin' us you're an actor. It would be funny, if it weren't unfunny…! Who are you?

(*A beat.*)

They've got to your head, Horace.

(*A beat.*)

Take a good look at yuhself. Earring in one ear, fat cigar in yuh han'. Who, or what are you supposed to be, a

gypsy or Fidel Castro? (*Pause.*) Man, who you tryin' to fool? Ah know, you've had to go through hell. Ah know dat. You've had to dance to dere tune fo' so long, your corns have got corns. But goin' aroun' in a cloud of fantasy, dat's no answer. Blacks love to talk about how dey're 'gettin' it together'. But half de time dey're not doin' shit. Isn't it about time we stop kiddin' ourselves?
(*A beat. HORACE sucks air, like a hurt boxer.*)

HORACE: You're a son uva bitch, boy.

WALKER: It's true, Horace. You know it.

HORACE: You can stick yuh job up yuh ass. (*HORACE goes.*)

WALKER: Horace!
(*HORACE has gone. COURTNEY rounds on WALKER.*)

COURTNEY: (*To WALKER.*) You shouldn't treat the man like that!
(*Pause. COURTNEY and WALKER look at each other.*)

WALKER: Courtney, don't get me more vex. Okay? Okay? I want dese trousers taken over to Mr Nat. Now…please.
(*COURTNEY gives WALKER a hard look. Then, without another word, COURTNEY takes the trousers. He goes. Pause WALKER turns to BUSTER.*)
Problems, problems, problems.

BUSTER: You sure fixed Horace, didn't you?

WALKER: You think I was jus' tryin' to hurt him?

BUSTER: Only you would know dat, Walker.
(*Beat.*)
Anyway, I soon gotto go as well. My wife's in hospital, an' ah haven't bin to see her all day.

WALKER: Buster, ah feel fo' some company.
(*Pause. They look at each other.*)

BUSTER: Okay, ah'll stay a bit longer.

WALKER: (*A smile.*) You used to go to matinee a lot?

BUSTER: (*Working.*) What?

WALKER: Matinee. Cinema: Filmshow.

BUSTER: What about it?

WALKER: Ah used to love goin' to matinee. Back home, School holidays. Saturday afternoons. Ah even used to skulk from school so as to go to de pictures. Two o'clock matinee. The sun outside hot, an' de cinema inside cool.

Remember John Wayne, eh? Eh? John Wayne an Montgomery Clift an' Randolph Scott. Where are dey now? When de English talk films dey talk about *The Sound of Music* an' *E.-frigin'-T.* When I talk about films I mean *The Magnificent Seven* an' *Red River* an' *The Spoilers.* Remember dat fight in *The Spoilers.* What a fight? More dan half de picture: jus' one fight. Ah mean all yuh had to do was sit back in yuh seat an' count de blows. When people talk about a landmark in the cinema, you can be sure of one thing – dey not talkin' about *The Spoilers.* An' what about *The Fiend Dat Walked De West.* (*He whips his fingers, happily.*) Boss. A boss film. De best thing about dat film was de title. An' de cinemas! What cinemas! What names! Cinemas wit' names like Metropole, Gaiety, an best of all, Rialto. Here all dey got is de A.B.C. Cinemas. Goin' to the cinema in Englan' is a bore.

(*A beat.*)

The pit. I used to sit in de Pit. If you couldn't afford a seat in de Pit, den, financially, you were really in a bad way. Ah used to sit wit' all dem bad boys. Sometimes ah used to be afraid. Damn right. Some uh dem boys jus' had to look at yuh an yuh teeth would chatter. Dey had one guy in particular. Bernie. No, no Barney. Dey used to say he buggered little boys. An' he wasn't no homosexual, neidder. Barney jus' used to bugger little boys as a punishment. Boy, some uh dem Guyanese boys were real bad, yuh know. Of course it wasn't true. No boys ever got buggered. It was part of the myth that's all. De day outside hot, an' dere we were in de cinema…in anodder world. (*Running down.*) Humphrey Bogart an' Peter Lorre tryin' to escape from Devil's Islan'… Alan Ladd, he was so short, they used to say they made 'im stand on a box, a box he was so short…an' who said – 'this is your last chance, Mr Parker.'? Dr Fu Manchu, of course. Dr Fu Manchu. All gone now. Passed away. Jesus, Jesus. Now films have aliens as heroes. Buster. Buster. To this day, I believe maybe I shouldn't have come to dis country.

(*A beat.*)

Yeah, yeah, yeah. I go on, I go on. (*Pause.*) The joke was on us. Buster, de joke was on us. Gary Cooper. John Wayne, Montgomery Clift, Widmark. Dey was all white. White heroes every one uh dem. Ain' dat de funnies' thing of all? We never even had our own heroes.

BUSTER: Well…ah suppose things are a bit better dese…

(*DARLENE is heard off.*)

DARLENE: (*Off.*) Anybody home?

WALKER: Darlene?!

(*DARLENE enters.*)

DARLENE: (*Panting a little.*) Boy, them stairs. (*Then.*) Hello, hello, long time, no see. (*Then.*) Buster, your wife had 'er baby yet?

BUSTER: I don't think so.

DARLENE: Why aren't you at the hospital, Buster?

BUSTER: (*Jumping up.*) You right. She might need me.

WALKER: Why don't you mind your own business, Darlene! Sit down, Buster. She's okay! Yuh wife's okay.

BUSTER: No, it's time fo' me to go, Walker (*He gets his coat.*)

WALKER: (*To DARLENE.*) See! I blame you fo' dis!

DARLENE: Me? What did I do?

WALKER: Buster, jus' half hour more, man.

BUSTER: Ah gone, Walker. G'night, Darlene.

DARLENE: Good night, Buster.

BUSTER: See you tomorrow, Walker (*He goes.*)

WALKER: (*Shouting at DARLENE.*) I hope you're satisfied.

DARLENE: (*Quiet plea.*) Don't shout at me, Walker.

(*Pause.*)

WALKER: You want some coffee? (*Without waiting for a reply, he disappears into back room. Plugs in kettle.*)

DARLENE: Where's Horace. Has he deserted you?

WALKER: (*Off. Laughter.*) Dese days one can never rely on de hired help. (*He returns.*) What were you tellin' me earlier, about job or something?

DARLENE: You wouldn't be int'rested.

WALKER: Doan let that stop you.

DARLENE: (*Irritated.*) Walker, what about dat money?

WALKER: We're goin' to have an argument, ah can see dat.

DARLENE: No, we're not goin' to have no argument.

WALKER: Ah can't pay yuh de money.

DARLENE: We're goin' to have an argument.

WALKER: Darlene, jus give me a little more time.

DARLENE: You've had time.

WALKER: You know how long ah've scraped, saved, denied myself.

DARLENE: Denied yourself!

WALKER: Denied myself! So one day I could afford my own business. Saturday nights an' weeken's ah've stayed home. Ah doan even back de horses any more. Ah deserve to get everything ah want.
(*A beat.*)
Dat's why I came to England – to get on. What was dere for me back in Guyana an' the West Indies? Nothing. Dere's a better chance for me here.
(*A beat.*)
My own business, girl. Dey like magic, dose words. Magic. I mean, girl, black people have tried revolution, at lease talkin' about it, an' we tried relyin' on white, liberal, money. Maybe we should try something else. Green power. Self help. Political clout. That means startin' our own business. Mini cabs, food stores, insurance offices, restaurants, de whole gaddamn works. If it's good enough fo' de Asians, an' de Jews, an' de whites, why ain' it good enough fo' us? Ah mean, what have we produced in dis country since we bin here? Ah'll tell yuh, a lottuh talk an' Reggae Music. Jesus Christ Almighty.

DARLENE: I know. I agree. Ah do. But jus' don't lock me out of yuh life, Walker.

WALKER: My mind won't leave me alone, girl.

DARLENE: (*Flirting a bit.*) Yuh mind won't…leave you alone, eh? You know what they do to men whose mind won't leave them alone? (*Then, softly.*) Big Ben. Mr Diff-i-cult. God. Why do we have to argue so much?
(*A beat.*)
You had it all, Walker. (*Their own special, secret word.*) Daddy. I tried to be the companion you always wanted.
(*WALKER and DARLENE embrace.*)
Walker…Walker.

(*DARLENE starts getting a bit carried away. She tries to unbutton his shirt. He puts up a sort of token resistance. But then MR NAT bursts in. In his hands are some of the trousers WALKER returned at lunch time. MR NAT is in a state of near panic plus he is out of breath.*)

MR NAT: Shoddy! Shoddy workmanship! (*He panics.*)

DARLENE: (*Fearful, she has never seen MR NAT before.*) Walker!

WALKER: (*He eases free from DARLENE.*) Mr Nat, come in, come in!

(*MR NAT, of course, is already in.*)

Make yuhself at home.

MR NAT: (*Brandishing trousers.*) Look at them! (*He pants.*) You – ! You've ruined me!

WALKER: Who ruin you? Who?

MR NAT: I'm come to take them back! All the trousers!

WALKER: What!

MR NAT: (*About the trousers in his hand.*) Look at these! It's just not good enough! You rushed through them you lot! More haste, less speed!

WALKER: (*Infuriatingly calm.*) You mind if I see dose trousers.

MR NAT: (*Trying to avoid WALKER.*) You've done enough damage!

WALKER: Lemme see dem, man. (*WALKER manages to get one of the trousers away from MR NAT. He inspects the trousers. Then.*) Oh God. I'll kill 'im. I'll kill dat Horace!

DARLENE: What's he done?

WALKER: Dese trouser bottoms – he's sewn dem together! (*DARLENE gives a snorting laugh. WALKER glares at her. She shuts up.*)

MR NAT: (*Almost incoherently.*) A godsend Walker! The man was a godsend!

WALKER: Who? Who?

MR NAT: Our Japanese friend! (*Then.*) I will not have you dragging me back to your level.

WALKER: Careful, Mr Nat. Careful. Be cool.

MR NAT: 'Be cool'? Be cool! I'm facing bankrupcy – the boot of my car is full of ruined trousers – and he's telling me to 'be cool'. I want my merchandise back!

WALKER: Don't keep sayin' dat.
(*MR NAT puts down the trousers he has brought back. He starts to collect the rest of the trousers.*)
MR NAT: Look, Walker, I'm taking them back! I'll let Panos fix them.
WALKER: (*Grabs for the trousers.*) Panos! No way!
(*WALKER and MR NAT each get hold of a trouser leg. They struggle over the trousers.*)
MR NAT: Let go!
(*They continue to tug at the trousers.*)
WALKER: Too hard!
MR NAT: I'll have the police on you!
WALKER: I've worked too hard!
DARLENE: Stop it! Stop dis foolishness, you two!
(*Her words get through to the two men. They stop struggling over the trousers. Both panting a little. Especially MR NAT.*)
WALKER: (*To MR NAT.*) Too hard, man. I've bin workin' too hard an' too long to stop now.
(*Suddenly MR NAT starts making hissing noises through his nose, in WALKER's direction.*)
MR NAT: Damn. Now you've gone and done it. (*He makes more hissing noises through his nose.*)
WALKER: Why you hissin' at me, Mr Nat?
DARLENE: I don't think he's 'hissin' at you, Walker. He's havin' an' asthma attack.
WALKER: (*To MR NAT.*) Oh, sorry.
(*MR NAT's asthma attack gets worse. His intake of air is quick but his exhalation is prolonged, and noisy. His face is flushed, pale.*)
MR NAT: My…my bronchodilator.
WALKER: (*To DARLENE.*) What's he sayin'?
MR NAT: (*Fighting for breath.*) My inhaler.
DARLENE: Where is it?!
MR NAT: Car…my car. Hurry!
(*DARLENE goes rushing off. We hear her running down the stairs. Then we hear her come running back up the stairs. She rushes back in.*)
DARLENE: Your car keys?!
(*MR NAT searches desperately for his car keys. All the while, he wheezes and wheezes. He finds the keys. He gives then to*

*DARLENE. She goes down again. Then she comes back up
again.)*

Which car is it?

MR NAT: Jaguar! Black Jaguar!

DARLENE: Be calm!

(*She runs off again. MR NAT's wheezing gets worse.*)

WALKER: Mr Nat, you have no idea how much dis job
means to me.

MR NAT: Not now, Walker! Not now!

WALKER: There's not time like the present, Mr Nat.

MR NAT: All this stress...my doctor says it's not good for me.

WALKER: Dis shop is my last hope.

MR NAT: Why is she taking so long?

WALKER: Why you keep interruptin' me, Mr Nat? (*Then.*)
Let's face it, I'm not gettin' any younger. But what the
hell? Better late dan never, right?

MR NAT: Where... Where is she? (*He wheezes and wheezes.*)

WALKER: She'll soon be here, be calm.

MR NAT: I am calm...!

(*DARLENE is heard on stairs – off.*)

DARLENE: (*Off.*) Hold on! I'm comin'.

(*DARLENE enters, waving bronchodilator.*)

MR NAT: Give...give me.

WALKER: (*To DARLENE.*) No, give me dat.

(*Before DARLENE can stop him, WALKER takes the
bronchodilator from her.*)

DARLENE: Hey!

WALKER: (*To MR NAT.*) Now, Mr Nat, about dose trousers.

DARLENE: Walker!

MR NAT: Wa... Wa... Walker.

WALKER: I'm sure we could come to some agreement
about the trousers.

MR NAT: Anything you say! (*He wheezes.*)

WALKER: Now you talkin'.

(*WALKER hands over the bronchodilator to MR NAT. MR
NAT puts the bronchodilator to his lips. He sucks on it greedily.
WALKER watches him. After a while, MR NAT's agonised
breathing starts to subside a bit.*)

WALKER: How you feelin', Mr Nat? You better now?

MR NAT: (*Wearily.*) It's not fatal.

WALKER: You coulda fooled me.

MR NAT: (*A weak smile in DARLENE's direction.*) Thank you, young lady.

DARLENE: Yuh welcome.

WALKER: Good, good. You okay now, Mr Nat? Can we get back to business now? Mr Nat?

MR NAT: Give me a minute, Walker. Please.

DARLENE: For heavens sakes, Walker!

WALKER: Keep outa dis, Darlene. (*Then.*) Mr Nat, about dese trousers with the sewn up bottoms...

MR NAT: (*Interrupting.*) Do me a favour, Walker, just let's forget we ever met.

WALKER: (*The nearest he will come to begging MR NAT.*) Fo' godsakes, man, I'm almost there. It's almost in the palm of my hand, I can feel it, taste it – a little success. Don't snatch it away now!

(*Pause. WALKER and MR NAT looking at each other.*)

MR NAT: Alright.

WALKER: (*About trousers MR NAT has just brought back.*) I'll unpick dese an' sew dem back for free. If! If by morning, I fix dem up, to your satisfaction, give me one more chance.

MR NAT: Who's going to help you?

WALKER: I'll do dem myself.

MR NAT: You'll have to work all night.

WALKER: Hey, let me worry about dat.

(*DARLENE still has MR NAT's car keys.*)

Give me dose keys, Darlene.

DARLENE: What?

(*WALKER takes MR NAT's car keys from her.*)

WALKER: Ah'll get the rest of the trousers. (*He goes.*)

DARLENE: Walker!

(*MR NAT Coughs. DARLENE turns to see what is happening with MR NAT. She is torn between WALKER and MR NAT. She finds a bottle of WALKER's scotch. She pours some for MR NAT.*)

Are you alright?

(*She hands the drink to MR NAT.*)

MR NAT: Very determined, isn't he?

DARLENE: Too determined.

MR NAT: Are you Walker's girlfriend?

DARLENE: His Wife. I think!

(*MR NAT sucks on the bronchodilator.*)

Should I phone your wife?

MR NAT: No point. She left me twelve years ago.

DARLENE: Oh, I'm sorry.

MR NAT: You're sorry! How you think I feel?

DARLENE: Do you miss her?

MR NAT: I don't think about it anymore.

(*A beat then he tells the truth.*)

In the hard times, she was a good wife. Just when I'd almost made it, she left me. I still can't understand it.

DARLENE: Maybe she was lonely…

MR NAT: Lonely? She had five kids. (*Then.*) Perhaps you're right. I lost her. I put business first.

DARLENE: Tell Walker that. I have tried to tell him. I am tired of tryin'. I get lonely, sometimes.

(*Pause. MR NAT pats her on the shoulder, a gesture of sympathy. WALKER returns. With the trousers from MR NAT's car.*)

MR NAT: Well, Walker, you fix those trousers by morning, and I'll reconsider my decision tomorrow. Take it or leave it, Walker.

(*Pause.*)

WALKER: (*Coldly.*) We'll play by your rules, Mr Nat always.

MR NAT: Good. (*To DARLENE.*) Young lady, thanks again.

DARLENE: G'bye.

MR NAT: Walker, see you tomorrow. Take care of her, Walker. (*He exits.*)

DARLENE: Did you hear dat, Walker. Take care of me.

WALKER: Yeah well – Okay let's go! Let's go! Work! Work! Help me unpick dese trousers.

DARLENE: You're incredible! You care more about dese stupid trousers dan you do about yuh own daughter.

WALKER: (*Getting organised.*) What? Look you take half, an' I'll take half. Use dat razor blade.

DARLENE: Ah can't talk to you. De way your mind works. It – it – Lord! You mix me up. Ah can talk to Horace, ah can talk to anybody. But not you. When ah talk to somebody like Horace, or even Buster, dey make my spirits rise up. Ah feel to smile. But you. You do as much good for my spirits as a fish hook does for a fish.

WALKER: Look, okay, maybe you're right, about me neglectin' de child. Help me finish dese an' I'll come home wit you tonight. Okay?

DARLENE: Tonight?

WALKER: (*Unhearing.*) Ah'll get to know 'er better. Dis weeken' ah'll take 'er to Clapham Common. Or de zoo. We'll walk hand in hand, me an' my daughter.

DARLENE: (*Completely mystified.*) What're you bablin' about?

WALKER: We'll be closes' fadder an' daughter in de whole wide world. (*Quiet cry.*) Ah'm 'er father. Sometimes ah feel so bad. Neglectin' 'er like dat. May God forgive me.

DARLENE: You gone crazy, boy?

WALKER: (*A plea.*) Let me come home wit' you tonight.

DARLENE: You are crazy. (*Then.*) Sleep alone. Dat's all yuh deserve. Ah hope yuh doan sleep at all.
(*DARLENE goes. Pause.*)

WALKER: Oh Jesus. Oh sweet Jesus. (*Then.*) De price of it all!
(*Pause. Blackout.*)

End of Act One.

ACT TWO

Scene 1

*Some early morning sunlight bathes the room. WALKER is slumped
over his sewing machine asleep. He is not immediately noticeable.
COURTNEY enters. He turns on the lights. He starts sweeping up.
Eventually he sees WALKER.*

COURTNEY: Walker! Fire! Fire!

(*WALKER sits up with a start.*)

WALKER: Where! Where!

(*COURTNEY laughs at WALKER. WALKER is not amused.*)
Very friggin' funny.

COURTNEY: Walker, don't you have a home?

WALKER: I worked until nearly five o'clock dis morning.

COURTNEY: For what?

WALKER: What you mean, 'for what?'

COURTNEY: What for? All this work, work, work?

WALKER: Boy, what you gettin' at? Look, I finished dose
trousers over dere. Bag dem for me. Now, please. Den
rush dem over to Mr Nat. Den bring back another load
of trousers from his warehouse.

COURTNEY: You never stop, do you, boss? You're mad.

WALKER: Bag, boy. Bag.

COURTNEY: (*Cool.*) Okay. Okay.

(*COURTNEY starts putting the trousers in plastic bags.
WALKER goes into the side room (off). We hear him brushing
his teeth.*)

WALKER: (*Off.*) Buster is late.

COURTNEY: Don't tell me, tell him.

(*WALKER finishes brushing his teeth. He comes out again.
He has battery operated shaver in one hand and a mirror in
the other. He hooks the mirror on a nail against the wall.
WALKER shaves. COURTNEY bags trousers for a while.
Neither speaks. Then.*)

WALKER: (*Raising his voice as he shaves.*) How're things at
that estate of yours?

COURTNEY: What?

WALKER: Dat estate where you live, how's it goin'?

COURTNEY: You used to live there too, remember.

WALKER: Used to. I'm makin' money now.

COURTNEY: You're not makin' all that much money, boss. Don't fool yuhself.

WALKER: Anyway, how're things?

COURTNEY: Before the riots, the police used to patrol the estate in twos. Now it's never less than twenty-twos.
(*WALKER switches off shaver.*)

WALKER: You boys.

COURTNEY: (*Hotly.*) What you mean, 'you boys'?

WALKER: Some of you boys don't even look West Indian. You're black, sure, but you not West Indian.

COURTNEY: The English say we're not English, you say we're not West Indian! What the hell are we?

WALKER: You're soldiers.

COURTNEY: Soldiers?

WALKER: Dat's right. Soldiers gettin' ready for a war.
(*COURTNEY thinks about WALKER's words. They please him.*)

COURTNEY: Yeah. Yeah. That's what we are. Soldiers.

WALKER: Outnumbered soldiers.

COURTNEY: At least we'll die on our feet, not on our knees.
(*Pause. They look at each other.*)

WALKER: (*Sadly.*) Courtney, Courtney, Courtney. You're wastin' yuh life how old are you? Eighteen? Nineteen? Dat estate, it'll poison You. Fo'ever.

COURTNEY: How would you know? You've already turned your back on us.
(*Pause.*)

WALKER: You wanna know the truth?

COURTNEY: What?

WALKER: Dat estate. It frightens me. It frightens me when I see what the whites are doin' to us on dat estate.
(*Pause.*)

COURTNEY: It never ends. Never. Never.
(*Pause. BUSTER enters.*)

BUSTER: Mornin' everybody.

WALKER: Afternoon, you mean.

BUSTER: I see. It's one of dose mornin's, is it?

WALKER: Courtney, take dose trousers over to Mr Nat. Don't bother to bag anymore.

COURTNEY: Whatever you say, boss. (*He collects the trousers. He starts to go.*)

WALKER: Don't be long.

COURTNEY: Yeah, yeah. (*COURTNEY goes with the trousers WALKER has worked on all night.*)
(*Meanwhile, BUSTER has taken off his coat but he is just sitting at his sewing machine. WALKER looks at him.*)

WALKER: You okay, Buster?

BUSTER: Yes, why?

WALKER: First you come in late. Den you jus' sit dere like something from the British Museum.
(*The phone rings. WALKER answers.*)

WALKER: 'Alterations' (*To BUSTER who still has not moved.*) Work, Buster. Da's why I'm payin' you.

BUSTER: Who the rass you think you talkin' to?

WALKER: (*Into phone.*) Oh, hello…what? No I was not home las' night, Liz…no, I wasn't wit' any woman. I was here, all night… I'm tellin' the truth, I was here. Look, Liz, I am very busy, today is my make or break day; I'll call you back later, okay? Bye. (*He hangs up. Then to BUSTER.*) Women, boy. Some uh dem can get jealous, eh?

BUSTER: You think ah'm your friggin' slave don't yuh?

WALKER: Could we row later, huh? Look at de time, Buster.

BUSTER: Frig the time!
(*A beat.*)

WALKER: Buster, what is it, eh? Yuh not gonna start takin' offence at a time like dis are you? I'm at bay, Buster.
(*A beat.*)
Jus' see me through dis one day, Buster. Courtney will soon be back wit more trousers. Even wit' de two of us, it's goin' to be a miracle but wit'out your help it would be bloody impossible.

BUSTER: (*A warning.*) Yuh better not push me den, eh?
(*A beat.*)

WALKER: Dis is my make or break day, Buster.

BUSTER: Yuh haven't even asked me if Hortense had 'er baby. What sort uh frien are you.

WALKER: Has she had 'er baby?

BUSTER: No.

WALKER: Well, dat's why ah din ask you. Ah knew she hadn't had de baby.

BUSTER: Yuh lie! Yuh too lie!

(*They laugh. BUSTER sits at his sewing machine. WALKER deposits a number of pairs of trousers on BUSTER's machine and an equal number of trousers on his own machine.*)

WALKER: All night I've bin up, thanks to Horace.

BUSTER: Why?

WALKER: The bloody ass sewed up the trouser bottoms. Sewed dem up.

BUSTER: What?!

WALKER: Not jus' one of dem – a whole batch. Mr Nat brought dem back.

BUSTER: Don't say I din' warn you. The man is more trouble dan he's worth.

WALKER: Dat's the understatement of the year.

(*They work.*)

BUSTER: Damn, it's like a friggin' trouser epidemic.

WALKER: (*At his sewing machine.*) Maybe we should open a trousers take-away. Like MacDonalds.

BUSTER: Ah'm glad you can joke about it.

WALKER: Let's work Buster.

(*They work.*)

BUSTER: Walker! If you do get dis place, what you plan to do with it?

WALKER: Ah know exactly what ah want.

BUSTER: Tell us den.

WALKER: Ah know de secret. We bound to make money.

(*BUSTER sews.*)

BUSTER: An' what's dis secret?

WALKER: Are yuh ready fo' dis?

(*BUSTER stops sewing.*)

BUSTER: Ah'm ready, ah'm ready.

(*WALKER leans forward slowly. Then.*)

WALKER: Suits is in.

(*A beat.*)

BUSTER: And?

WALKER: Dat's it

BUSTER: Suits is in? Dat's it?

WALKER: Dat's right

BUSTER: 'Suits is in'? (*Loudly.*) It's not even proper grammar, Walker!

WALKER: Bugger grammar. Ah'm serious, Buster. Ah plan to start makin' suits. My own suits. No more alterations.

BUSTER: Suits, eh? Yuh rass. Yuh see all dem young white people out dare wearin' denim, Jeans! – an you're tellin' me about suits? Suits!

WALKER: Ah'm not talkin' about middle-aged suits. Ah'm talkin' about suits fo' trendy, successfully young guys.

BUSTER: Walker, we doan know any trendy, successful young guys!

WALKER: Buster, if Christopher Columbus had had you fo' a frien', he'd 'ave stayed home! (*He glances at his watch.*) Oh hell, look at de time. We're talkin' too much, Buster.

BUSTER: We? You, yuh mean. You're do only one running off at de mout'.

WALKER: (*Working.*) We're slippin' behind. Ah mean we haven't even finished dis lot yet.
(*They work.*)

BUSTER: We still got to press dem as well.

WALKER: Forget pressin' dem.

BUSTER: Mr Nat won't be pleased.

WALKER: Fock Mr Nat.
(*They work – then.*)

BUSTER: Walker, we're beginnin' to panic!

WALKER: Speak fo' yuhself.
(*They work.*)

BUSTER: Walker!

WALKER: (*Still working.*) What now?

BUSTER: Ah jus' remember.

WALKER: (*Working.*) Remember what?

BUSTER: Ah hate trousers!
(*Blackout.*)

Scene 2

Both WALKER's and BUSTER's sewing machines going furiously. Then COURTNEY enters with another load of trousers.

Immediately BUSTER stops working. He jumps up. WALKER stops as well.

BUSTER: Oh Gawd! Not more trousers!

COURTNEY: (*Pretending to crowd BUSTER.*) Move! Move!

BUSTER: I'm not in yuh way, boy!

(*COURTNEY laughs. Deposits trousers.*)

WALKER: Courtney, leave Buster alone. (*He inspects trousers.*) Good, good. More trousers. Great. I'm glad to see he kept his side of the bargain. What did he say?

COURTNEY: (*Winding WALKER up.*) Who?

WALKER: Mr Nat! What did he say?

COURTNEY: Say? He din say nothing. People don't talk to me. All I do is fetch an' deliver. Fetch dis, deliver dat. Talk to me! Dey don't even see me. In fact –

WALKER: Courtney!

(*COURTNEY shuts up.*)

Is dis all the trousers?

COURTNEY: There's more in the van.

(*COURTNEY goes. BUSTER disappears in to back room .he puts on kettle.*)

WALKER: Buster! where yo' goin'? I hope you're not stoppin' fo' no calls of nature now. We can't afford to stop fo' no calls of nature.

(*BUSTER appears in doorway.*)

BUSTER: Listen, Hitler, ah'm makin' us a cup of coffee. Even Big Business allows dey employees to stop fo' a cup uh coffee every once in a while.

WALKER: Ah'm at bay, Buster.

BUSTER: What does dat mean, you're at bay?

WALKER: It means ah got my back to de wall.

BUSTER: Den walk away from the wall. (*He goes back into backroom.*)

(*WALKER is busy dividing the new batch of trousers. Some for him, some for BUSTER.*)

WALKER: We're not gonna be able to make it. We need somebody extra.

BUSTER: (*Off.*) Go an' phone Horace, he might come back.

WALKER: Over my dead body!

BUSTER: (*Off.*) Horace would like dat! (*He returns with two cups of coffee.*)

WALKER: T'anks (*Still anxious.*) Who can we get? (*Pause.*) Never ends, never ends.

WALKER: Let's get back to work, Buster.

BUSTER: Hold yuh horses. Dis is called a tea break. An' dat's what ah'm takin'. A tea break.

(*COURTNEY returns with more trousers. BUSTER sees trousers.*)

Lord, have mercy –

COURTNEY: (*Seeing coffee.*) Where's my coffee?

BUSTER: Dere's hot water in dere.

(*COURTNEY goes into backroom. BUSTER produces a newspaper.*)

Hey, you read dis one. Dey interviewin' people at work an' on de street. The subject is 'today's race problem'.

WALKER: To dem, when they talk about it, it's a problem. But to us, what they're talkin' about is you an' me.

BUSTER: Yeah. Anyway, listen, nuh. To be fair to dis woman she's not a racist.

WALKER: (*Crying out.*) Ah'm at bay, Buster!

BUSTER: Ah know, ah know. Listen – says here…

WALKER: Jesus, Jesus.

COURTNEY: (*Off in backroom.*) Didn't you hear the man, Buster? He's at bay, whatever that means.

BUSTER: (*To WALKER.*) Says here – she's a canteen worker dis English woman. She says: 'The woman next door is West Indian. When she moved in last year the kids used to chant 'Wogs, Wogs'. Well I wasn't having that, I can tell you. I soon put a stop to that. She's a good neighbour. The other day her grandson, he's two, wanted me to lift him up. Well, I'd never lifted a little coon before. I did though'. (*He laughs dryly.*) Rass, boy.

(*WALKER HAS started sewing again. BUSTER looks at him, momentarily.*)

BUSTER: Take a rest, Walker!

(*WALKER stops sewing. COURTNEY returns from backroom.*)

WALKER: You're right.

(*He gets up. He moves away from sewing machine.*)

Boy, I dunno. Seems a waste of time, doan it? I mean, so what, if I own dis shop? What will be prove? Buster, I itch sometimes. Itch! An' I dunno where to scratch. All I know is dat things could be better. Lord, man. I got dis hunger. But fo' what? Ah don't know. I feel like ah'm doomed fo' ever to wander dis fockin' earth. Where am I welcome? I jus' want to be able to open de newspaper once wit'out havin' to read dat I'm a problem. Jus' once.

BUSTER: Boy, dat'll be the day. Dat'll be the day.

COURTNEY: You know the trouble with you two? You hope it'll blow away, like smoke.

WALKER: What?

COURTNEY: The problem. You hope it'll jus disappear. Magic.

BUSTER: You reckon I should pray fo' things to get worse?

COURTNEY: (*To WALKER.*) Look at you. You work yuh guts out. Even weekends. You hope money will protect you. Jus' like the Asians.

WALKER: At least dey can pay their bills.

COURTNEY: The next time you see any Asians take a good look at dem, they work hard, harder than you – yet the Whites still attack dem. They will always find a reason to attack us. We're not the problem. Dey are the problem.

WALKER: Money! Makin' money is the best revenge I know.

BUSTER: (*Rounding on COURTNEY.*) Shoutin' 'Move! Move!' at everybody! You reckon dat's the answer?

COURTNEY: You're worse dan him. You keep your head down in the hope dey won't notice you.

BUSTER: (*Crying out.*) I keep my head down to hold my head up!

COURTNEY: The only thing dey understans is strength.

BUSTER: What's your idea of strength? Mugging ole people? Shopliftin'? Sellin' ganga? You yout's give us a bad name.

COURTNEY: Listen to dis pussy-cat man! Yout's! Don't get me vex. How would you know about 'yout's'? Dey got you so afraid you don't even go in the pub anymore.

BUSTER: I'm not afraid of dem…!

COURTNEY: We don't all mug ole people! We don't all steal. We don't all deal in drugs! Where do you get all your facts from? Alf Garnet?

WALKER: Buster, he's right. You gettin' jus like an ole man. (*To COURTNEY.*) Dere's only one solution. One. We got to get on our bikes.

COURTNEY: Bikes? What bikes? I can't afford a bike.

WALKER: (*Not wanting to pursue it.*) Anyway. Time fo' me to get on my bike. (*He stretches. He is ready to work again.*) 'When the goin' gets tough, the tough get goin'.'

COURTNEY: (*Shouting.*) I'm not finished yet!

WALKER: (*Quietly. Deadly.*) Don't raise yuh voice at me, Courtney.

(*A beat.*)

COURTNEY: Neither of you got any idea – what it feels like to be young in Englan' now. I don't mean young an' Black, I'm jus' talkin' about being young. Jus' dis once let's forget about being Black. You don't know how it is to be young in Britain today! No idea. On yer bike, you say. But go where? Where? Where are all these jobs? I open my papers an' I read how young people today don't really want to work. Bollocks! I read about hundreds of jobs goin' beggin. It's all bollocks! I mean, if things are so good, what am I doin' in dis job? Van driver! A no-hope, dead-end kiss-me-ass van driver!

WALKER: I'm glad you think so highly about yuh job.

COURTNEY: (*Pain.*) Who wants to be a van driver for life? (*A beat.*)

WALKER: (*Some sympathy.*) Okay, okay, look, you don't have to be a van driver for ever. Stick with me, Courtney, help me get dis shop, den the sky's the limit. As long as I get on, you'll get on.

COURTNEY: You don't understan', do you? I don't want to be like you – to jus' make my pile an' move to Guildford! You add to the problem.

(*Pause.*)

WALKER: (*Cold as ice.*) I think dis tea break is over.

(*WALKER returns to his sewing machine. BUSTER collects dirty coffee cups. He takes them back in to the side room. Then he re-appears. He sits at his sewing machine. All this in silence.*)

COURTNEY: Walker.

(*WALKER begins sewing, ignoring COURTNEY. COURTNEY raises his voice.*)

Boss!

(*No reply.*)

How about me takin' back another batch of trousers to ole man Nat?

(*WALKER ignores him. BUSTER answers instead.*)

BUSTER: Courtney, wait. Dere's not enough fo' anodder van load.

COURTNEY: I'm sure Walker would like it if I was to piss off for a while.

(*WALKER gives COURTNEY a hard look.*)

WALKER: As far as I'm concerned, you could piss of for good.

COURTNEY: Is dat what you want?

BUSTER: Walker!

(*Pause. WALKER holds his tongue. BUSTER turns back to COURTNEY.*)

Okay, Courtney, take dat lot to Mr Nat. Den come back straight away. You hear me, Courtney.

COURTNEY: Buster, Buster.

BUSTER: Don't 'Buster, Buster' me, boy. Now go.

(*COURTNEY collects all the appropriate trousers. He starts to go.*)

COURTNEY: Bye Walker.

(*COURTNEY goes. BUSTER looks at WALKER.*)

BUSTER: Congratulations, man. Keep on the way you're goin'. You soon won't have anybody workin' fo' you.

WALKER: It's my fault?! How is it my fault? How is it my fault? I was offerin' him a stake in the future.

BUSTER: Boy, you would use anybody. Friends, co-workers, anybody.

WALKER: You too, Buster?

BUSTER: I 'too' what?

WALKER: You feel ah'm usin' you.

BUSTER: Damn right.

WALKER: Buster, we're in dis together.

BUSTER: Even I am not dat bloody stupid.

(*Pause.*)

WALKER: (*Serious.*) Buster. I'd be the firse to admit I'm a son of a bitch, but, boy, ah'm not a total son of a bitch.

BUSTER: Sez who?

WALKER: You're jokin' aren't you? Say you're jokin'. You're my friend, we're partners.

BUSTER: We're not partners.

(*A beat.*)

We bot' know dat. What sort of damn fool you take me for? (*Pause.*) You know half our trouble? Not jus yours an' mine, ah mean all of us. We're all out fo' number one. De moment one black man gets ahead he doan give a damn fo' nobody else.

WALKER: But it doesn't always have to be like dat!

BUSTER: I know I don't always have to be like dat. I know dat, but do you know dat?

(*Pause HORACE enters.*)

HORACE: (*Holding out his fat cigar.*) Surprise, Walker. Dis is your lucky day!

(*WALKER rises. He is not exactly pleased to see HORACE.*)

WALKER: What're you doin' here?

HORACE: You hear dat, Buster? You hear the welcome in his voice?

WALKER: I almost lost my contract wit' Mr Nat, thanks to you.

HORACE: Me, my good man?

WALKER: What did you think you was doin' to me? You think you could break me dat easily? Well, you didn't I stayed up all night, I undid all your – handiwork. Let's face it, you hate me, don't you? Dat's why you're back. You hate me. Right?

HORACE: Dat's not why I'm back.

WALKER: Den you want your money. Is dat why you're back?

HORACE: No.

WALKER: (*Unhearing.*) I refuse to pay you a penny until you finish the whole job. Not a penny. (*Then, looking away from HORACE.*) Buster give me a good reason why I shouldn't strangle dis man?

BUSTER: You need him.

WALKER: Yuh right. Dat's three good reasons. (*Then.*) Horace, it's madness, but I still need you.

HORACE: Dat's not why I'm here, either.

WALKER: What! You're not here to work?

HORACE: In a word, no.

BUSTER: (*To HORACE.*) Den why the ass are you back here? (*Both WALKER and BUSTER close in on HORACE. HORACE backs off, nervously.*)

HORACE: Well.

WALKER: Speak up! (*HORACE looks for an avenue of escape. There is none.*)

HORACE: I'm thinkin', I'm thinkin'…

WALKER: (*Sticks a pair of trousers in HORACE's hand.*) Here, make yuhself useful while you're thinkin'. (*He leads HORACE to one of the sewing machines.*) Whistle while you work! (*HORACE allows himself to be manhandled.*)

HORACE: Okay, Walker. But doan forget: nothing's fo' free, Walker.

WALKER: (*Raw hurt.*) No-one ever gave me nothing free in my life! Never! (*Pause.*)

HORACE: (*Dislike.*) Good. Den we understan' each other.

BUSTER: What's the price, Horace?

WALKER: (*To HORACE.*) Yes, what's the price?

HORACE: You'll see. All in good time, Walker.

WALKER: (*Amusing to him.*) My soul, perhaps? My soul, Horace? Is dat it? Is dat what yuh want?

HORACE: (*Some contempt.*) What would anybody want wit' your soul, Walker?

(*BUSTER laughs.*)

Yuh hear dat, Walker? He feels better fo' seein' me.
Ah'm a tonic. I make people want to smile. Can you say de same, Walker.

(*Pause. HORACE and BUSTER work. WALKER irons. Blackout. Blues: 'Dust My Broom' by Elmore James.*)

Scene 3

WALKER at BUSTER's sewing machine, sewing. HORACE at WALKER's sewing machine, sewing. BUSTER ironing. After a moment, COURTNEY enters with more trousers.

COURTNEY: Move! Move! The last batch! The last batch!
(*He puts the trousers down.*)

WALKER: You hear dat, Buster? The last batch.

BUSTER: It look like one hell of a large, last batch to me.

COURTNEY: (*To WALKER.*) Ole man Nat wants dis lot back by four o'clock.

BUSTER: Four! Four o'clock. The man mad!

HORACE: Walker, ah want to talk to you about yuh wife.

WALKER: (*Busy, preoccupied.*) Darlene?

HORACE: Yuh got more dan one wife?

WALKER: Why should you want to talk about Darlene. Not even I talk about 'er. An' I'm de one who's married to 'er.

HORACE: Dat's no way to talk about y'wife. She's a good woman, loyal.

WALKER: Ah know, Horace, as ah said, I'm the one who is married to her (*Then.*) Buster, you know what dey say about marriage?

BUSTER: No. What?

WALKER: A man is incomplete until he's married. After dat he's really finished.

HORACE: (*Trying to interrupt.*) Walker, I'm tryin' to talk to you.
(*Phone rings.*)

BUSTER: Ah'm a father! Ah'm a father! (*He leaps to the phone.*) Hello. Buster Gibbs speakin'. (*He listens.*) Who?…
Oh, yeah, hold on. (*He puts his hand over mouthpiece.*)
Bloody hell! (*To WALKER.*) It's fo' you. Liz.

(*WALKER stops work. HORACE too.*)

WALKER: Ah can't talk to her now.

BUSTER: (*Into phone.*) Hello, Liz…!

WALKER: Hold on, ah'll speak to 'er

BUSTER: Make up your mind, Walker.

(*WALKER leaves his sewing machine. Takes phone from BUSTER. BUSTER returns to his ironing.*)

WALKER: (*Into phone.*) Hello, baby…yeah, listen, ah' on de las lap, can ah call yuh back…what? fo'chrissake, Liz, yuh not still goin' on about las' night, are you…ah was not wit' my wife… Christ, yuh like a drill…yes, I think that's a good idea, we'll talk to each other later, when we've both cooled down…bye. (*WALKER hangs up.*)

HORACE: She don't sound very stable, Walker.

HORACE: Funny you should say dat…ah was thinkin' de same thing m'self. –

BUSTER: He likes un-stable blondes. Don't you, Walker?

HORACE: (*To WALKER, irritatingly.*) Disgustin'. Disgustin'. (*A beat.*)

WALKER: It's like that now, is it? De two uh you gangin' up on me.

HORACE: Gangin' up on you? Dear boy, ah doan go in for group sex.

WALKER: Ah happen to know one white woman.

HORACE: No need to apologise, Walker.

WALKER: (*Not amused.*) Boy, you're a joke to me.

HORACE: Yeah? Glad to be of service.

WALKER: Ah remember one Sunday at dat pub at Shepherd's Bush. De pub wit' dat calypso band. You an' some readhead. (*To BUSTER.*) You should've seen 'im, massagin' her bones right in front of de whole pub.

HORACE: You should talk. Put blonde hair on a box of biscuits, an' you'd jump it!

WALKER: You friggin' dumb-assed, son of a bitch.

HORACE: (*Face to face.*) Doan you call me a friggin', dumb-assed son of a bitch!.

BUSTER: What's de matter wit you two guys?

COURTNEY: Yeah. Wha' the rass wrong with you two?

WALKER: (*To HORACE, sucking his teeth.*) Look at you. A big nothing. Zero. I could buy you. At lease I got –

HORACE: Buy me?

WALKER: I got a shop – you got nothing.

HORACE: Buy me!

WALKER: I own a shop! I own something.

HORACE: You think dis little nasty insignificant cough drop box of a shop counts for anything out there? Haul yuh ass, boy.

WALKER: It could grow into something bigger. It has potential.

HORACE: (*A contemptuous little laugh.*) Suddenly he's a pillar of de White Establishment. One friggin' shop an' he's de best thing dat ever happened to the Conservative Party. One friggin' little shop.

WALKER: Jealousy! You're all jealous of me. Everyone of you!

COURTNEY: Jealous? Who's jealous?

HORACE: Oh God, yuh hear dat, Buster? Yuh hear dat? We're jealous of him.

WALKER: Poser! Dat's all you are. A gaddamn poser. Babblin' in de dark to keep from screamin'. You've done nothing in dis country since you been here. To them you're jus invisible. You can't do it. You can't get through. Dis country has whipped your ass. Crippled you.

COURTNEY: Walker!

HORACE: (*To WALKER.*) I'll tell you – I'll tell you why I stand here an' take all dis crap from you!

BUSTER: Shut up. Both uh you!

WALKER: (*To HORACE.*) Go on. Tell me.

BUSTER: Will you two shut up! (*Pause.*) Ah mean, Jesus, man. Christ. If you could've seen yourselves. The, the bile. Bile. Why do we have to fight each odder? Yuh head is being messed up! (*To WALKER.*) Ah'm surprised at you, Walker. Ah mean you should know better, man. Okay, so it looks pretty certain you gonna get dis shop An' yuh deserve it. But you couldn't 'ave done it alone. Doan fool yuhself, you need us.

(*A beat.*)

(*To HORACE.*) As fo' you. He's right. When are you gonna stop performin'! an' start gettin' it togedder. All dis jivin'. Pretendin' to be Mr Big. It's crap.

HORACE: (*Pain.*) Why should I let de white man see the naked me?

(*A beat.*)

BUSTER: Well, dat's where yuh got me, brother. Ah can't answer dat one. All I know is when we firse got off the boat, we used to support each other. We don't anymore. We've become like dem. Dog eat dog. Crabs in a basket.

(*A beat.*)

COURTNEY: Nice. Nice one, Buster. Maybe I was wrong about you.

WALKER: Imagine dat. A lecture by Buster of all people.

HORACE: (*To BUSTER.*) Ah thought you wanted to see us fight?

BUSTER: Dere's a difference between de two of you fightin' each odder an' hatin' each odder.

HORACE: He's de one hates, not me. He hates 'imself. It's called self hate.

(*Pause. We see WALKER is hurt by HORACE's words.*)

WALKER: Boy, ah can't be boddered wit' you. Let's work.

(*They work. Lights go down.*)

Scene 4

WALKER and HORACE at their respective machines, sewing. BUSTER and COURTNEY bagging some of the finished trousers. Nearly all the trousers have been done now.

COURTNEY: Walker, it's almost four o'clock.

(*WALKER jumps up.*)

WALKER: Okay, okay – we've almost finished. Here, take dis lot back to Mr Nat. Tell him he can collect the rest when he brings my cheque.

COURTNEY: I'll see yo all tomorrow. By the time I get over to Nat, it'll be time to go home.

WALKER: G'night, Courtney.

BUSTER: (*To COURTNEY.*) See yuh.

(*COURTNEY goes, taking a large batch of trousers. WALKER is feeling very good.*)

WALKER: Onward! Onward Christian Soldiers!

BUSTER: Walker, you sound drunk!

WALKER: Let's have some music. 'If music be the food of love, play on.' You hear dat, Horace? You're not the only one who's familiar wit' Shakespeare. (*He fusses with his cassette.*)

HORACE: Walker! No more of dat howliri' noise. Ah beg you.

WALKER: Something not too heavy. Hudie Leadbeter. Leadbelly to you.

(*The music plays for a while.*)

HORACE: (*Standing up.*) Walker, if you doan mind me askin' you dis…wat de fock is dat man sayin'? Yah, yah, yah. What sorta singin' yuh call dat. Only some dumb-ass, intellectual, white liberal would like music like dat.

WALKER: Sit down, Horace. Your ignorance of a man like Leadbelly is a crime. Don't make matters worse by being not only ignorant but proud of your ignorance as well. Leadbelly. 'The King of The Twelve String Guitar players of The World.' The man, as dey say, was larger dan life. He was twice pardoned fo' murder. Two separate murders. De man was a violent man, no doubt about dat. Both times he – sang his way to a pardon. –

BUSTER: Nice. Nice one.

WALKER: The second time he got off it was due to the efforts of the man we have to thank fo' most of the recordings made by Leadbelly. A white man of course. Since not many black people really want to know about blues music. To dem it's loser's music. Too depressin'. Anyway, dis white man managed to get Leadbelly paroled. Pardoned. But hear, listen. Dis responsible carin' liberal gentleman took Leadbelly wit' him up North to Washington an' there he used to show him off at parties. You understan' where I'm comin' from. Cocktail parties. Dressed up in 'is convict clothes. Can you jus' see it? Can you see it? All those fat-cat types callin' out to Leadbelly in their cocktail voices: 'sing "Midnight Special". Sing "Goodnight, Irene". He's so…natural, isn't

124

he?' (*Pause.*) An' the worst part of all, the worst part…ah bet he thought dat that proved dey loved him. (*Pause.*) You think you know everything about me, Horace. Don't you? You think all I care about is me. Numero Uno. Well, you dunno shit. You dunno what I feel about nothing. (*Looks at Leadbelly's picture on his wall. A positive declaration of faith.*) They ain't gonna make me dance! They ain't gonna make me sing! An' dat's why dis shop means so much to me. It's my protection. Whatever this shop costs me, whatever de price, I'll pay it.

(*DARLENE enters. Panting a little from the stairs. She has gone to a lot of trouble to make herself look her best. The Phoenix has risen. HORACE whistles his appreciation when he sees her.*)

HORACE: The Queen! The Queen Bee!

DARLENE: Have you told him yet?

HORACE: Darlene, I didn't have a chance.

WALKER: Tell me what?

DARLENE: Horace wants to marry me.

WALKER: What?

DARLENE: Horace wants to marry me.

WALKER: (*To BUSTER.*) What is she saying?

BUSTER: Me? You askin' me?!

DARLENE: Why're you sittin' there workin', Horace? You said you were goin' to tell my husban' you wanted to marry me.

HORACE: I got sidetracked.

WALKER: Darlene, a joke's a joke – !

DARLENE: It's true. We want to get married. Me an' Horace.

WALKER: Woman, you married to me.

DARLENE: Horace, say something, huh.

HORACE: My dear, I don't think your timin' is quite right.

WALKER: Say it's a joke, Darlene!

DARLENE: Ah want a divorce, Walker.

WALKER: (*Some fear now.*) Why are you sayin' dis to me?

DARLENE: You doan love me any more, husban'. Admit it.

WALKER: You're jus' sayin' all dis to punish me, right. Because uh de chile, an' de money an' everything.

DARLENE: De money was de las' straw. But no, ah'm riot tryin' to punish you.

WALKER: Den yuh doin' it to spite me. Cos nobody in dey right mind would want to marry Horace. Except to spite me!

HORACE: No need to get personal, Walker.

DARLENE: (*To WALKER.*) Lord, boy, yuh love yuhself don't you?

WALKER: (*A plea.*) Darlene. Darlene, say it isn't so. Say it, girl. It isn't, is it?
(*A beat.*)

DARLENE: Walker, ah doan want to hurt you.

WALKER: Ah'll break apart, ah'll break apart like a walnut when yuh hit it wit' a hammer. (*Then.*) You're my wife. (*Then.*) Look, look, let's go fo' a walk or something. (*Then.*) Ah'm panicin'! (*Then.*) Oh no. Dis is not really happening to me!
(*A beat.*)

DARLENE: Ah never really thought you'd take it dis bad.

WALKER: Let's go fo' a walk, Darlene.

DARLENE: It won't do any good, Walker. Ah've made up my mind.

WALKER: Aw, shit. (*To BUSTER.*) What do dey want? What do women want?

DARLENE: Doan get me angry, Walker. 'What do women want?' What about yuh white girl? What's 'er name, Liz? An' yuh daughter? How much does she mean to you? Horace comes to see her more often dan you do!

WALKER: (*Terrible rage.*) He does what.! You've introduced my daughter to dat son uva bitch!

HORACE: Hey, hey.

DARLENE: Walker, stop it.

WALKER: (*Fearsomely.*) He's breakin' up my home!
(*WALKER lunges at HORACE. He strikes him a terrific blow. They wrestle. Fall to the floor. They fight like dogs. WALKER striking and striking HORACE. HORACE tries to fight back.*)

DARLENE: Oh God, oh God!

WALKER: Bloody murder! Bloody murder! (*He butts HORACE. Once…twice.*)

HORACE: Get 'im off me!

DARLENE: Buster!

(*BUSTER grabs hold of WALKER. Pins him in a hammer lock. Drags him off HORACE.*)

BUSTER: Enough, Jesus, Walker!

(*WALKER struggles. Then eventually ceases to struggle.*)

WALKER: Okay, okay. Okay, ah said!

(*A beat. BUSTER releases him. WALKER faces BUSTER.*)

The man breakin up my home, Buster.

(*A beat.*)

DARLENE: You doan want me anymore, Walker. Lemme go: Ah beg you.

WALKER: (*To BUSTER.*) The man breakin' up my home.

BUSTER: (*To HORACE.*) Yuh better go.

HORACE: He butt me. You saw it. He butt me.

BUSTER: Yuh rass. If was me I'd a kill yuh.

(*HORACE sucks his teeth, turns away.*)

DARLENE: (*To BUSTER.*) What about me? What about my feelin's? He doesn't want me anymore. Why shouldn't ah look to somebody else?

BUSTER: You're 'is wife. Dat's all I understan'.

DARLENE: I got feelin's too, yuh know.

HORACE: Let's go, my dear. De're stone-age men, those two. Stone-age men.

(*HORACE and DARLENE start to leave shop.*)

WALKER: Darlene.

DARLENE: (*A plea.*) Walker, lemme go.

WALKER: (*Loudly.*) Yuh can't jus' walk out on a marriage like yuh walkin' out on a filmshow yuh doan like.

DARLENE: (*Close to tears.*) You did it first. What about Liz?

(*A beat.*)

Yuh only want me, cos yuh can't bear for anodder man to have me.

WALKER: Ah can change. Ah will change. You'll see.

DARLENE: Oh Walker.

WALKER: Let's go fo' a walk. Jus' you an' me, girl.

DARLENE: (*In tears.*) Ah doan want no walk. Not wit' you, not anymore.

(*A beat.*)

WALKER: Baby, doan talk like dat. Not in front of other people.

DARLENE: (*Still looking at WALKER.*) Horace...there's nothin' more here fo' us. We might as well go. (*Painfully.*) You lose, Walker.

(*Pause. DARLENE and HORACE exit. Pause.*)

WALKER: Ah'm a dead man, Buster. Ah'm a dead man.

BUSTER: She'll come back. If yuh really want 'er back, she'll come back.

WALKER: Yeah, sure. (*Pause.*) Yuh never miss yuh water till yuh well run dry.

BUSTER: We still got to finish dese trousers. Come on ah want to visit de hospital.

WALKER: How is Hortense? Any news?

BUSTER: Your guess is as good as mine.

WALKER: Phone dem. Ah'll phone dem.

BUSTER: Let's finish here firse.

WALKER: (*Sucking his teeth.*) Trousers? Trousers, boy? If ah never see anodder pair uh trousers it'll be too soon.

BUSTER: Look, ah'll do dem. Dey almos' done, anyway.

(*BUSTER works. WALKER reaches blindly for the phone. Knocking a dirty cup that is next to the phone.*)

BUSTER: Get yuhself together, Walker!

(*WALKER dials anxiously. Gets an engaged signal.*)

WALKER: She's engaged. Dis is intolerable! (*He slams down the phone.*)

BUSTER: Who is? Liz? Only one more pair uh trousers to finish.

(*WALKER picks up phone again. Dials.*)

WALKER: Extension two-five... Liz, it's me...look, look, what yuh doin' later...oh no, don't say dat... (*He twists himself away from BUSTER so BUSTER won't hear his pleading tone.*) Liz, look, ah want to see you tonight It's important to me, dat's why! Baby, listen...will you listen Liz, please...ah jus' bought dis shop...yes, it's mine now, it's a big day in my life, but oh God, ah got nobody to celebrate with...ah don't want to spen tonight alone, girl... Liz? Liz?

(*A beat. He looks at BUSTER. Tries to laugh it away.*) We must got cut off, Buster.

(*A beat.*)

BUSTER: Ring 'er back den.

WALKER: Naw. Naw. (*He hangs up.*) Ah'll ring 'er back later. Let 'er suffer for a bit. Eh? Dat's de way to treat women, ain' it? Make dem suffer. Dey love you more for it. Right? (*Pause.*) Well answer me! Ah'm right, aren't I?

BUSTER: Look at de time. Ah got to get to de hospital.

WALKER: Not yet. Not yet, Buster.

BUSTER: Ah got to go, Walker.

WALKER: Tell yuh what, tell yuh what, ah'll phone de hospital fo' you, okay? Okay?

(*A beat.*)

BUSTER: If yuh want, Walker.

(*WALKER lifts the phone.*)

WALKER: What's de number?

(*BUSTER hands a piece of paper with the number on it. WALKER dials. WALKER suddenly hangs up.*)

Okay, okay, you win! Maybe I can't do it on my own.

BUSTER: Do what? What yuh talkin' about? Are you phonin' or not.

WALKER: I can't do it on my own. Okay?

BUSTER: Tomorrow. Let's talk about it tomorrow.

(*A beat. WALKER dials again.*)

Ask for the maternity ward.

WALKER: (*Into phone.*) The maternity ward, please...hello, am, I'm speakin' on the behalf of Mr Gibbs, Buster Gibbs, his wife is expectin' a baby...eh? Say that again...great, great... I'll pass the news on. G'bye. (*He hangs up.*)

BUSTER: Well? Well? What?

WALKER: She had a son. Yuh wife had a baby boy.

BUSTER: A son? A son?

WALKER: (*Tired smile.*) Congratulations an' all dat.

BUSTER: A son? A son?

WALKER: (*Wearily.*) Doan keep sayin' dat, Buster.

BUSTER: A son. Imagine dat. (*He brings out a pick. Begins combing the back of his head.*) A boy. Ah feel so happy ah could cry.

(*Pause. WALKER looking at BUSTER. BUSTER not aware. BUSTER puts away pick. Only then does BUSTER turn to WALKER.*)

Ah'll see you tomorrow, Walker. (*He rubs his hands together.*) Oh God, boy. Oh God. I'm a fadder. See yuh, Walker.

WALKER: (*A plea.*) Buster, wait!

BUSTER: Not now, man. Ah see you, Walker.

(*BUSTER waves, goes. WALKER alone.*)

WALKER: Christ, man. Christ.

(*WALKER looks around the shop. Suddenly he grabs the broom. He starts trying to smash up the shop with broom, the bench, the chairs, the sewing machines. Unseen by him, MR NAT enters.*)

MR NAT: Walker!

(*WALKER stops. Faces MR NAT.*)

A one man riot. How fascinating. Calm down, calm down. I've brought your cheque. (*He does not produce the cheque.*) Somehow, I thought you'd be happier than this.

WALKER: I've lost my wife fo' good, an' probably my daughter as well, but apart from dat I'm fine.

MR NAT: I'm sorry to hear about your wife.

WALKER: Tell me something, Mr Nat. Do you have a lot of friends?

MR NAT: Not a lot. Business acquaintances, mainly. Why?

WALKER: Was it worth it? You're a rich man, was it worth it?

MR NAT: The English love an underdog. Is that what you want, to be an underdog all your life?

WALKER: No way!

MR NAT: Then don't ask stupid questions. (*Then.*) You're not like your friends. You can offer them work. They can't offer you work.

WALKER: I'm my own boss. At last.

MR NAT: Look at it this way. You may have lost a wife, but you've gained a shop!

(*They laugh. MR NAT produces the cheque.*)

Here's your cheque, signed, sealed, delivered, it's yours.

WALKER: (*Taking cheque.*) I like it! I like it!

MR NAT: By the way, in case you're interested, I've found another buyer for another room full of trousers. A Chinese this time.

WALKER: You're on! I'll start on Monday.

(*They shake hands on the deal. Then MR NAT brings out a big, fat cigar. He sticks it in WALKER's mouth.*)

MR NAT: Welcome to the club, Walker Holt. (*Then.*) Got to go now. G'night.

WALKER: G'night, Mr Nat.

(*MR NAT goes. WALKER lights cigar. Then picks up receiver. He dials. Into phone.*)

Hello, is that Cheshire, Woods an' Company? It's Walker Holt here, lemme speak to Mr Woods. (*He puffs on his cigar.*) ...oh hello, Walker Holt here, it's about dis shop, sixty-five B Carnaby Street...yes, ah've finally got the money, what time can ah come in an' see you...yeah fine... (*He writes down the time.*) ...right, okay, see you tomorrow...excited? Yeah, sure, after all, it's all I've ever wanted. But the price, yuh know. Dere's always an extra price. Isn't dere? Well see yuh later, Mr Woods.

(*He hangs up. He then crosses to a window. He opens the window. He sticks his head out the window. Shouts.*)

I've beaten you, you bastards!

The End.

IN THE MOOD

Characters

ORRIN HARRIS

T.D. MAXWELL

SONIA HARRIS

KATE SMOLLETT

TREVOR BISHOP

In The Mood was first performed at the Hampstead Theatre on 1 October 1981, with the following cast:

ORRIN, Norman Beaton

T.D., Allister Bain

SONIA, Mona Hammond

KATE, Marty Cruickshank

TREVOR, Stefan Kalipha

Director, Robin Lefevre

Designer, Sue Plummer

ACT ONE

Spotlight on bare forestage. On two middle-aged West Indian men in uniform. Both ex-Royal Air Force. The two men are laying a wreath. ORRIN HARRIS and T.D. MAXWELL. ORRIN is the lean one. T.D. the heavier one.

They lay wreath.

Bugle sounds off-stage. The National Anthem is played. The two men stand to attention.

Black out.

Lights come up on set behind. A living room, A large room, two rooms knocked into one. The Harris' living room. Quite a well appointed living room: the Harris's live pretty well. But nothing old or antique. The three piece suite is the sort of stuff to be found in any large furniture store, usually overpriced. A number of small cushions scattered about the room. Small red cushions, blue, brown ones, plain colours, not stripes or polka dots, Not excessively colourful either. The Harris's see themselves as being able to afford a middle class lifestyle, to them excessive use of colour is working class. Up right is their dining table, There is also a small piano in this room against the left wall. On the piano and on the mantelpiece are a number of colour photographs, family, friends, holiday snapshots, most of them taken back in the West Indies. Hanging on the walls are one or two paintings, of certain well-known Guyanese landmarks, in particular Kieture Falls, the Stabrock Market. Also a large photograph, group of West Indian soldiers during the second world war.

There is something else in a prominent position on the left wall: a Luger pistol in a proper holster and belt belonging to some long dead German soldier. What else is in this room? A stereo set. Also a lovely bar, built to ORRIN's specifications, ORRIN's pride and joy. There is a window in the right wall. Only one door in or out of this room.

SONIA HARRIS enters. She starts to lay the table. SONIA: West Indian, late forties. Smartly dressed for her guests. A cut above her husband, ORRIN, and we must feel that this is what he has paid for, her 'respectable middle classness'. She does not hold with loudness or untidiness or smut. Her sense of humour is her saving grace, even though she can be quite caustic at times.

After a moment or two, we hear somebody at the front door – off. Then we hear ORRIN in the hall – off.

ORRIN: (*Off.*) Woo! Woo! We're back! We're back!
  (*ORRIN and T.D. enter living room. Coats over their uniforms. T.D. is carrying a suite on a hanger. A brown suit he will change into later. T.D. looks a bit upset over something ORRIN has said to him.*)
  (*On entering.*) General Eisenhower an' Sir Winston Churchill.
  (*ORRIN: successful West Indian. Fifty-five years old. Owns 'Blitz' an emergency plumbing service. An effervescent man but not a particularly loud man. Like his wife, he too believes in respectability.*
  T.D. MAXWELL: West Indian. Same age as ORRIN. Loves to pontificate. A wine snob. A food snob. But T.D. is not a buffoon and must not be played as a buffoon.)
T.D.: (*Savouring the word.*) Felicitations, Sonia.
  (*They kiss.*)
ORRIN: (*Quite pleased about it.*) T.D.'s in a bad mood.
T.D.: (*On his dignity.*) I am not in a bad mood.
ORRIN: He's angry as hell at me.
T.D.: I am not angry at you. This is your house after all.
ORRIN: All I said, T.D. was that the only thing you talk about these days is Politics.
T.D.: That was not all you said.
ORRIN: Oh yes, that's right. I called you a bore as well.
  I do apologise. I didn't mean it.
SONIA: (*Pouring oil on troubled waters.*) So how is Councillor Maxwell?
T.D.: I'm not a Councillor yet, Sonia. So far I'm only one of a number of possible candidates. The actual elections aren't until next year. (*He starts taking off his coat.*)
SONIA: Tell me something, how come you're a Labour Party candidate? You've been votin' Conservative for years.

T.D.: You know that. But the Socialists, they don't know that.
(*T.D. who has taken off his coat, holds it out to ORRIN. ORRIN turns away at that exact moment…*)

ORRIN: Let's slip out of all this politics an' in to a nice, cold drink. (*He moves to the bar.*)

SONIA: I'll take your coat, T.D. Your suit too.
(*She takes T.D.'s coat and suit, ORRIN holds out his coat for her to take. She grabs his coat from him, but at the last moment gives him a smile.*)

ORRIN: What can I get you, my dear?

SONIA: (*Fondly.*) A little sherry. An' when I say a little, I mean a little.

ORRIN: I'll use an eye dropper, dear.

SONIA: (*Going, pleased.*) Wicked. So wicked. (*She exits with coats.*)

ORRIN: How about you, T.D.?

T.D.: (*Still seething a little.*) A scotch, old boy.

ORRIN: (*Out to tease.*) You still vex with me, T.D.?
(*ORRIN is very particular about his drinks. Very theatrical. He takes ages. A production.*)

T.D.: You called me a bore. I shan't forget that in a hurry.
(*T.D. remains standing. As yet no-one has sat down. SONIA returns.*)

SONIA: Do sit down, T.D. (*She sits.*) That's why we have chairs.

T.D.: (*Glaring at ORRIN.*) I prefer to stand. (*Then to her.*) How is Brenda? When did you last see her?

SONIA: Last weekend. She's in Los Angeles now. (*Then.*) What about Kate? What time is she comin'?

T.D.: She should have been here by now. (*Pompously.*) When it comes to being on time some Europeans are as bad as some West Indians.

ORRIN: You tell them, T.D.

T.D.: What're you doing with those drinks?

SONIA: (*To T.D.*) Anyway, how is Kate? Is she still writin' her West Indian cookbook? And is she plannin' any more 'simply marvellous' Caribbean holidays? I still remember her last holiday – to where was it? The

Bahamas? She came back all red an' purple an' peelin'. Like one of Mae West's grapes.

(*ORRIN laughs quietly.*)

T.D.: Sonia, I don't think you like Kate.

SONIA: Tell me, T.D. when're you goin' to get married?

(*ORRIN brings over the drinks, on a tray.*)

ORRIN: (*Serving SONIA.*) Get married? T.D.?

T.D.: (*Again irritated by ORRIN.*) Why not? What's so funny about that?

(*ORRIN serves T.D. ORRIN sits. T.D. remains standing. He is peering at his drink.*)

What is this?

ORRIN: What is what, dear friend?

T.D.: What's in this glass?

ORRIN: Scotch, T.D. Scotch,

T.D.: Yes, I know, but what's swimming in it? Looks like a frog.

ORRIN: That's watercress.

T.D.: Watercress! Watercress! Watercress in a scotch? I asked for a drink, not a salad.

ORRIN: Why not watercress? I'll try anything once.

T.D.: Not in my glass you won't. (*Holds out his glass to ORRIN.*) Here take it out.

(*ORRIN sighs, rises. Takes T.D.'s glass. Then he looks at his wife.*)

ORRIN: (*In SONIA's direction.*) He really is a bore, isn't he? (*And returns to bar.*)

T.D.: (*Seeking support.*) Sonia!

SONIA: Ignore him, T.D. Just think of him as a mild headache.

(*ORRIN fishes out the watercress from T.D.'s glass. With a swizzle stick. Then returns to T.D.'s side. Hands over drink.*)

ORRIN: There. Happier now?

T.D.: I'm glad to see you didn't use your finger.

(*ORRIN sits.*)

ORRIN: Put my finger in your glass? I have too much respect, for my finger.

SONIA: (*Getting in quickly.*) How did the parade go, T.D.? You all had a good time?

T.D.: With all due respect, Sonia…one does not pay a visit to the Cenotaph on November fifth to have a 'good time'.

SONIA: You mean yo-all march past the Cenotaph, year after year, to have a bad time?

T.D.: Did you see us on Television?

SONIA: Sorry, no. I was too busy, T.D. Sunday lunch doesn't cook itself.

T.D.: (*Trying to make her feel guilty.*) Remembrance Sunday is the Sunday of the year.

SONIA: I tell you what. Next Remembrance Day I'll go marchin' an' you two can stay home an' cook the food.

T.D.: (*Going quiet.*) Point taken.

SONIA: (*Gently.*) Sit down. Come on.

T.D.: (*Looking at ORRIN.*) Well… (*He sits. To SONIA.*) Did you find those records we talked about last time?

SONIA: What records?

T.D.: The Master! The Master!

SONIA: The Master?

ORRIN: He means Glenn Miller.

SONIA: Oh, him. They're upstairs, somewhere. I'll have a look later.

ORRIN: (*To T.D.*) Old Sir John was at the parade. Did you see him? Still every inch a soldier.

T.D.: The man's a gentleman. They don't make Englishmen like him any more. More's the pity.

ORRIN: Roll on next year.

T.D.: (*Testing him.*) Incidentally, what's your, am, decision?

ORRIN: Decision?

T.D.: About giving me your support.

(*T.D. draws his chair closer to ORRIN.*)

I don't mean to press you, of course.

ORRIN: T.D.…

T.D.: (*Leaning forward.*) Yes?

ORRIN: You're pressin' me.

(*T.D. is offended.*)

SONIA: What decision? What are you talkin' about?

T.D.: I want your husband to help me in the elections.

SONIA: In what way?

T.D.: In this borough the West Indian vote could make or break a politician.

ORRIN: T.D., it's Sunday, why do you have to talk about politics?

T.D.: Why shouldn't I talk about politics?

ORRIN: When it comes to politics, that's all you do about it. Talk about it. Like most West Indians.

T.D.: And what do you do about it?

(*Pause. ORRIN made uncomfortable rises, crosses to bar. To freshen up his drink. After doing so he remains standing behind bar.*)

SONIA: What do you think Orrin can do to help you?

T.D.: Your husband is a successful man. He knows most of the West Indians who have any influence here in Clapham.

(*SONIA notices ORRIN has not rejoined them.*)

SONIA: (*To ORRIN.*) Dear, what's the matter? What're you doin' over there?

ORRIN: Leave me alone, Sonia.

SONIA: What's eatin' you?

ORRIN: Politics, politics, politics. (*He sucks his teeth.*) There're two topics that cost the most bloody trouble in the world. Politics an' race. The two most bloody topics.

T.D.: (*Magnanimously.*) If it makes you happy, I'll drop the subject. (*Then hand up.*) But – before I do, give me your promise. Endorse me publicly. That way I will be assured of the black vote.

ORRIN: Just by me endorsin' you publicly? You have such faith in me.

T.D.: I do have faith in you, old boy.

ORRIN: I'm touched. Either that or you're touched. In the head.

T.D.: This might come as a surprise to both of you, but I've been very busy these last few months. Very busy. I go to meetings regularly – I deliver leaflets – I've delivered so many leaflets the Guinness Book of Records is considering devoting a whole page to me.

ORRIN: That's all very well an' good, but what do you believe in?

T.D.: I believe in fighting the Left Wing faction tooth and nail.

ORRIN: The Left Wing faction? T.D., your enemy is the Tories, not the Labour Left. (*Then.*) T.D. as a politician, what do you stand for? Do you even have any catchy political slogans?

T.D.: How about 'I fought in the Second World War.'

ORRIN: What's wrong with this man? The Second World War was nearly two generations ago. Not even Biggles could win an election with that slogan.

T.D.: Okay, okay. How about 'I stand for Law 'n' order.'

ORRIN: Now yuh talkin'. You can fool a lotta voters with that one. The whites think you mean to arrest the Blacks, an' the Blacks will think you mean to arrest the Whites. How can you lose?

T.D.: (*Getting quite carried away.*) I got a better one. 'I'll stand firm on job opportunities.'

ORRIN: Woo! Woo! I like it. It doesn't say you'll help anybody find a job. All it says is that you'll stand firm on the question of job opportunities. That could mean any goddam thing.

T.D.: (*Loudly.*) With all due respect – I am being serious.

ORRIN: T.D.… I know you are. That's what worries me.

T.D.: (*Raising his voice.*) I'm not playing at it! I'm not playing at politics!

ORRIN: (*Shouting.*) I thought we agreed to drop the subject.

SONIA: Stop shouting, you two. You're not in Brixton or Harlem now. Now stop it.

T.D.: You're perfectly right, Sonia. I apologise. You can always tell a man who lacks refinement and breeding he invariably resorts to shouting. (*He gives ORRIN a look. To make sure ORRIN has got the message.*)

ORRIN: Shout? Me? You know how much I pay to live in this neighbourhood. In this street, they don't sell houses to shouters.

(*ORRIN returns to his seat, Even T.D. sits down.*)

T.D.: It's funny. Funny peculiar. At the Cenotaph…during the march past… I was thinking about George. George Lucas.

SONIA: Dear George. I wonder how he is these days? I wonder if he's still happy being back in Trinidad.

T.D.: I don't suppose in Trinidad they have such things as 'Remembrance Sunday'.

SONIA: (*Sad.*) He stopped writin'. Haven't had even a Christmas card in years.

T.D.: Our reunions no longer seem the same. Not without old George. Remember how he used to love wearing all his medals.

ORRIN: (*Some jealousy.*) So he won a few medals! So what? I won a few medals too.

(*The doorbell is heard. T.D. rises.*)

T.D.: That'll be Kate. I'll let her in.

(*T.D. goes out to answer the door.*)

SONIA: You think she will ever marry him?

ORRIN: She's a teacher, Sonia. She deals with children all day. She doesn't want a child at night as well.

SONIA: I'm surprised they're still together. What makes her stay?

T.D.: (*Off.*) Give me your coat.

KATE: (*Off.*) I hope you've noticed I'm wearing a dress for a change. I don't suppose you'd like it.

T.D.: (*Off.*) Yes, yes, come on, come on in.

(*KATE SMOLLETT enters. With T.D.*
KATE: English. Thirty-five. Daughter of a vicar, a provincial vicar, not a trendy vicar. Tall, attractive enough. At first it is difficult to say what she is doing with T.D. Gushes when nervous. Wearing a sensible dress but one that shows her legs, her best point, when she sits down. SONIA and ORRIN rise as they enter.)

SONIA: Hello, Kate.

KATE: Oh, hello, Sonia – Orrin – been ages hasn't it? Yonks. Did T.D. tell you last month he narrowly missed death?

ORRIN: Missed death? What's this? Why do you keep such good news to yourself, T.D.?

KATE: Yes – missed death – yet again – fell asleep at the wheel most likely –

T.D.: I did not!

KATE: Put him behind the wheel of a car and he automatically goes to sleep.

T.D.: Once! One time!

ORRIN: (*To SONIA.*) They're having a lovers quarrel, dear. Restores your faith in romance, doesn't it?

KATE: (*A smile, a little less nervous.*) You haven't changed, have you?

ORRIN: You look like you could do with a drink.

KATE: Could do… Dry Martini and tonic, thank you.
(*ORRIN goes behind the bar.*)

T.D.: I was not asleep at the wheel.
(*KATE ignores T.D. She moves over to Luger on wall.*)

KATE: You still have this pistol? It's against the law of England. To have a real gun in your possession. (*Then.*) So, Orrin, how is the emergency plumbing business empire?

ORRIN: Can't complain. Another…small sherry, dear? And how about you, T.D.? Another scotch? I'll leave out the watercress this time.
(*SONIA hands her glass to T.D. T.D. takes their two empty glasses over to ORRIN.*)

KATE: When a businessman says he can't complain, business must be very good, indeed.

SONIA: Sit down, Kate.

KATE: Sorry, what? Oh. (*She sits down.*)

ORRIN: I can still remember when it was just me an' one helper. Now I got over twenty plumbers workin' for me. Woo, woo, don't forget my motto.

KATE: (*Smiling.*) What motto?

ORRIN: 'It's not the streets of London that are paved with gold, it's the blocked sinks an' the toilets'!
(*KATE laughs. ORRIN has poured KATE's drink. He hands it to T.D.*)

SONIA: How is school? Or shouldn't I ask?
(*T.D, hands KATE her drink.*)

KATE: Thank you, T.D. (*To SONIA.*) School is rapidly driving me to thoughts of mass murder. Apart from that everything's fine.

ORRIN: I passed by your school the other day.

KATE: Did you? Why didn't you drop in, say hello?

ORRIN: At your school? I couldn't afford the bodyguards. There were one or two specimens hangin' aroun' the school gates. Swearin' an' carryin' on. An' they were only the teachers.

KATE: (*To SONIA.*) Does he ever stop?

SONIA: I don't know girl. I've only been married to him for twenty four years.

(*T.D. hands SONIA her sherry. He takes his own scotch. T.D. sits. ORRIN comes from behind bar. He remains standing.*)

KATE: (*To ORRIN.*) We have seventeen different nationalities at our school, West Indians, Pakistans, Greeks, Africans –

ORRIN: What, no English?

KATE: Some English, of course.

ORRIN: Sounds like the English at your school are an endangered species.

KATE: Africans, Irish, Saudi Arabians –

T.D.: Saudi Arabians? No doubt they want to buy the school? Ho, ho, ho.

KATE: Chinese, Maltese –

ORRIN: They come in a box, don't they?

KATE: Gypsies. I know I shouldn't say this but they're the most trouble. The Gypsies. The other kids are usually quite clean. But we often have to send home the Gypsies. It's their hair. The nits. Covered in nits. We have to think of the other children.

ORRIN: Let's hear it for the gypsies.

SONIA: Personally I think you should send home some of those young West Indians who cause trouble. The ones who go around with their hair plaited. Makes them look so untidy.

KATE: We've even had some Vietnamese children recently.

ORRIN: Yeah? Vietnamese?

KATE: They're adorable, aren't they?

ORRIN: Adorable? Not when you're fightin' them. Ask the Americans.

KATE: (*A laugh, she knows ORRIN is teasing.*) I'm being serious! They're so well-behaved. They've helped considerably to raise the tone of our school.

ORRIN: Woo! Woo! What do you think of that, Sonia? They've got to import Vietnamese children to raise the tone of their school.

KATE: (*Cheerfully.*) Stop it, you. (*Then.*) Anyway, it's a lovely school. All those nationalities help to make it special. Not the sort of school I was accustomed to in Dorset.

(*For a moment they all go quiet, picturing KATE at her school in Dorset.*)

T.D.: (*Abruptly.*) A school is like the political arena. Sometimes calm, sometimes intimidating, but always fascinating.

ORRIN: (*Moving away.*) He's back on politics again!

T.D.: Sonia, you could help me as well.

SONIA: Me?

T.D.: You're very good at organising functions and things.

SONIA: What about Kate here?

KATE: He's got me doing other things.

SONIA: Well, I must say I do see myself as a good hostess. A born organiser. Not that I'm trying to blow my own trumpet, but I am.

KATE: I blame myself for all these delusions of his.

T.D.: I beg your pardon! What delusions?

KATE: I'm the one who first suggested to him that he join the Labour Party.

ORRIN: The Labour Party may never recover.

KATE: (*To SONIA.*) How is Brenda?

SONIA: Fine. We never see her but she's fine. She's always over the Atlantic.

KATE: Over the Atlantic?

T.D.: She's a stewardess, dear.

KATE: (*A laugh.*) Oh yes. Of course. How stupid of me.

ORRIN: Sometimes I wonder if Brenda isn't just carryin' on with some married pilot. I imagine them up there demonstratin' life jackets and things an' sayin' to each other: 'we really can't go on meetin' like this.'

(*KATE gives a soft, pleased laugh.*)

KATE: (*To SONIA.*) He never fails to make me laugh.

SONIA: Yes. So I've noticed.

(*Pause. None of the others quite know how to take that one.*)

KATE: (*Trying to fill the awkward vacuum.*) Um, Orrin, do you still have your, um, gadget. The one you showed me

147

last time. (*To SONIA.*) He took out his gadget and showed
it to me.

SONIA: My husband did what?

KATE: Oh Lord, that's not what I meant!

SONIA: He took his gadget out an' showed it to you?

ORRIN: Sonia, you know Kate means that new electronic
gadget I bought, the one that opens the garage door.

SONIA: Oh, that thing.

KATE: (*Quietly.*) Don't worry, Sonia, I can take a little joke.
You can too, I hope?

(*Pause. ORRIN suddenly jumps up.*)

ORRIN: (*Acting a bit strange.*) Woo, woo, I got it in my coat,
the gadget. Excuse me. (*He leaves the room.*)

KATE: Very American, isn't it? An electronically controlled
garage door! What next?

T.D.: He's too lazy.

(*ORRIN returns, gadget in hand.*)

ORRIN: Who're you callin' lazy? (*He crosses to window.
Points gadget out, He presses button on the gadget. Presumably
the garage door (off) opens.*) Open sesame! (*He works gadget
again.*) Close, sesame! (*To T.D. and the others.*) Like 'Magic
Roundabout', ain' it? (*He moves away from window. Crosses
behind bar. Puts away the gadget.*)

SONIA: Forgive my husband. He's crazy.

(*ORRIN rejoins them.*)

ORRIN: Okay, I'm back. You can start talkin' again.

SONIA: (*Some mischief here.*) So, Kate, how is it coming
along? Your West Indian cookbook.

KATE: I made some souse recently.

SONIA: Souse? You made souse?

KATE: I did. You gave me the recipe, remember?

SONIA: You made souse?

KATE: Well, it's not that incredible, is it?

SONIA: Souse? You're a real Guyanese now, aren't you?

KATE: No thanks to T.D. He's the so-called Master Chef in
our house but he never cooks anything even remotely
tropical. Believe me, it can get a bit weird, living with a
West Indian who only cooks Polish food.

T.D.: I don't only cook Polish food.

ORRIN: Talkin' about food, Sonia.

SONIA: (*Rising.*) I know, I know. I made some patties, I'll get them.

KATE: Oh, can I help?

SONIA: No, sit down. (*Then.*) Orrin, we can't eat until your friend gets here.

T.D.: Friend? You've invited somebody else?

ORRIN: He's our friend, Sonia.

SONIA: Trevor Bishop? Not my frien'.

T.D.: (*Getting up.*) Trevor! Trevor Bishop!

SONIA: (*To ORRIN.*) To me he's a hustler an' a drunk. Even sober he's a hustler an' a drunk.

T.D.: That con man is coming here?

SONIA: You mean Orrin didn't tell you?

KATE: (*To T.D.*) He's not a con man. He used to be a teacher.

T.D.: You think because he was a teacher he cannot be a con man? You don't know many teachers, do you?

SONIA: I'll get those patties. (*She leaves the room.*)

T.D.: Why didn't you tell me you'd invited Trevor Bishop?

ORRIN: He invited himself.

T.D.: Invited himself? Who is he? Royalty?

ORRIN: He phoned, said he's in trouble. He only comes to see me when he needs to borrow money.

T.D.: You know how I feel about Trevor.

KATE: Here we go again.

T.D.: (*Rounding on her.*) I'd keep quiet if I were you.

KATE: What is that supposed to mean?

T.D.: To listen to Trevor you'd think there's nothing he can't do. He's a teacher, an actor, a singer. Last time I saw him he was goin' on about yet another of his wild schemes. A disco, this time. He drinks so much, that man.

ORRIN: All I know is that he had a part in some musical that they were tryin' out in Brighton or somewhere.

T.D.: I suppose he has a half-decent singin' voice. He can't sing, he –

KATE: He can sing. Very well too. He sings a lot like Nat King Cole.

T.D.: If you know so bloody much about Trevor's singing voice, what other parts of him do you know about? (*Pause.*)

KATE: Do you realise what you're saying, T.D.? Do you? Especially in front of a mutual friend. (*Pause.*)

T.D.: I think I'll go upstairs, change in to my suit.

KATE: Good.

T.D.: (*To ORRIN.*) Just going upstairs. How about you?

ORRIN: I'll stay like this. You never know, somebody might declare another war. I'd be ready to go immediately.

(*T.D. goes to the door. Stops. Turns. Glares at KATE, then goes. Upstairs – off.*)

He gets very jealous about you, doesn't he?

KATE: It's getting worse. He even believes there's something going on between Trevor and I.

ORRIN: Is there?

KATE: No. You know that, Trevor is not my sort. (*Pause.*) What do I do about T.D.? I don't want to hurt him but, recently, I have been thinking a lot about leaving him.

ORRIN: And what have you decided?

KATE: I was going to make my decision today.

ORRIN: Today?

KATE: My only worry is…going out with T.D. is marginally better than the alternative. Not going out at all.

ORRIN: What? An attractive woman like you.

KATE: You forget, I'm thirty-five years old.

ORRIN: What about all those men teachers?

KATE: What men teachers? Don't make me laugh.

ORRIN: Well, so much for men teachers.

KATE: I went home to Dorset for a week. I haven't seen you since. Have I?

ORRIN: How was Dorset?

KATE: White. White and Protestant. Middle England personified. Do you realise? Do you realise that before I came to London I had never even seen a black person. I mean I wouldn't be surprised if it isn't against the law to be black in places like Dorset and Cornwall.

ORRIN: Perhaps it's only a local ordinance.

KATE: (*Ignoring that one.*) I can remember when my father was still a vicar in Stormington Newton.

ORRIN: Stormington where?

KATE: No, Newton. (*She smiles.*) Stormington Newton. It's a market town. Anyway, my father would often make an appeal on behalf of the poor, black babies in Africa. Everybody was always remarkably generous yet many of us had never even laid eyes on an actual black baby. African or otherwise. Why am I telling you all this?

ORRIN: I was just about to ask you that very same question.

KATE: Yes, well. (*Pause.*) I taught in Dorset for a while and then came to London. What a difference. During my very first week in London they threw me in the deep end. That school in Notting Hill Gate of all places! A bit like going from a convent to Cambodia.

ORRIN: (*Drily.*) You deserve an Iron Cross, at the very least.

KATE: You're making fun of me. I've grown up a lot since then. Now I think I know more about black people than T.D. does.

ORRIN: That's not sayin' much. Even Snow White knows more about black people than T.D.

KATE: (*Abruptly.*) Has T.D. been on to you about the elections?

ORRIN: Yes, at great length.

KATE: And will you help him?

ORRIN: I haven't made up my mind.

KATE: How do you rate his political chances?

ORRIN: T.D.! A Councillor! What chances?

(*Pause, She gets up. Moves around.*)

KATE: I suppose I feel a bit responsible for T.D.

ORRIN: Why?

KATE: If you helped him then I'd find it easier to leave him.

ORRIN: You want me to help T.D. become a Labour Councillor, just so you can turn around an' leave him?

KATE: I didn't mean it that way. All I mean is that he wouldn't need me as much if he was elected a Councillor.

ORRIN: Women love to think men need them, don't they?

KATE: T.D. needs both of us. You and me.

ORRIN: You've changed your tune, haven't you? Just about two months ago, you were sayin' I should stand for Councillor.

KATE: I still feel you should.

ORRIN: You even got some of your Socialist friends to see if I'd be interested.

KATE: And why not? You've been a member of the Labour Party for some years.

ORRIN: Yet all of a sudden you're headin' the 'T.D. For Councillor' Campaign. How come?

KATE: That's his fantasy, not mine...! Does he know?

ORRIN: Know what?

KATE: About my friends? My 'Socialist Friends', as you call them. Does he know they've been in touch with you?

ORRIN: No, I have not told him.

KATE: I see.

(*A beat.*)

Why haven't you?

ORRIN: Because I haven't decided what I'm goin' to do.

KATE: You've had more than enough time to make your mind up.

ORRIN: I run a business. People expect a Councillor to be at their beck an' call twenty-four hours a day. I'd rather be a rich immigrant.

KATE: (*A bit upset.*) Don't say that! It lessens you. (*Then.*) I blame Sonia. You'd do far more if you had the right woman behind you.

ORRIN: (*Warning her.*) Kate, don't go over that again, please.

KATE: I have a theory about you and Sonia. Don't you want to hear my theory?

ORRIN: I don't want to hear any theories, Kate.

(*Pause.*)

KATE: (*Abruptly, made nervous.*) I had a dream last night. Can I at least tell you about my dream? I dreamt about the Cheese Counter in Selfridges.

ORRIN: Selfridges! The Cheese Counter?

KATE: I always reckon the Cheese Counter in Selfridges is a good place to be picked up. Always providing that one wants to be picked up, of course.

ORRIN: Oh, of course.

KATE: Anyway, I dreamt I met this man there – this American – at the Cheese Counter in Selfridges –
(*ORRIN sighs.*)

KATE: – a very tall, very rich American. Very tall. A freak. About seven foot.

ORRIN: Only seven foot?

KATE: He was sort of embracing me. He had to lift me up to kiss me. A freak. About seven foot. God, it was awful. (*Then.*) Don't be cross with me.

ORRIN: I'm not 'cross' with you. Why should I be 'cross'?

KATE: Because of what I said about Sonia. (*Then.*) Well, I'm not sorry.
(*He moves to bar, a bit irritated by her. Pours another drink.*)
You were cross last week when I rang you. You hung up on me.

ORRIN: You know why! We both agreed. To forget.

KATE: You agreed.
(*She moves near to him. She makes a move to touch him. Stops herself. Pause. He moves away.*)

ORRIN: Just don't ring me, Kate. Please.

KATE: (*Becoming nervous.*) I just rang. So what if I rang – just the other night a man rang me – a heavy breather – took me ages to even find out what the hell he wanted – it turned out he wanted to borrow my knickers – I told him to buy his own knickers.

ORRIN: Kate, what the hell are you talkin' about?

KATE: (*Moving towards him.*) You don't allow people to be human.
(*Again he moves away.*)

ORRIN: What? What do you mean?

KATE: (*Pain.*) You're like all men!

ORRIN: I give up. Not even Freud or Mickey Mouse, could make sense of this conversation.

KATE: (*Some dislike.*) One day I'll be the one who's laughing, not you.

ORRIN: Laughin'? Do you see me laughin'?

KATE: There is only one reason I continue to see T.D. so I can continue to see you. (*Pause.*) I don't even have a physical relationship with him anymore.

ORRIN: Kate, please keep your voice down. (*Cornered laugh.*) I'm not sayin' I don't still like being near you…

KATE: (*Offended.*) Thanks very much.

ORRIN: Kate, admit it, what happened between us, it's been very short.

KATE: All the more reason why it needn't end so quickly.

ORRIN: You know what would happen if Sonia found out? She'd do two things. She'd kill you once. Then she'd kill you a second time! You, not me.

KATE: (*Firmly.*) Maybe so. Let me worry about Sonia.

ORRIN: No, I worry about Sonia.

(*A beat.*)

I told you that from the very start.

(*Pause, T.D. returns. Has changed into his suit. A sort of cravat tied at his throat, rather than a tie.*)

T.D.: I'm back again, was I missed?

(*KATE sits, sighing.*)

ORRIN: Missed is hardly the word, T.D.

T.D.: Pardon, old boy?

ORRIN: Want another drink, T.D.?

T.D.: No, I'm perfectly fine.

KATE: (*Getting up again, restless.*) May I help myself?

ORRIN: Be my guest.

(*KATE crosses to bar.*)

T.D.: Have you given it any more thought, my political aspirations?

ORRIN: Persistent, aren't you, T.D.? Jesus. Anyway, you have political aspirations? Why didn't anyone tell me?

T.D.: We could win!

ORRIN: We?

T.D.: Me! Me! Me!

ORRIN: (*To KATE.*) I like the way he says 'Me, me, me!' He's beginnin' to sound more an' more like a politician every minute.

T.D.: I'd make an exemplary black politician. I'd never be drunk. I'd never be found with my fingers in the till – black people would never need to feel ashamed of me.

ORRIN: Is that it? Is that the full extent of your political platform? The fact that black people would never feel ashamed of you?

T.D.: Don't knock it. Compared with some of the politicians around today, both black an' white, that's saying a lot.

ORRIN: That's all very well an' good, T.D. But this is Clapham. Okay, so I live in the up-market part of Clapham, or so they tell me. However just a couple of bus rides away from here is Clapham Junction. Or Clapham Jungle, as some people call it. But if you expect them to vote for you, what do you hope to do for them?

T.D.: I thought we'd been over this ground already.

KATE: No, you haven't T.D. There are a number of things you've been quite blithely ignoring. You're depending on black voters, how do you plan to help them in return? Deprivation breeds deprivation. You have to find a way to break that circle.

T. D.: Everybody knows where I stand on the pertinent social issues of the day!

ORRIN: That's exactly it, we don't know!

T.D.: As I see it, we need to go back to the old truths: humanity, brotherhood, decency. An' there's one certain way to re-introduce those ideals in to our society. Bring back hanging.

KATE: We're being serious.

T.D.: An' you think I'm not being serious?

KATE: God.

ORRIN: T.D., you're a politician for all seasons. A Socialist outside, an' a Conservative inside. The English will love you.

T.D.: (*Crying out.*) What do you want from me?

ORRIN: Open you eyes, T.D. that'll do for a start.

T.D.: What's eatin' at you, man?

ORRIN: I'm in my fifties…! Every evenin' all I do when I come home from work is that I pour a glass of Scotch, then I park myself down in front of the T.V.

T.D.: So?

ORRIN: I keep thinkin' I should be contributing in some way.

T.D.: In what way?

ORRIN: Forget it. You don't understan' a word I'm sayin'. (*Shouting.*) Sonia! What're you doin' with those patties?

Trainin' them to walk? (*To KATE.*) Any moment now we'll be invaded by a band of strollin' patties.

(*KATE and ORRIN exchange a smile. Pause. T.D. crosses to Luger hanging on the wall.*)

T.D.: When are you goin' to get rid of this old thing?

ORRIN: Why?

(*T.D. takes down pistol, holster, and belt. Straps them around his waist.*)

KATE: You really should have a licence for it.

ORRIN: Licence? I don't even have bullets for it.

(*T.D. is strutting around with the pistol on his hip. Trying out his first draw.*)

ORRIN: Look at him. He thinks he's hopalong Cassidy.

T.D.: (*Miffed.*) You're very offensive sometimes.

ORRIN: I'm jokin' T.D. Lord, man.

T.D.: (*To KATE.*) You know how he got this, don't you? He won it in a poker game. A poker game.

ORRIN: Here, give me that!

(*ORRIN snatches pistol back from T.D. ORRIN returns gun, belt and holster to wall. SONIA returns. Bearing a plate of patties, savoury mince beef patties.*)

Where've you been, Sonia? Calcutta?

(*ORRIN moves to piano.*)

SONIA: (*To KATE.*) Will you have a patty?

KATE: (*Taking one.*) Thank you. (*Tastes it.*) Mmm. Wonderful. Wonderful.

ORRIN: (*Picking out a few notes to go with his words.*) They're Guyanese patties. Good for fatties!

(*T.D. helps himself to two patties.*)

KATE: What's the difference between a Guyanese patty and, say, a Jamaican patty?

(*SONIA brings plate over to ORRIN.*)

ORRIN: (*Helping himself.*) Thank you, darling. (*Then to KATE.*) A Jamaican patty is much bigger. You can always tell a Jamaican patty. It looks like it wants to fight you.

KATE: May I have another?

SONIA: (*Pleased.*) Just help yourself.

(*KATE does so.*)

KATE: T.D., why don't you make patties like these?

T.D.: Because, my dear, I'm known for my Polish patties.

SONIA: What the hell is a Polish patty?

T.D.: That's a meat patty made entirely with potatoes.

ORRIN: Joke! Joke! T.D.! T.D.! Remember this? (*He plays, sings 'We'll meet again'.*) We'll meet again…
(*T.D. joins in. They sing together.*)
Dunno where, dunno when…
(*They sing quite a bit of the song. KATE and SONIA applaud, even if somewhat ironically.*)
Woo! Woo! The good old days, T.D.

T.D.: Fun an' comradeship.

ORRIN: (*Playing piano like a mad concert pianist.*) Fun an' comradeship. Toodle-dum an- Toodle-do. Thank God for World War Two. (*He ends with a flourish.*)

SONIA: My husban', the Mad Pianist.

T.D.: (*To ORRIN.*) Remember those two black G.I.'s

ORRIN: Who?

T.D.: The two black American soldiers. Met them in a pub. We were stationed in Warwick at the time. 1943.

ORRIN: Young! One of them was called Young.

T.D.: That's right! What was the other one called? Oates? Otis!

ORRIN: Woo! Woo! Otis! Otis!

T.D.: (*To KATE and SONIA.*) One night the four of us were in this pub-five, George was there too, of course. (*To KATE.*) You've heard me talk of our friend, George Lucas, haven't you? Anyway, the five of us were the only non-whites in the pub, at the time. An' this was a time when Coloured people weren't exactly a common sight in the streets of Britain. We were playing darts, I recall. Darts. Ah. Wonderful, English game.

ORRIN: Get on with it, man.

T.D.: Otis went to the bar, To order another round of liquid refreshments. At the bar he had an altercation with a white American G.I. The white American started it first. He made some racial remark to Otis. A quarrel ensued.

ORRIN: Young meanwhile was still playin' darts with us. He used to always wear his army coat. Even playin' darts. I mean, he never took dat coat off.

157

T.D.: That night we finally found out why. (*To KATE and
SONIA.*) Young was in the middle of throwin' a dart,
when all of a sudden he heard his friend's voice behind
him, raised in anger. He threw the dart at the board an –
(*He acts it out.*) an' spun around an' by the time he'd
turned around he had a gun in his hand.

ORRIN: Man, you should've seen how that whole pub went
quiet. Woo. Woo.

T.D.: He'd pulled it from inside his coat. A forty five. Fast.
Magic. Magic.

ORRIN: Talk about Wyatt Earp.

T.D.: Then there was this click. As Young thumbed back the
safety catch.

ORRIN: (*A laugh.*) Man, I was so scared. Don't forget I was
only around eighteen at the time. Only I know, from the
state of my underwear, jus' how scared.

SONIA: Orrin!

T.D.: He wasn't foolin', either. Young had that automatic
pointed straight at that white GI's heart.

KATE: What happened? What happened?

ORRIN: Luckily someone hurriedly called two American
MP's. They were in a jeep outside the pub.

KATE: Was anyone arrested?

T.D.: The white American. All the English people in the
pub agreed he'd started the trouble.

ORRIN: America, America. The Land of the Brave and the
Free.

KATE: (*To SONIA.*) Quite exciting, wasn't it?

SONIA: I've heard that story a hundred times. Every year
they tell it. (*To T.D. and ORRIN.*) Don't you? (*Pause.*) An'
it's not even that special a story. Nobody even got shot.

T.D.: (*His feelings hurt.*) I'm sorry. I'll throw in a few dead
bodies next time.

(*ORRIN's mood, meanwhile, has changed. Something about
all this reminiscence has made him sad.*)

ORRIN: (*Turning away.*) Yeah, well. There you are. It's all
water under the bridge now. (*He sucks his teeth. Goes to
drinks cabinet.*) Another drink, Kate?

KATE: Please. (*She brings her glass over to ORRIN.*)

T.D.: What're you sayin', old boy? Water under the bridge?

ORRIN: A drink, T.D.? Sonia?

T.D.: Not for me.

SONIA: Nor me.

ORRIN: T.D., something like twenty thousan' West Indians fought in the Second World War. Twenty thousan', fought for Britain. But who remembers? (*Loudly.*) I was in the RAF, T.D. We both were. Yet, often when I tell people that, they look at me shocked. Stunned.

T.D.: That still does not devalue what we did. We answered a call, Britain was at war. The British way of life was being threatened.

KATE: Here we go.

T.D.: Threatened. By the Fascists. The greatest menace to have evolved since the days of Sparta.

ORRIN: Sparta? How'd we get on to Sparta?

T.D.: We in the Colonies answered a call.

ORRIN: (*Loudly.*) But did we make the right choice, man?

T.D.: Choice? What choice?

ORRIN: Comin' here in the first place. Comin' to England.

T.D.: (*Facetious.*) Well, it's a bit late now, my friend.

ORRIN: You can say that again.

T.D.: The Mother Country needed us in those days.

KATE: (*Quietly.*) The Mother Country?

T.D.: (*Snapping at her.*) Yes, the Mother Country.

ORRIN: (*Loudly.*) An' does the Mother Country need us now? (*Pause.*) I should've gone to the States, man, like my brother, Carl. I could've lived in New York.

SONIA: Orrin, you not goin' to start about New York now, I hope?

ORRIN: New York is a twenty-four city. Over here by midnight London Transport starts to shut down.

T.D.: You can't buy English culture in New York, old boy. Not for love nor money.

ORRIN: I wouldn't go to New York to buy English culture. I promise you that. (*Then.*) The whole pace of New York is so vibrant, man. Instead I stay here. (*To SONIA.*) I'll tell you who'd have benefited the most if we'd moved to New York. Brenda.

SONIA: Brenda?

ORRIN: Yes, Brenda! Our daughter would've had more black friends. They are successful young black people in New York. She might've married one of them. The poor girl is lonely here. Wherever she goes, she's always the only black face in a roomful of whites.

SONIA: Orrin, I don't think this is the time for us to discuss our daughter.

ORRIN: She's a total stranger to us, Sonia! Fo' godsake, woman, admit it. (*To KATE.*) You were askin' about Brenda, Okay, I'll tell you about her. My daughter. Sometimes I look at her an' I don't recognise her. If you see the make-up she wears these days. Thick, thick make-up. She puts it on with a trowel. Eyelashes out to here like she wants to stab you to death with them. Some days it's like sittin' down next to a porcupine. As for the men in her life. She's got this white man, T.D. He's married. That's what depresses me more, man, the fact that he's married, not 'is colour. Also the man is almost as old as me. I swear to God, T.D.

SONIA: The man is not as old as you. Talk sense.

ORRIN: T.D., the only reason I'm not sure how old he is is cos he's always wearin' jeans. Fifty years old an' he's wearin' jeans. What sort of mature man is that? Apparently he's something at the B.B.C. Up to now I dunno what. An' T.D., T.D., I got no idea what he does to Brenda but she always looks tired. Exhausted! T.D., Mr Jeans has got my baby daughter doin' things to him in bed that weren't even invented in my day. Yet how come they say we're the erotic ones? How come they call us sex maniacs? They're the ones who buy all the 'How to do it' books, complete with photographs. Not us. (*Pause.*) We could've gone to New York. A nice house in Flushin' or Queens…two Alsatian dogs to keep friends an' enemies at bay…the muggers an' the cops takin' it in turns to beat us up. (*He sings.*) 'New York, New York!' (*Then.*) I can't think of any other place I'd rather be.

SONIA: Well, maybe you can't but I can.

(*Doorbell is heard off.*)

About time too!

(*ORRIN gets up.*)

T.D.: (*To ORRIN.*) I dread this. I dread this! Why have you invited that man?

(*ORRIN goes out.*)

SONIA: I bet you I know what that Trevor will ask for the minute he enters this room. 'A large scotch'. Mark my words.

ORRIN: (*Off.*) The Bishop! The Bishop!

TREVOR: (*Off.*) What's happenin', banner?

ORRIN: Enter. Enter.

(*TREVOR and ORRIN enter the living room.*

TREVOR BISHOP: a West Indian about forty. Something very dapper about him. Not just the way he dresses but his whole manner. He has this wonderful smile as well. Very plausible. Very disruptive. Carries one of those executive cases around with him.)

TREVOR: Guests, Guests. How exceedingly civilised. T.D.! If I knew you'd be here, I'd 'ave taken elocution lessons, banner.

(*T.D. sighs. Moves away.*)

An' Kate. Yuh lookin' good, girl. Yuh lookin' good.

Sonia. Oh God, Sonia. Give us a hug.

(*SONIA pushes him away. Sucks her teeth.*)

SONIA: No chance.

TREVOR: (*To KATE.*) You wouldn't believe it but Sonia is my bigges' fan,

KATE: You're right, I wouldn't believe it.

TREVOR: How about a drink? I bin here a good twenty seconds an' no-one's offered me a drink as yet.

ORRIN: What would you like?

TREVOR: Ah. A large Scotch would do me fine. Plus…

SONIA: Plus? Plus?

TREVOR: Plus a beer chaser, if I may.

SONIA: On the waggon, are you?

(*ORRIN has gone to the drinks cabinet. TREVOR sits down next to KATE. Runs his eyes over her.*)

TREVOR: Kate! Kate! At the garden gate! Lord. Look at the legs on dis woman.

KATE: Oh, Trevor, you are a fool. But tell me more, if you insist.

T.D.: With all due respect, may I interrupt you two.

TREVOR: (*Cheerfully.*) It's okay, banner, I'm not gun steal 'er away, man. (*In ORRIN's direction.*) I only jus siddown, skunt, an' already the banner wants to beat me up, skunt! Oh God!

SONIA: (*The first warning.*) Trevor, mind your language, please.

T.D.: (*To TREVOR.*) I did not say you were goin' to steal Kate away. (*To the others.*) Did I say anything of the sort?

ORRIN: I heard you.

TREVOR: (*To T.D. mischievously.*) Yuh mean to pick a quarrel wit me, don't you? Man, yuh difficult. Difficult.

T.D.: (*Loudly.*) I am not tryin' to pick a quarrel.

TREVOR: Now you're shoutin'. You know Sonia doesn't like loud black people.

T.D.: You'd turn me into a gibberin' idiot.

TREVOR: No, no, Nature beat me to it a long time ago.
(*ORRIN hands TREVOR his two drinks.*)
Aah. Good man, good man.
(*TREVOR drinks. Like a man who has just returned from a desert. The others watch him, fascinated.*)

T.D.: My God.
(*TREVOR finally comes up for air.*)

TREVOR: (*To ORRIN.*) Siddown, nuh, banner.
(*ORRIN sits near to him.*)
How're things, banner? How is, what's the name of yuh company, 'Blitz'? I hear dere's no stoppin' you dese days. Yuh's a star of the Western Plumbin' World! A pity Sean O'Casey is dead. Cos he's the only man who would do your biography justice.

ORRIN: (*To SONIA.*) Listen to this man. Listen to him.

SONIA: I wish I didn't have to listen to him, I tell you that.

TREVOR: (*To ORRIN.*) Plus I hear yuh bought yuhself a new Mercedes! What yuh did wit the ole one? Why don't yuh give it to me?

(*Immediately ORRIN starts to move away. TREVOR catches hold of him.*)

I'm only jokin'! Tell me something, how come a man like you buys a German car? Why don't you buy British?

ORRIN: I'll tell you why. If the English police see a Black man in a big, black Mercedes, they wave him on, they think he's a foreign diplomat. But let them see a Blackman drivin' in a Rolls Royce an' they're sure to think he's stolen it.

TREVOR: Say no more! I dig it, I dig it!

T.D.: Might we ask how things are with you? On the…'theatrical front'?

TREVOR: Have you heard I'm in a musical? Well, it's goin' in to the West End.

KATE: Well, I am pleased for you, Trevor.

TREVOR It couldn't have happened to a nicer person.

ORRIN: The West End! The West End! You'll have to give us free tickets.

TREVOR: (*To KATE.*) You wouldn't believe dis man is rich.

ORRIN: You an' T.D. are really movin' up in the world. Have you heard the lates' about T.D.?

TREVOR: What lates'?

ORRIN: T.D.'s goin' in for politics. Today Clapham, tomorrow the world.

(*TREVOR jumps up, shock, horror.*)

TREVOR: (*To T.D.*) Politics! Say it isn't so, T.D.!

T.D.: Very funny!

SONIA: (*To TREVOR.*) T.D., wants to be a councillor.

TREVOR: Councillor T.D. What nex'?

T.D.: I see nothing hilarious about it!

KATE: He has a secret weapon.

TREVOR: No offence, T.D. But you'll need one.

T.D.: Orrin is my secret weapon. He knows a lot of businessmen in this area, with his support I could be a force to be reckoned with.

ORRIN: (*To TREVOR.*) I keep tellin' him if I'm his secret weapon then he's really in trouble.

TREVOR: No, no, maybe he's got a point dere. (*To T.D.*) Yuh right, y'know. (*With a nod in ORRIN's direction.*) The banner here is the one man who could make even you look good.

T.D.: (*On his dignity.*) I doubt if I'd go quite that far.

TREVOR: Maybe you wouldn't, but I would.

SONIA: (*Getting up.*) I think I better see about food.

(*SONIA collects the patty plate.*)

KATE: I'll come with you.

T.D.: What's the menu, Sonia? Titillate my palate, my dear.

ORRIN: Not in my livin' room she won't.

T.D.: The menu, the menu, Sonia.

SONIA: (*To T.D.*) I'm startin' with green peppers stuffed with crab.

T.D.: I approve! I approve!

TREVOR: Hear dat? T.D. approves.

SONIA: For main course Molong Pork. Or for those who don't like pork there's Creole Chicken.

TREVOR: An' what about dose who don't like pork or chicken?

(*SONIA makes a face. Ignores him.*)

SONIA: (*Rounding on ORRIN.*) Orrin, you plan to come to my dinin' table dressed like that? In your cowboy suit?

ORRIN: This is not a cowboy suit, Sonia.

SONIA: (*Calmly but meaning it.*) Please go an' change, Orrin. Now, please.

(*ORRIN rises.*)

ORRIN: (*Pacifist.*) Awright. Awright. (*To TREVOR.*) At first me an Sonia used to fight about who is boss an' who wears the trousers in this house. But we've learned to compromise. Now I wear the trousers an' she's the boss.

(*ORRIN goes upstairs, laughing. Then SONIA and KATE go off to kitchen. T.D. and TREVOR alone in living room.*)

TREVOR: Looks like we're alone, T.D.

T.D.: A very astute observation, Sherlock Holmes.

TREVOR: (*Rising.*) Nice scotch he's got there, man. Shall we have another? (*And is already at the drinks cabinet.*)

T.D.: Good Lord. Your glass was half-full a minute ago. Neat scotch.

(*TREVOR helps himself to more whisky. As he pours he clears his throat. Hawks and hawks. Loudly. A man with terrible catarrh. T.D. endures as much of it as he can. Finally.*)

For godsakes, man!

TREVOR: What's the matter, T.D.?

T.D.: Nothing. Nothing.

TREVOR: So how, nuh, banner? You awright? (*TREVOR crosses to luger on wall.*) He still has this empty, ole thing?

T.D.: Trevor, I have a bone to pick with you.

TREVOR: (*Not liking the sound of that.*) What's all dis about you an' politics?

T.D.: I only want to be a councillor. From everybody's reaction, you'd imagine I wanted to be President of the United States Of America.

(*TREVOR moves towards T.D.*)

TREVOR: (*So sincerely.*) Well, banner I'll keep my fingers crossed for you. I mean that from the bottom of my heart.

T.D.: (*Believing it.*) I say, that's kind of you.

TREVOR: You're very welcome, T.D. By the way, banner… if an' when you become a councillor, there's a little favour you could do for me.

T.D.: (*Not so pleased with TREVOR any more.*) I beg your pardon!

TREVOR: I want a house.

T.D.: A house?

TREVOR: A council house.

T.D.: What! I can't believe I'm hearing right.

TREVOR: As a councillor you could use your influence –

T.D.: You do have to be joking, Trevor…!

TREVOR: I'd be prepared to accept a council flat.

T.D.: (*Sarcastic as hell.*) You would, would you? That's terribly decent of you.

TREVOR: The truth is I'm havin' a spot of bother at the moment. A temporary embarrassment as it were…
I would appreciate a place to stay right now. Could you put me up for a day or two?

T.D.: I really couldn't, old boy. Sorry an' all that.

TREVOR: (*Serious.*) You'd have my company, T.D., what more could you ask?

T.D.: The offer is tempting, but I must refuse.

TREVOR: Well, it's your loss. An' don't forget I'll soon be in the West End. Then you'll wish you'd put me up in your flat.

T.D.: Yes, well. (*Genuinely.*) I'm glad they're going to be doing your play in the West End.

TREVOR: The West End, skunt! Ah gone wit dem, banner. I play the lead, spar. As I said, it's a musical. About dese three woman. Black. All sisters. Dey live in Georgia. Atlanta, Georgia. But dey dream of escapin' to New York. It's my big break, banner. Dat show is goin' to make me a star.

(*T.D. looks sceptical.*)

No crap, T.D. I've been around failure long enough to smell success a mile off. Believe me, it smells differently. A star! Ah gone wit dey skunt, banner! I'll be able to do all the things I ever wanted to do. Like go to rich clubs an' get drunk an' smash up the place. Amusin' things like dat. When dey t'row m'skunt out I'll accuse dem of not likin' me because uh my colour.

T.D.: (*Deep dislike.*) I don't like you. I never liked you.

(*Pause.*)

TREVOR: What's the matter wit you, man?

T.D.: You offend me. Offend. Appal. Nauseate me.

TREVOR: (*Almost surprisingly sad.*) We're like chalk and cheese, aren't we, banner?

T.D.: Every time I open the papers you're either goin' in or comin' out of some police station.

TREVOR: I'm a popular man, banner.

(*A beat. Dislike between them.*)

T.D.: What you do in your life is your business, your affair. But when you start sniff in' around what's mine, my friend, that becomes my business.

TREVOR: I dunno what yuh mean, Sorry.

T.D.: You've been phoning Kate, annoying her.

TREVOR: I could do wit anodder beer. (*He returns to drinks cabinet to get himself another beer this time.*)

T.D.: (*Painfully.*) You leave Kate alone.

(*TREVOR's head turns sharply to look at T.D.*)

TREVOR: Banner, what crap yuh talkin', eh?

T.D.: (*Steeling himself.*) Did you an' her...

TREVOR: Did we what?

T.D.: You have, haven't you? The two of you.

TREVOR: (*Becoming tough, ugly.*) Who the skunt you think you're talkin' to, eh? Who the skunt?
(*He moves closer to T.D. Grabs the front of T.D.'s suit with one hand. Draws back his other hand as if to strike T.D. T.D. flinches.*)

TREVOR: (*To T.D.*) You know how many men better dan you have tried to mess wit me. (*Drawing his hand back again.*) Yuh skunt, yuh.
(*Just then ORRIN walks in. Sees what is happening. ORRIN is no longer in his uniform.*)

ORRIN: What the hell's goin' on?
(*ORRIN pulls TREVOR away from T.D.*)
Have you gone mad?

TREVOR: It's the banner who's gone mad.

T.D.: He's been sniffin' around Kate! (*To TREVOR.*) If I'd had a real gun I'd have shot you dead!

TREVOR: (*Struggling to get to T.D.*) You want more trouble, skunt?
(*ORRIN holds TREVOR.*)

ORRIN: Enough. It was only a joke.

TREVOR: A joke. Who sez it was only a joke?

ORRIN: (*Quiet warning.*) I say so.

TREVOR: (*To T.D.*) Banner, don't tear yo'self up inside like dat. Love is not worth it.
(*A beat. KATE appears in doorway. A bottle of wine and a cork screw in her hand.*)

KATE: Will one of you two open this?
(*T.D. rushes over to her. Grasps her arm.*)

T.D.: Did he make a whore of you?

KATE: (*Trying not to raise her voice.*) T.D., have you lost your senses? (*She frees her arm.*)

TREVOR: (*Cheerfully.*) The banner has gone totally crazy, skunt! Totally.
(*T.D. rushes to the luger on the wall. But does not take it from holster.*)

T.D.: If only this blasted thing was loaded!

KATE: T.D!...

TREVOR: But it's not loaded, is it?

T.D.: I'd like to see your life's blood splattered all over this floor, Your blood, your intestines, your life.

KATE: (*Not loudly.*) Oh no, T.D., no, no.

TREVOR: (*To T.D. quite surprised, hurt.*) You hate me that much?

T.D.: I'd see you dead if I could.

(*Pause. SONIA appears pushing a trolley groaning with dishes of food on it.*)

SONIA: Lunch is...what's the matter?

(*ORRIN still has his hands on TREVOR.*)

ORRIN: Nothing. Woo. Woo. We were only learnin' to dance, me an' Trevor.

TREVOR: Do you come here often?

(*ORRIN and TREVOR start to dance. KATE laughs. A release of tension.*)

SONIA: Will you two stop your foolishness? Lunch is ready.

(*ORRIN and TREVOR separate. T.D., KATE and TREVOR sit down.*)

ORRIN: Lunch, boy. Lunch.

(*Blackout.*)

End of Act One.

ACT TWO

Scene 1

About an hour, two hours later. All of them still sitting at dining table. Eating a sort of orange-coloured ice cream, mango ice cream. They have finished their main course. SONIA has already removed some of the dirty dishes. Still on the table, apart from ice cream dish and bowls, is a bottle of wine, glasses etc.

TREVOR will help himself to the wine frequently, continually, he does not stop talking whenever he helps himself.

TREVOR: (*In full flow.*) Uncle Van! Uncle Van! Dat's the name of the guy I'm playin'! The uncle of the three girls. A real straight creep, banner! The very first song I sing sums me up. It's a number called 'I wear black cos' I'm in mournin' for my life'. Nice. Nice title. Yuh like it? Yuh like it? Dey loved it in Brighton, spar. Heavy, heavy number, boy! Oh God. All about my unrequited love for anodder man's wife. Wait till the London critics hear it. Ah gone wit dey skunt. Heavy, heavy!

SONIA: Trevor, your language, please.

TREVOR: (*Not hearing her.*) An' listen to the name of the play. 'Black Sister'. Heavy, heavy. Chosen by the white director an' the white producer. Of course, they are white. The actors are black, but everybody else connected with the show is white. Isn't dat always the case? (*Then.*) Anyway, a smash hit, banner... It's bound to be a smash hit. It'll run as long as dat South African musical. The one that proves once an' for all, what a happy time the Blacks have in South Africa. All bare tits an' knees-up tribal dancin'. Anyway, 'Black Sister' is bound to be a hit. Bound to. West Indians will hate it, of course, but the English will lap it up.

T.D.: There's no pleasin' some people. The years you've waited for success, now it looks like it might happen, an' instead of you being grateful...

TREVOR: (*Harsh.*) Grateful? I know I've been waitin' years, I've got the grey hairs to prove it. But even I aspire to

something a bit higher dan a dancin', singin' all-black minstrel version of a Russian play. Grateful? Dat's a very white word. But dat's your sort of word, isn't it?
(*Pause.*)

SONIA: (*Trying to fill the awkward silence.*) Am, anybody want some more ice cream?

KATE: A teeny bit more. Wonderful, wonderful. This is another recipe I'll have to get from you.
(*SONIA serves KATE. Serves ORRIN.*)

ORRIN: Woo! Woo! Mango. Mango ice cream. You scream. I scream, we all scream for ice cream.

SONIA: Thank you. Thank you, Orrin.

KATE: Trevor, is it really just a minstrel show? This musical of yours. It can't be that bad, surely not?

TREVOR: (*Cheerful disgust.*) Can't be dat bad? Firse it was Black Shakespeare, den it was black Gilbert an' Sullivan, now it's black Chekhov. What next? Black War and Peace, I suppose? Skunt! Such crap. It's so dishonest an' patronisin' to us. I'm not talkin' about the occasional black actor tryin' to prove he can play Brutus or Othello. I'm talkin' about where Blacks are exploited to sell a play. Too many producers would radder stage an all-black tap dancin' version of 'Sinbad the Sailor' dat has nothing to do wit black people, dan put on one black play dat jus' might help further some sort of understandin' between the races. Disgustin'.

KATE: What will they think of next? How about...how about an all-black musical about Hitler and Eva Braun? Can't you just see it? Jokes about blacks and Jews. It would run for years.

T.D.: (*To TREVOR.*) Anyway, he wasn't. He was not black.

TREVOR: Who wasn't 'black'? Yuh gettin' difficult again man.

T.D.: Othello was not black.

TREVOR: Did I say he was black? Anyway, he was black.

T.D.: With all due respect –

TREVOR: If you say dat once more I'll scream.
(*TREVOR helps himself to more wine.*)

SONIA: (*Wearily.*) An' if you drink anymore I'll scream.

TREVOR: (*Toasting her.*) I'll drink to your scream. (*Drinks.*)
(*SONIA sighs. Tut tuts.*)

T.D.: With all due respect, he was an Arab, Othello.

TREVOR: Arab? Black!

T.D.: An Arab! Any student of English Shakespearean
culture is familiar with that fact.

TREVOR: Don't talk to me about English culture. Haul yuh
ass. Don't hand me none uh dat skunt.

SONIA: Trevor, I told you, I will not have such language at
my table.

TREVOR: The banner gettin' me vex, skunt.

SONIA: Trevor!

TREVOR: Vex, vex. Tellin' me O'tello was an Arab. The
man was a flickin' black man.

T.D.: (*Rising.*) Will you excuse me, Sonia. I want to use your
loo.
(*T.D. leaves the room. Everybody silent for a moment or two.*)

TREVOR: Oh God. Is gone he gone? The banner can't take
a joke at all, y'know.

SONIA: Enough is enough, Trevor!
(*SONIA starts clearing up everybody's ice cream bowls.
Regardless of who has finished and who has not.*)

ORRIN: I wanted some more.

SONIA: Well, it's too late. It was too late from the moment
you invited that man there. (*And points at TREVOR.*)

TREVOR: Me? What did I do?

SONIA: Kate, excuse me, I'm jus' goin' to wash these up
quickly.

KATE: Do sit down, Sonia.

SONIA: No, no, I want to do it.

KATE: (*Rising.*) Then let me help you.
(*KATE starts helping SONIA. Loading dirty dishes onto
trolley.*)

SONIA: I don't need any help, really.

KATE: I insist.
(*SONIA and KATE go off with trolley into kitchen – off.*)

TREVOR: (*To ORRIN.*) Boy, I don't understand why your
wife doesn't like me.

ORRIN: I wanted some more ice cream. I'm the one who pays for the food, an' I can't eat as much as I want. Go figure it.
(*TREVOR rises.*)

TREVOR: Shall we retire in to the drawin' room proper for the Port.

ORRIN: Port? What port?

TREVOR: You don't have Port, banner?

ORRIN: Port?

TREVOR: You're supposed to pass it to the man on your left.

ORRIN: I haven't got any port to pass to any man on my left or right!

TREVOR: Port tastes horrible in the wrong sort of glass. Always remember dat.

ORRIN: I will. I will.
(*They have moved into living room section now. They do not sit immediately. And then ORRIN sits first.*)

TREVOR: Nice meal, banner.

ORRIN: (*You'd think he'd cooked it.*) Ah. Thank you.
(*A beat.*)

TREVOR: Can we talk about why I'm here.

ORRIN: I wondered when we'd get to that bridge.

TREVOR: I want to borrow some money.

ORRIN: Surprise. Surprise.
(*ORRIN sits.*)

TREVOR: A thousan' pounds.
(*ORRIN rises.*)

ORRIN: I know I didn't hear right.

TREVOR: Banner, I'm in bad, bad trouble. Okay, make it five hundred.

ORRIN: What am I? The Ford Foundation?

TREVOR: You mind if I help myself to yuh Scotch, banner?

ORRIN: It's none of my business but you're drinkin' a lot.

TREVOR: You're right. It's none of your business.

ORRIN: Let's put it anodder way. It's not my business but it's sure as hell my Scotch.

TREVOR: (*Helping himself.*) Okay, I won't have a double, I'll settle for a single. How about you?

ORRIN: No, I'm fine.

(*TREVOR returns over to ORRIN's side.*)

TREVOR: I'm in heavy trouble, Orrin. Dey mean to lock m' skunt up dis time. I got two days to come up wit a thousan' pounds.

ORRIN: Talk to your bank manager. Tell him you're soon goin' to be a star.

TREVOR: I've already consulted my bank manager. The man runs from me every time he sees me now.

ORRIN: Maybe I should do the same.

TREVOR: 'Mr Bishop', he says to me. 'Mr Bishop, you're clearly insolvent.' Tellin' me I'm insolvent.

ORRIN: Your bank manager said this to you?

TREVOR: (*He is at a certain level of drunkenness by now.*) Yuh not listenin', banner. Not the bank manager. The official of the Bankruptcy Court.

(*TREVOR drops into a chair.*)

ORRIN: Bankruptcy Court?

TREVOR: Din I tell you. I starred recently at the Bankruptcy Court.

ORRIN: Woo! Woo!

TREVOR: I was tryin' to organise a heavy-weight boxin' match.

ORRIN: A heavyweight boxin' match?

TREVOR: I had the right backers an everything. But certain Jewish promoters were jealous of me. Sabotaged me.

ORRIN: Sometimes I wonder how you ever find the time to be any kind of actor.

TREVOR: 'Clearly insolvent,' he says to me. So I said to him. 'I know I'm insolvent. I wouldn't be here otherwise'.

(*TREVOR giggles happily.*)

ORRIN: I bet that put 'im in his place for a moment or two.

TREVOR: Wha'?

ORRIN: Nothing.

(*TREVOR suddenly gets to his feet.*)

TREVOR: I'm like an epic movie. Epic! 'The Towerin' Inferno'. Only I'm a movie dat steps out of the screen an' says: What's happenin, banner?' Dats me. A real life epic movie.

(*Pause.*)

ORRIN: That's how you see yuhself. But how do others see you? (*Pause.*) Sit down.

TREVOR: Banner, like I can't sit down for very long. Like I can't stop spinnin'. You know what I mean?
(*A beat. TREVOR sits.*)
Christ, banner, Christ.
(*Pause.*)

ORRIN: Weren't you supposed to be gettin' a little money from Guyana? After they sold your father's house?

TREVOR: (*Trying to focus.*) What? My fadder's house? Oh, dat ole house. I din't get a red cent.
(*A beat.*)
My ole man, boy.

ORRIN: Your father was a good man.

TREVOR: (*A sigh.*) I know. I know, banner. A good man. An' a disappointed man. Disappointed cos of me.
(*Pause. Then cheering up again.*)
Boy, you should seen some of the letters he used to write me. Five page lectures. Epistles. My fadder could've taught St. Paul a thing or two.

ORRIN: What were they about, his lectures?

TREVOR: I used to read dem over an' over again. I knew whole chunks of my ole man's letters by heart, skunt!
(*Begins to quote from some past letter.*) 'Boy, the older I get, the more I see how little I know. Be humble.' Yuh like it. Be humble. (*Sucks his teeth.*) My ole man.

ORRIN: Carry on.

TREVOR: 'Dere's another food shortage or maybe it's the same old one from before. From about five o'clock in the mornin' people queuein' up. For chickens. If you don't get dere in time you out of luck. All you hear is: full up, full up. Thank God some things never change. Every midday there's still 'Portia Faces Life'.

ORRIN: Portia faces what?

TREVOR: Life.

ORRIN: Life? She faces life? Why would she want to do a thing like dat?

TREVOR: It's a radio programme back home. Never heard of it?

ORRIN: Never.

TREVOR: It has no beginnin', an' certainly no end.

ORRIN: Like inflation?

TREVOR: Exactly.

ORRIN: Anyway, continue.

TREVOR: 'Son, I detect from your las letter dat you're again in some sort of trouble. I take it you're ashamed to come right out an' tell me about it. I only wish you were ashamed enough not to get into trouble in the firse place. Your drinkin' is nothing short of a disgrace. Sometimes I just feel like sayin' to you, I never want to see you again. But I can't. For better or for worse, you are my son. Boy, when are you goin' to come to your senses? Well, it's gettin' late. I better go an' lie down. It's not me dat's weary. It's the back of my body dat's weary. God bless you. Your lovin' fadder.'

(*Pause.*)

ORRIN: Sounds like the sermon on the Mount, Part Two.

TREVOR: Help me banner. I need dat money. I've been livin' like a wolf recently. A bloody wolf.

(*ORRIN sighs. He goes to drinks cabinet. Helps himself to a drink. TREVOR joins him. Helps himself.*)

Is dis all the Scotch you got?

ORRIN: If you'd given me enough warnin', I'd have bought two cases of the stuff.

(*He moves away. TREVOR follows.*)

TREVOR: No, no, but seriously, if I can't raise dat money in time, I shan't be in the musical. I can forget dat play.

ORRIN: Why?

TREVOR: I'll be in jail.

ORRIN: Jail? It's that bad?

(*Pause.*)

TREVOR: Dey want to get me for deception. The magistrate, the police, everybody – the Church for all I know. Deception. As if I'd ever deceive anybody. Would I do a thing like dat? Would I? (*Pause.*) I said –

ORRIN: I heard you, I heard you.

(*Pause.*)

TREVOR: I blame my bank.

ORRIN: Is it ever your fault?

TREVOR: I'm a busy man, busy, busy, I can't keep track of every penny I spend.

ORRIN: Sorry, are we talkin' about pennies or a thousan' pounds.

TREVOR: I have six bank accounts, man.

ORRIN: Six?

TREVOR: I believe in spreadin' the load.

ORRIN: Spreadin' the load? What load? What are you talkin' about?

TREVOR: (*Nakedly.*) Banner, I got nowhere else to turn… will you help me?

ORRIN: (*Pause.*) How will you pay me back?

TREVOR: From the money I make in dis West End musical of mine.

ORRIN: 'Black Sister' eh? (*Then.*) If I lent you the money you'd have to sign a banker's order.

TREVOR: A banker's order?

ORRIN: That's right. Every week part of your salary would come directly to me. Through your bank, not through you.

TREVOR: (*Cheerfully.*) Like you don't trust me at all, banner.
(*ORRIN produces his cheque book.*)

ORRIN: What's the name of the man you owe money to?

TREVOR: Make the cheque payable to me.

ORRIN: No way. I couldn't forgive myself if I put such temptation in your way.

TREVOR: Banner, yuh hard as nails, you know dat? Okay, you win. His name is Lew Leonard.
(*ORRIN writes cheque out. Hands it over to TREVOR. TREVOR sees the amount is not quite as much as he had hoped to receive.*)
Is dis all?

ORRIN: What I've given you there ought to be enough to keep you out of prison.

TREVOR: You can always tell the rich. Dey hold on to dey money like dey chained to it.

ORRIN: Give me it back then.
(*ORRIN makes a grab for cheque. TREVOR laughs, pulls it back. TREVOR puts the cheque away.*)
What has happened to T.D.? (*He calls.*) T.D.! (*He sits.*)

TREVOR: Is the banner really serious about becomin' a Councillor?

ORRIN: He's serious. The question I want to know is: 'is the Labour Party serious?' Anyway, it's all conjecture. The election is not until next year.

TREVOR: I've been thinkin'. Why don't you stand for Councillor instead of T.D.?

ORRIN: Who? Me?

TREVOR: You'd be a far better choice.

ORRIN: Forget it.

TREVOR: You belong to the Labour Party, don't you?

ORRIN: Yes, but no, include me out.

TREVOR: Hasn't anybody ever approached you to stand for Councillor?

ORRIN: Well. The Treasurer of our local branch has sort of mentioned it.

TREVOR: Dere you go.

ORRIN: No, no no. It's not worth the effort.

TREVOR: (*Bluntly.*) About time you pulled your finger out. You sit on the fence too much.

ORRIN: (*Irritated.*) Sit on what fence?

TREVOR: You take the easy route.

ORRIN: (*Getting up.*) I don't take any easy route!

TREVOR: You've done well fo' yuhself, yuh oughta be doin' more fo' our community, the Black community.

ORRIN: (*To TREVOR loudly.*) Why is it every time a Black man becomes successful the whole blasted world expects him to do something for his community? The only thing a well-off White Man is expected to do for his community is keep up with the Jones!

TREVOR: (*Moving closer to ORRIN.*) It's time you became more politically aware.

ORRIN: What is this? Hyde Park Corner?

TREVOR: No matter how hard you try to be accepted you'd always stick out like a fractured thumb!

ORRIN: What're you talkin' about? Who's a fractured thumb?

TREVOR: You can't pretend to be anything but black!

ORRIN: (*Shouting.*) Since when did I pretend to be anything but black!

TREVOR: You can't say to hell wit other Blacks.

ORRIN: I've never said that!

TREVOR: Your motto is: 'if I can do it, den other Blacks can do it, so to hell wit dem'.

ORRIN: That's not my motto! That's not my bloody motto!

TREVOR: Well, den prove it! Stand fo' Councillor. You've got your Mercedes, now think about somebody else for a change!

(*Pause. TREVOR crosses to Luger and holster on the wall.*)

Talkin' about T.D. He's lucky I didn't make him eat dis.

ORRIN: T.D. is alright.

(*TREVOR handles the Luger.*)

TREVOR: Why do you still keep dis here, eh?

ORRIN: It's just a decoration, man.

TREVOR: (*Facing ORRIN.*) A gun is not a decoration.

ORRIN: (*Firmly.*) I like it. Some people hang flyin' ducks on their wall, I hang guns.

TREVOR: (*Sucking his teeth.*) Bloody empty gun. These days the Black man in Africa has got both guns an' bullets. The Black man in America has got both guns an' bullets. Trust the Black man in Englan' to have an empty gun.

(*TREVOR looks at ORRIN. Pause.*)

ORRIN: (*Goaded to anger.*) How do you know I don't have bullets?

(*A beat.*)

TREVOR: (*Intrigued.*) You have bullets, banner?

ORRIN: It's a different story now, ain't it? Give me the blasted thing.

(*ORRIN snatches the gun from TREVOR's hand. ORRIN takes the gun behind the bar. Rests gun down. Produces a small box from behind the bar. He takes top off the box. Holds box up to show TREVOR that it is a box of bullets.*)

TREVOR: I dig it, I dig it!

(*ORRIN loads Luger. Then slowly he points loaded Luger at TREVOR's legs.*)

ORRIN: Now what were you sayin' about an empty gun?

TREVOR: What the skunt is the matter wit you?

(*Pause.*)

ORRIN: (*Without raising the gun higher.*) Suppose I was to point this gun higher an' pull the trigger, you'd never again have to worry about such problems as impotence.

TREVOR: Dat's very kind of you, banner. But I promise you I don't worry about such problems now. (*Pause.*) I'm not sayin' I don't have such problems, I'm jus' sayin' I don't worry about dem.

(*ORRIN laughs. He stops pointing gun at TREVOR. He begins to unload gun.*)

Christ, I ought to break your neck. For a minute dere I thought you were goin' to play 'Gunfight at O.K. Corral' on my kneecaps.

(*ORRIN has finished unloading gun. NOTE: There must be some doubt about how many bullets he has removed from gun. ORRIN moves from behind bar. He returns Luger to its holster hanging on the wall. He returns behind bar. He puts box of bullets away.*)

ORRIN: Have I shown you my gadget?

TREVOR: Yuh what, spar?

(*ORRIN produces his remote control that works his garage door. He holds gadget up for TREVOR to see.*)

ORRIN: My gadget Kate calls it. (*He comes from behind bar. Takes gadget to window. Signals to TREVOR.*) Come closer, as the spider said to the fly.

(*TREVOR joins ORRIN at window.*)

See the garage.

(*TREVOR looks.*)

TREVOR: I'm not blind.

ORRIN: Hey, presto.

(*ORRIN presses button on gadget. Presumably this opens the door of the garage – off.*)

TREVOR: (*Blase.*) Yeah, yeah. Magic, magic.

ORRIN: (*Put out.*) You're not impressed?

TREVOR: (*Bored.*) I'm impressed.

ORRIN: Look, look, I can close it as well.

(*ORRIN presses button again. Checks to see garage door (off) has closed. Then pulls at TREVOR's sleeve.*)

Well, what d'you think?

(*TREVOR yawns.*)

TREVOR: Excuse me.

ORRIN: Go to hell.

(*ORRIN turns away from window, puts gadget down on one of the tables and stalks out of the room. Heading for kitchen.*) Sonia, what're you doin', still washin' up?

(*He disappears down the hall (off). TREVOR laughs a little. He waits for a moment. Then he tiptoes over to the gadget on the table. Picks up the gadget. He returns to the window taking gadget with him. He starts playing with it like a young boy. He presses button. He looks out the window.*)

TREVOR: (*Pleased.*) Oh skunt! (*He presses button again. Looks.*) Nice! Nice!

(*T.D. comes down the stairs. Enters living room. TREVOR, oblivious, works button again.*)

Magic, skunt! Magic.

T.D.: Having fun, Flash Gordon?

(*TREVOR spins round, guiltily.*)

TREVOR: I was jus', am, tryin' it out for Orrin.

T.D.: That thing is not a toy, you know.

TREVOR: It's still open out dere.

T.D.: Close it then. Close it.

(*TREVOR turns back to window, points gadget in direction of garage. Presses button. Outside, door closes. TREVOR then puts gadget back on table.*)

Where's everybody?

TREVOR: Why? Isn't my company good enough fo' you? I'm hurt, man.

T.D.: (*Ignoring that one.*) I wonder if Sonia remembered to look for those records?

TREVOR: What records?

(*KATE enters.*)

KATE: (*Entering.*) That goes for you two as well.

TREVOR: Now what?

KATE: West Indian men think washing up is women's work.

TREVOR: What do you know about West Indian men?

KATE: Sonia and I did all the washing up. You men could at least have offered to help.

TREVOR: If I ever get married I'd make a pact wit my wife. Once she allows me to do all the drinkin', I'll allow her to do all the cookin' an' the washin' up.

KATE: (*Moving closer to him, annoyed.*) In other words you're concerned about the way Blacks are treated in this country but you're not concerned about the way women are treated.

TREVOR: Dat's not true. I'm very concerned about the way women are treated in dis country. Very concerned. Especially when I see the way some men get down on their knees to women – more dan concerned – disgusted! (*He laughs happily.*)

KATE: Trevor, if that's supposed to be funny, then I've missed the point!

TREVOR: (*Moving away but unrepentant.*) I'm sorry I spoke.

T.D.: (*To KATE, a bit pompous.*) My dear, take no notice of him. In fact I've been thinking of making that one of my election manifestoes.

TREVOR: What? That men should help women wash up dishes?

T.D.: (*Loudly.*) You are ridiculous!

TREVOR: Calm down, T.D. No call to shout, jus cos you find me ridiculous!
(*ORRIN returns from the kitchen. T.D. rounds on him the minute he enters the room.*)

T.D.: (*To ORRIN.*) Why did you invite that man here!
(*ORRIN takes a step backwards, throws up his hands in mock horror.*)
Is Sonia still in the kitchen?

ORRIN: Yes.

T.D.: Good. I'd go mental if I had to endure another minute in his company.
(*T.D. strides out of the living room. Goes to kitchen – off.*)

TREVOR: (*To ORRIN.*) I think the banner's tryin' to tell me something.

ORRIN: Nonsense. T.D. likes you. He likes you so much he leaves the room every time he sees you.

TREVOR: Talkin' about leavin' the room I have some bodily functions to attend to. Excuse me. (*He starts to leave the room.*)

KATE: (*As if addressing a favourite naughty child.*) Trevor! Really!

(*TREVOR disappears up the stairs.*)

He gets worse. (*Then.*) What is Sonia doing now?

ORRIN: Makin' coffee for everybody.

KATE: Never stops, does she?

ORRIN: Do you think West Indian women spoil their men?

KATE: Spoils them? Well, I wouldn't really know. I think of them as always busying themselves around their men. You know what I mean. Being busy around them. I don't think of it as actual spoiling.

ORRIN: Maybe that's why we seldom ever talk to each other, Sonia an' I. She's always so busy being busy.

KATE: Can I ask you a question now?

ORRIN: You can ask me any question you like.

KATE: What am I to you, just a bed partner?

ORRIN: Woo! Woo!

KATE: Whenever anyone says something that makes you feel uncomfortable, you say 'woo, woo'.

ORRIN: (*Jokingly.*) Woo! Woo!

KATE: It's a defence, pure and simple.

ORRIN: I stand accused.

KATE: Anyway, you haven't answered my question. Am I? Just your idea of a bed partner?

ORRIN: (*Quietly.*) No. (*Then.*) No. I've grown since I've known you. I've benefitted, knowin' you.

KATE: Oh good!

ORRIN: In a way, you've…awakened a social conscience in me. Well, maybe re-awakened is a better word.

KATE: What does Sonia really feel about all of this re-awakened social conscience of yours?

(*SONIA enters followed by T.D. Between them they are carrying the coffee things. SONIA has an expensive coffee set. Not just expensive, ostentatious. SONIA looks at her husband and KATE. Then SONIA puts her tray down.*)

SONIA: What does Sonia feel about what, Kate? I'll tell you my first reaction to most things. Disapproval.
(*A beat. Then ever so sweetly.*) Coffee…everybody?

T.D.: I'd love some, Sonia,

SONIA: Kate…how about you?

KATE: (*A sigh.*) Yes, please.

SONIA: (*To ORRIN, a bit coldly.*) And you?

ORRIN: (*Mischievously.*) Dear, I'd walk a mile for your coffee.
(*Coffee is poured. Handed around.*)

KATE: T.D., tell Orrin and Sonia about last Saturday, when you cooked that meal. (*To ORRIN and SONIA.*) My sister, Sarah, came down from Dorset – she's married to a real creep – anyway, T.D. invited us over to that flat of his where he proceeded to give my sister indigestion.

T.D.: I did not give her indigestion! I can't help it if she's not acquainted with Polish food.

SONIA: A West Indian who only cooks Polish Food! T.D., you're in a class by yourself.

KATE: T.D. had a wine list.

ORRIN: A wine list! Only three of you to dinner an' he had a wine list!

T.D.: I served a different wine with each course. By the time the meal was over her sister was on the floor.

KATE: The amount of wine you served, we were all on the floor.

ORRIN: Woo! Woo! Orgy. Orgy.

KATE: Orgy? You obviously don't know my sister.

T.D.: Anyway, you have to admit she at least liked the sweet I provided.

KATE: True. True. Though she did think it was rice pudding.

T.D.: (*To SONIA.*) I cooked her 'Pashka'. 'Pashka' for godsakes – an' the silly woman thought it was rice pudding!

SONIA: What the hell is 'Pashka?"

ORRIN: Sounds like an aphrodisiac, if you ask me. T.D., what were you tryin' to do with Kate's sister? Feed 'er or have sex with her?

T.D.: It so happens, old boy, that 'Pashka' is a Polish dessert.

ORRIN: That's worse. A Polish aphrodisiac. My Lord.

T.D.: Made with cream. Pashka. With the Pashka I served my most expensive bottle of claret! I'd bought it at a wine auction.

SONIA: A wine auction? My, my. I'm impressed. (*To ORRIN.*) How come you've never been to a wine auction, dear?

ORRIN: (*With a wave in T.D.'s direction.*) I leave such things to the expert here.

SONIA: Anyway, what was this…claret that you served with your Polish dessert?

T.D.: (*Proud as punch.*) A Lafitte forty five.

ORRIN: A forty five? You served a gun with yuh puddin'? Woo! Woo!

T.D. You are becoming as distressing as Trevor.

(*ORRIN tries to keep a straight face.*)

ORRIN: I'm sorry, T.D.

T.D.: I have no doubt in my mind, even the Nineteenth Century French aristocracy would have deemed my meal a gastronomic miracle.

ORRIN: That may be so, T.D., but would they have eaten it, that's the question.

(*TREVOR returns.*)

TREVOR: (*Entering.*) Time for a political discussion, T.D.!

SONIA: (*A sigh.*) Oh, Lord.

TREVOR: (*Ignoring her.*) If you're contemplatin' enterin' the political arena, you must have some political views. What are your political views? Do you even have any political views?

T.D.: I'm a politician who believes in people not policies.

TREVOR: (*Agitated.*) T.D., don't get me vex again, man. You have a golden opportunity to tell it like it is…out dere. Tell dem.

T.D.: Like it is? What is? Tell them what?

TREVOR: Dat dis is a racist society.

T.D.: I beg your pardon?

TREVOR: Deeply racist. Make dat the basic premise of your campaign.

SONIA: You reckon that's the best way for T.D. to win the English vote? He must tell them they're all racists.

T.D.: Trevor, in this election I have every intention of sweeping the polls. If I followed your advice. I'd end up sweeping the streets. (*To SONIA.*) And this man used to be a teacher, mark you.

TREVOR: T.D., I'm not against you enterin' politics! The more West Indians who enter politics the better. Anyway, what's it got to do wit anything, the fact dat I once was a teacher? I was a damn good teacher as well.

SONIA: Especially when you struck your head master.

TREVOR: He was the Deputy Head, not the Head.

SONIA: I stand corrected.

TREVOR: An' I didn't hit 'im. (*Rising. Demonstrating.*) I jus' grabbed the dog by 'is jacket. 'Come here' ah said to 'im an' ah jus' draw m' fist back like Muhammed Ali.

KATE: You didn't! Gosh. Really? Wonderful.

TREVOR: (*Drawing his fist back to commit murder.*) Boy, I was all set to put some licks in his skunt. He would have remembered me fo' life. Bup! Bup!

ORRIN: Woo! Woo! Blackboard Jungle! (*To TREVOR.*) Thank God not all teachers are quite so pugilistic.

TREVOR: He deserved it, skunt. Tellin' me how he didn't know Blacks knew anything about socks in the West Indies.

ORRIN: Woo! Socks! I never heard a better reason for anybody hittin' a Deputy Headmaster.

TREVOR: (*Trying to keep calm.*) I did not hit the banner, Anyway, dere were other things. He couldn't bear to touch the black kids.

ORRIN: Touch them? Touch them up, you mean? I should hope not. What sort of school was that.

TREVOR: (*Being very serious for him.*) Come on, banner, you know what I mean. I'm not referrin' to his sexual preferences. He would laugh an' joke an' put his arm around the white kids, but the black kids he treated differently. He could never bring himself to touch them.

KATE: I've known one or two teachers like that. It's quite odious.

TREVOR: Dere are things being done to black kids in some English schools – boy, I tell you. Would make you weep. Damagin' dem…inside. Dose kids aren't stupid. Dey know when a white teacher can't bear even to touch dem.

ORRIN: Makes you sick.

T.D.: Race, race, race. There's only one race: The Human Race!

TREVOR: (*To ORRIN.*) He's like a child, ain't 'e? A two year old. (*TREVOR turns to T.D.*) Banner, the time has come fo' me to tell you one or two unpleasant truths.

T.D.: Such as?

TREVOR: You were sayin' earlier dat if you didn't have Orrin's support, the voters wouldn't even elect you 'dog ketcher'.

T.D.: I never said anything of the bloody kind.

TREVOR: Don't let's mince words, T.D., dat's the bottom line, skunt, as far as you're concerned.

T.D.: I don't have to listen to this.

SONIA: Why don't you leave T.D. alone, Trevor?

TREVOR: Anyway, I've made a different suggestion to Orrin.

ORRIN: Trevor, don't.

TREVOR: I suggest dat Orrin ought to stand fo' Councillor instead of merely being your crutch.

T.D.: (*On his feet.*) What!

SONIA: (*To TREVOR.*) Orrin?

ORRIN: (*To T.D.*) It's no more than a suggestion.

TREVOR: (*To T.D.*) He'd make a better Councillor than you any day.

T.D.: You Judas!

KATE: T.D., at least listen to him.

T.D.: (*To TREVOR.*) You drunken Judas!

(*TREVOR a bit wounded. He is always a bit wounded when anybody draws attention to his drink problem. Even though he covers up quickly enough we must always see this vulnerability in TREVOR.*)

TREVOR: Okay. Okay, man. So I drink. But jus' cos I drink dat don't make what I say any less true. Anyway, I'm not betrayin' you. Cos I was never on your side.

KATE: Speaking personally…speaking personally. I too consider it a good idea.

(*T.D. horrified turns to her.*)

T.D.: I beg your pardon!

KATE: I'm sorry, but I do think Orrin would make a splendid Councillor.

T.D.: You are three times a Judas!

KATE: Come off it, T.D.

T.D.: (*Shouting at her.*) I've worked hard! Writing speeches – campaigning. Worked!

KATE: (*Remaining cool.*) T.D., I've been to more political meetings than you have. It's a joke to you.

(*TREVOR gives a little, infuriating laugh.*)

T.D.: It is not a joke to me! I am thoroughly, resolutely, vigorously serious about my political ambitions!

SONIA: T.D., cool down. Admit it, one minute you're votin' Conservative, the next you're callin' yourself a Labour Candidate. It's enough to give a body eye-turn.

T.D.: Sonia, you too? You?

SONIA: Nobody's perfect, T.D.

T.D.: (*Shouting at all of them.*) I shan't give in without a fight, I'm warning all of you!

TREVOR: Face facts, T.D. as a politician you couldn't give Mickey Mouse a run for his money. An' that's being kind.

(*Pause. T.D. gives a sort of sobbing sound. He draws back his hand as if to slap TREVOR. TREVOR stares him down. T.D. lowers his head. T.D. leaves the room, hurriedly.*)

SONIA: T.D.!

(*We hear front door (off) slam. Pause.*)

TREVOR: (*Surprisingly sad for him.*) Well. Even I can't think of anything funny to say.

SONIA: (*To KATE.*) Do you think he's gone home?

KATE: (*Unsure.*) I shouldn't think so.

ORRIN: This has gone far enough. I'll go an' talk to him. Excuse me.

(*ORRIN goes. We hear him go out front door – off.*)

SONIA: Poor T.D.

KATE: Do you think I should go after him as well?

(*Pause. KATE does not move.*)

TREVOR: (*Walking up and down the room.*) I wasn't tryin' to hurt the banner's feelings, but between the two uh dem, Orrin is by far the better man for the job.

KATE: Sonia, you should push Orrin more.

SONIA: Push him? Push him where?

KATE: He knows many of the right people in this community. He may have quite a political career ahead of him. But you should be more of a help to him.

TREVOR: She's right, you know Sonia.

SONIA: (*Not pleased.*) Is she?

KATE: I know it's none of my business, Sonia, but how often do you two talk to each other?

SONIA: Who says I don't talk to him?

KATE: I mean, talking to him about trying to do something for others. He's done quite well for himself, he can afford now to spare a thought for others. Others who aren't as fortunate.

SONIA: (*Irritated.*) I don't talk to him about such things. He doesn't talk to me about them either.

KATE: Your husband needs someone to talk to. Do you think you two talk enough?

(*Pause.*)

SONIA: You got a lot of nerve.

KATE: I deserve that, I suppose.

SONIA: A lot of nerve. Do me a favour. Don't concern yourself with matters between me an' my husband.

(*KATE sighs.*)

TREVOR: (*Quietly.*) Oh, skunt.

SONIA: (*Not looking away from KATE.*) I tell you what you should be concerned about. About T.D. The poor man's out there now all upset. Shouldn't you go an' see how he is? (*Then cold bloodedly.*) Or is carin' for a man considered to be old fashioned these days by you an' your sort of friends?

(*Pause.*)

KATE: I'll see how he's getting on.

(*KATE leaves the room. We hear her at front door.*)

TREVOR: Sonia. Sonia, boy. A pity dey put an end to the S.S. You missed yuh callin', girl.

(*SONIA turns and faces him. Gives him a look of displeasure. Then.*)

SONIA: Trevor, don't you have a home to go to?

TREVOR: Funny you should say dat, Sonia girl. I was goin' to speak to Orrin about dat, but den I thought I'd ask you first.

SONIA: Ask me what first?

TREVOR: I'm a little inconvenienced at the moment, when it comes to havin' a place to stay. I was wonderin' – !

SONIA: (*Cutting in.*) No way.

TREVOR: You should at least give me a chance to finish, Sonia.

SONIA: As far as I'm concerned you are finished.

TREVOR: I need a place to stay, Sonia. You'd see me homeless?

SONIA: I'd close my eyes.

TREVOR: (*Loudly.*) You got three, four extra rooms in this house an' you'd have me walkin' the streets?

SONIA: Try not to shout at me in my own home, Trevor.

(*TREVOR moves over to her.*)

TREVOR: West Indians should help one another. Especially in England.

SONIA: You should learn to help yourself, Trevor. Especially in England. Now get out of my way. I'm goin' upstairs to find those records for T.D.

TREVOR: Stay. Don't leave me by myself down here, girl.

SONIA: Act your age, Trevor.

TREVOR: (*A sigh, then.*) Yeah. Yeah. What records?

SONIA: Glenn Miller.

TREVOR: Glenn Miller? What yo-all havin'? A wake?

SONIA: (*Disgruntled.*) Remind me to laugh tomorrow.

(*SONIA exits. Goes upstairs. TREVOR left alone. He looks at bar. He goes to bar. He pours himself a stiff scotch. Then pours himself a beer as well. Drinks some of both. A great wide grin of contentment appears on his face. He finds a box of ORRIN's cigars. Lights one up. We must feel TREVOR is behaving as if it's his home. He pulls happily on his cigar. Somebody is heard at front door. TREVOR comes quickly from behind the bar. He hides cigar behind his back.)*

TREVOR: Who is dat?

(Pause. Then KATE appears.)

KATE: Hello.

(Pause. TREVOR seeing it is only KATE stops hiding his cigar.)

Into cigars now, are we?

TREVOR: *(Ignoring that one.)* Where's T.D.?

KATE: He didn't want my company.

TREVOR: T.D.'s loss is my gain.

KATE: I don't know if I like the sound of that.

TREVOR: My dear, would you care for one of my brandies? Or a vodka? Or just a liqueur, perhaps?

KATE: Perhaps I'll try one of your brandies. *(She sits on sofa.)*

TREVOR: *(Posh, English voice.)* Oh, absolutely, absolutely.

(TREVOR goes behind bar. Finds brandy bottle. Pours some in a brandy glass. He brings drink over to KATE.)

KATE: Thank you. Where is, am, Lady Macbeth?

TREVOR: She went... *(He points.)* ...upwards mutterin' as she went about some damned spot or the other.

KATE: I suppose I'm being horrible, am I?

TREVOR: You are.

(He returns to bar to pick up his whisky and his glass of beer. Then carrying the two drinks he joins her on the sofa.)

KATE: Do you always drink as if you're expecting a drought?

TREVOR: One never knows, do one? Do you think Orrin will take a chance...an' stand for Con... Con... Councillor?

KATE: Would you say you were getting intoxicated?

TREVOR: I wouldn't, no. Mainly cos I can't even pronounce the word.

KATE: Actually I think Orrin's thinking about it.

TREVOR: About being intox...intox...intoxicated? Then why isn't he here drinkin'?

KATE: I meant about him standing for Councillor, silly.

TREVOR: Oh. *(But his mind is on other things now. Her legs for example.)* Oh God. Legs, boy. Legs. Look at dose legs.

KATE: I assure you, I only have two, Trevor, like everyone else.

TREVOR: What would yo do if I put my hand on yuh thighs?

KATE: Panic, I suppose.

(*TREVOR puts his hand on her leg. Pause.*)

TREVOR: You see, no panic.

KATE: (*Abruptly.*) My aunt used to drink a lot – she was a matron in a hospital. She only drank in bouts – she was reputed to – it was said – she said she only drank in bouts. The only trouble was that the bouts became more and more frequent – eventually becoming one, long continuous bout.

TREVOR: Kate, guess what?

KATE: What?

TREVOR: You're panickin'.

KATE: I know.

(*Pause.*)

TREVOR: Relax.

KATE: I'm relax.

TREVOR: No, you're not.

KATE: It's a bit difficult to relax with your hand on my leg.

TREVOR: What you doin' later? Why don't I come back to your flat? Jus' you an' me an' your flat.

KATE: (*The words rushing out again.*) She used to blame her job – she was stuck in Stevenage. Well, you'd drink too if you were stuck out in Stevenage. She was prone to accidents – when she drank, I mean – all kinds of accidents. At my sister's wedding –

TREVOR: Kate!

(*Pause.*)

KATE: At my sister's wedding she had this tremendously cut knee.

(*Pause. TREVOR removes his hand from her thigh. Takes her arm. He pushes back the sleeve of her dress, exposing her forearm. He begins to massage the back of her forearm near her elbow.*)

Don't be annoyed at me, but…what're you doing?

TREVOR: Shh. Don't you like what I'm doin' to you?

191

KATE: Yes, but…

TREVOR: But what?

KATE: (*Shivering away.*) It's ticklish!

(*He sits up angry, or pretending to be angry. Pause.*)

Now I've made you annoyed.

TREVOR: I'm wastin' your time.

KATE: No, you're not. In fact, I find all this…terribly dark and attractive.

TREVOR: What the hell does that mean?

KATE: It means this beats being in Dorset, thank God.

TREVOR: Now you're talkin'. Why don't we cut out of here? We could go in your car to your flat. Could you put me up for a while? Only a day or two. Well, a week. Well, say a few weeks. I don't mean to impose, of course.

KATE: What are you talking about?

TREVOR: Kiss me.

KATE: I couldn't. Orrin and T.D. will be back any minute.

TREVOR: We'd hear the front door. (*He puts his arms around her.*)

KATE: (*Twitching away.*) I can hear Sonia!

TREVOR: One kiss. Come on.

KATE: I need to get my raincoat cleaned. There's this little man in Hampstead –

(*TREVOR puts his hand over her mouth. Pause. Takes his hand away. Kisses her. He kisses her for a little while – she does not return the kiss but she does not act as if she hates it. ORRIN enters. T.D. behind him. They have come in the back way.*)

ORRIN: What're you two doin'?

T.D.: Kate?!

(*KATE jumps up.*)

KATE: Oh God.

(*TREVOR is more cool.*)

TREVOR: (*Rising.*) What's happenin', banner?

(*ORRIN crosses to KATE.*)

ORRIN: What was he doin' to you?

KATE: Nothing Orrin, I'm sorry, I'm sorry.

TREVOR: (*Putting a hand on ORRIN's arm.*) Hey, cool it, man.

ORRIN: (*Knocking TREVOR's hand away.*) Parasite.

TREVOR: What the hell's the matter wit' you? How come you're the one who's so upset?

(*ORRIN rushes over to Luger hanging in its holster. He rips Luger from its holster. Points gun at TREVOR.*)

ORRIN: In one second you're a dead parasite!

KATE: Orrin, no.

T.D.: Orrin.

TREVOR: (*To ORRIN.*) Banner, dat thing is empty.

ORRIN: Wrong. I left one bullet in.

TREVOR: Yuh jokin'.

ORRIN: (*Cold as death.*) You think I'm jokin'?

(*Pause.*)

T.D.: Bullet? Bullet?

KATE: (*To ORRIN.*) But you haven't any bullets! Do you?

ORRIN: (*Not taking his eyes off TREVOR.*) You forgot. One thing you forgot. One small miscalculation. You forgot I fought in a war. A World War.

TREVOR: What's dis man talkin' about?

ORRIN: I'm still as much man as you any day!

KATE: It's not loaded. Say it isn't.

TREVOR: (*Not looking away from ORRIN.*) It's not. It can't be loaded. I'm goin' to take it away from you. (*He does not move.*)

ORRIN: Come on. Try me.

TREVOR: Don't make me take it off you.

(*Pause. He does not move.*)

KATE: Do something, T.D.

T.D.: Orrin. Am. Orrin.

(*ORRIN cocks the hammer of the Luger.*)

TREVOR: (*Very afraid.*) Oh, skunt.

(*SONIA enters. Sees that ORRIN is holding a gun in his hand.*)

SONIA: (*A tone of authority.*) Just what is goin' on here?

(*ORRIN still has the Luger pointed at TREVOR. ORRIN pulls the trigger. A loud click. Quick curtain.*)

Scene 2

About half an hour later. T.D. and TREVOR alone in living room. TREVOR, pacing. Surprisingly there is no glass in his hand. Luger back on wall.

TREVOR: I still can't get over it. Nobody treats me like dat.

T.D.: Look let me pour you a fresh drink. (*He goes behind bar.*)

TREVOR: Everyone thinks I'm jus some dumb-ass drunk.

T.D.: (*Quietly.*) I wonder what gives them that idea?

TREVOR: (*Belligerently.*) What? What was dat? I din hear dat.

T.D.: I said... I wonder what they're doing up there. Orrin and Sonia, I mean.

TREVOR: You want to hear the dif...the diff'rence between us? I lay it on the line.

T.D.: What? Lay what on what line; old boy?

TREVOR: My life! I lay my life on the line. Out dere. On the streets. To alluh you I'm jus a drunk. But I go out dere an' I lay my life on the line. On the friggin' line! (*T.D. comes from behind bar with Trevor's glass of Scotch.*)

T.D.: Here. Here's you life line.

(*TREVOR takes drink from T.D. KATE appears in doorway. She has been getting her coat from the cupboard in the hall (off). She has the coat over her arm now. It is ORRIN and SONIA who are upstairs. T.D. sees KATE.*)

T.D.: What are you doing?

KATE: I think I'd better go, don't you?

T.D.: Why?

KATE: If I left it would make Sonia happy.

T.D.: If he left it would make everybody happy. (*To KATE.*) What makes you think Sonia would be happy if you go?

KATE: I can't help feeling she blames me for what happened.

T.D.: Rot. Why should she?

KATE: Don't you blame me?

T.D.: Of course not. You've done absolutely nothing to reproach yourself about.

KATE: (*Ruefully.*) Oh, T.D. What can one do with you?

T.D.: What? Do with me? (*Then pressing blithely on.*) What flummoxed me, what flabbergasted me, was Orrin's reaction.

TREVOR: (*Drily.*) Yes, I was a bit flabbergasted myself. In fact… (*He looks at KATE.*) …I've been wonderin' about it ever since. He did…overreact a bit, didn't 'e? You got anything to say, Kate?

KATE: Me? I'm as much at sea as you two. (*She looks down at her coat, nervously.*) The state of this coat – I'll give him a ring – my little man in Hampstead.
(*Pause. She looks up to see TREVOR is still looking at her suspiciously. But he remains unsure.*)

T.D.: (*Abruptly.*) What is happening up there?

KATE: (*To T.D.*) What should I do? Go or stay?

T.D.: Perhaps we should both go. Would you like that? I could come back to your place for a little while.

KATE: Well, actually…actually, I've reached a decision, T.D. I better let you know right now what I've decided.

TREVOR: Oh skunt. I don't like the sound uh dat, T.D.

KATE: I do wish you'd keep quiet, Trevor…at least occasionally.
(*TREVOR pretends to look contrite.*)
T.D., why don't we go in the kitchen?

T.D.: The kitchen?

TREVOR: Tell 'er yuh not hungry, T.D.

T.D.: (*To KATE.*) Why the kitchen?

KATE: (*Anger.*) Oh, you are so obtuse, sometimes? You deserve whatever happens to you.
(*Pause.*)

T.D.: Maybe…maybe there are some things I would rather not find out.

KATE: I no longer feel any love for you, T.D. None. I'm sorry.
(*Pause. TREVOR turns away from T.D. as if even he feels embarrassed for T.D.*)

T.D.: (*A plea.*) You can't possibly mean that…can you?

KATE: Yes, I do, T.D. Please.

T.D.: Did you have to tell me now? Like this? In front of him? (*Pause.*) Aren't women supposed to be kinder than men?

TREVOR: (*Not loudly, almost an aside.*) Not dese days, T.D.
(*KATE crosses to T.D.'s side.*)

KATE: (*Gently.*) T.D.
(*T.D. brushes her aside.*)

TREVOR: Watch it. Dey comin' back.
(*KATE moves away from T.D. SONIA and ORRIN enter. SONIA is carrying a bottle of champagne, the very large size. ORRIN is carrying some old Glenn Miller records.*)

SONIA: (*Entering.*) Sorry we took so long, everybody.

TREVOR: Champagne! Oh God! An' look at the size of it! Are we goin' to drink it or christen a ship wit' it?

SONIA: Oh, be quiet, Trevor.

ORRIN: First things first – I'm sorry everybody…if I've been a bit odd all day. I've been tryin' to make a decision.

SONIA: We have an announcement to make, my husband an' I. Orrin has decided that if the Labour Party is interested he will be happy to stand for Councillor of this Ward. An' I, I am goin' to help him.
(*A pause.*)

KATE: Well. I see. Well, that's, am, that's good, Sonia.

SONIA: (*Treating KATE to a knife-like smile.*) Yes, Kate, it is isn't it? An' don't forget. It was you who put the idea in my head in the first place.
(*SONIA and KATE look at each other.*)

TREVOR: (*To ORRIN.*) I won't be votin' fo' you. You're too trigger-happy, skunt.
(*Only then does T.D. manage to put his feelings into words.*)

T.D.: (*To ORRIN. Not too loudly at first.*) Thanks. First her an' now you. Thanks a lot.

ORRIN: What? What's this?

T.D.: You promised to help me!

ORRIN: I never promised any such thing.

T.D.: Now all you're doin' is helping you bloody self.

ORRIN: You know as well as I do, in Local Elections, every party puts up three candidates for each ward. The LABOUR Party could still choose both you and I as two of the three candidates.

T.D.: They could, but they won't.

ORRIN: I'm sorry, T.D., but I'm doin' this for me.

T.D.: You can say that again!

ORRIN: (*Loud confession.*) I have not liked me for years.

T.D.: What is that supposed to mean?

ORRIN: It means I've been a taker long enough. For a change I want to do what I can for others.

T.D.: What a fine way to start, by betraying me!

ORRIN: (*Vexed.*) I'm not betrayin' you, man.

T.D.: I can't take it. I can't take any more of this. First she says she no longer loves me, now you say the same thing.

KATE: Oh, honestly, T.D.

ORRIN: Who says I don't love you?

SONIA: We all love you, T.D.

T.D.: (*Loud, despairing cry.*) I'm being sold down the river here...!

SONIA: T.D., look what Orrin has for you. I found them. The old Glenn Miller records... Now isn't that nice?

T.D.: To hell with Glenn Miller.

SONIA: Now, now, T.D., there's no reason to take that sort of attitude.

KATE: T.D., no one wants to sell you down the river.

T.D.: (*He has not really looked away from ORRIN.*) My friend. My friend, Orrin. I used to think: whatever happened my friend would never break faith with me.

ORRIN: What can I say? I have not broken faith with you. (*TREVOR crosses over to T.D.*)

TREVOR: T.D., listen to me.

T.D.: (*Avoiding him.*) Get away from me, you smell like a brewery. Disgustin'.

TREVOR: I have something serious to say! (*Pause.*) The only reason the Labour Party would put you up as a candidate, you or any other Black man, is cos of one thing. The Black grassroots vote. Y'know what dat is?

T.D.: Of course I do.

TREVOR: As quietly as it's kept dey are now enough Blacks in certain areas of dis country to elect MP's much less Councillors. Slowly but surely all...three political parties are beginnin' to…app…app…to recognize dis fact. Un…fortunately dey not gun vote fo' you. Blacks at grassroot level won't vote fo' you, T.D. You an' dem don't even speak the same lang…language.

(*Pause.*)

SONIA: (*Holding out bottle of champagne to T.D.*) Tell you what. Give me a hand with this, T.D. Be nice, T.D. For me. Okay?

(*Pause. He does not take bottle.*)

ORRIN: (*Quietly.*) Leave him alone, Sonia.

(*T.D. moves away from SONIA.*)

SONIA: (*Abruptly, baffled.*) Why can't everybody be nice?! Why all this, this – upset? We have…worked…we have got on in this country…improved ourselves…why then can't we just enjoy the fruits of our labour? Why can't we just say thank God at least we can afford a little champagne? Eh? Tell me that? Why? Why not? Why should white people have all the good times?

TREVOR: (*Toasting her with his drink.*) Spoken like a true, Black Tory, Sonia.

(*He is ignored.*)

ORRIN: (*To T.D.*) I never broke faith with you. That's unfair. Unfair.

T.D.: Everybody always expects good old T.D. to be nice. Nice T.D. Good T.D. Bad T.D. Up, T.D. Down, T.D. Sit, T.D. Don't make a fuss, T.D. (*Plaintively.*) With all due respect, I'm sick to death of being nice! (*To TREVOR.*) You think I don't feel things like anybody else? Sometimes I want to turn to some of my colleagues at work an' I want to say: smile…please smile…be nice, say something friendly…welcome me…a smile, a welcome, a leaf instead of a stone.

(*A beat.*)

Sometimes T.D. is fed-up of being nice an' polite. (*Pause.*) The man from whom I buy my wines…he has a little place in Fulham Road… I used to go in there an' chat to him about wines…one day I overheard him discussin' me with a friend. It seemed to amuse him that I, a West Indian, should know so much about wine.

(*A beat.*)

I am aware that to some people I am but a joke.

(*Pause. ORRIN moves over to T.D.'s side.*)

ORRIN: T.D.…friend…if it hurts you that much I won't put my name forward for Councillor.

T.D.: It's a free country, do what you want.

ORRIN: T.D., our friendship was forged by a war. A war that killed millions. Man, I'm too old now to let politics destroy our friendship.

T.D.: Are you still my friend…are you sure?

ORRIN: Of course I'm yuh friend, man.

TREVOR: (*Abruptly.*) Tell me, Orrin! What made you change yuh mind? About being a Con… Con… Councillor?

ORRIN: Haven't you had enough to drink?

TREVOR: (*Loudly.*) You're always makin' me out to be such a drunk! I am sick of it. I lay my life on the line!

SONIA: What is he talking about?

T.D.: (*To ORRIN, abruptly.*) No! No, I won't! I won't just accept it!

ORRIN: Now what, T.D.?

T.D.: For once I refuse to be a gentleman. I will fight you, damn you.

TREVOR: (*To ORRIN.*) What made you change your mind?!

ORRIN: (*Rattled, sounding on TREVOR.*) Who the hell you think you're shoutin' at?

KATE: Everybody, please. Is all this emotion necessary?

TREVOR: (*To ORRIN.*) You wanted to shoot me…! (*He points at KATE.*) Because of her. A white woman.
(*Everybody goes silent. Pause. TREVOR turns to T.D. and SONIA.*)

He wanted to shoot me cos of her.

SONIA: Trevor. Careful. Careful what you say about my husband an' another woman. I'm warning you.

T.D.: Trevor, there's really no reason to bring Kate's colour into this.

TREVOR: (*To ORRIN.*) Dat's what made you change yuh mind, skunt. Her! Kate!

ORRIN: (*Quietly.*) You better leave my house, Trevor.

KATE: Perhaps I better go.

T.D.: No, not you. (*Pointing at TREVOR.*) Him.

SONIA: (*To ORRIN.*) Why do we put up with this man an' his insults?

ORRIN: (*Looking at TREVOR contemptuously.*) Because he's a professional West Indian. Being a West Indian is a full-time profession to someone like Trevor. He trades on the fact that, as a fellow West Indian, I'll never turn him away from my door.

TREVOR: Don't avoid the question, banner. How come you changed yuh mind?

ORRIN: Go on, Trevor. Get your coat.

SONIA: Yes, goodbye, Trevor.

T.D.: No, no. I want to hear the answer too. Why did you change your mind, Orrin?

ORRIN: I don't have to answer any fool questions!

TREVOR: Gave you a shock. Skunt, you, you would've shot me over her. No wonder it shocked you.

ORRIN: I dunno what you mean. Must've rotted your brain. All that liquor.

SONIA: (*Rounding on TREVOR.*) You shut up, you hear. Shut up! Shut up! (*Pointing to KATE.*) She means nothing to my husband. Nothing.

KATE: Don't make me angry, Sonia, please. It's because of me that you two have suddenly come together.

SONIA: Keep out of my marriage, Kate.
(*Pause.*)

ORRIN: (*Quietly.*) Oh, my God.

T.D.: (*To ORRIN and KATE.*) Maybe there is something going on between you two.

TREVOR: (*To ORRIN.*) No one waves guns at me. Nobody...!
(*TREVOR's ignored.*)

T.D.: Is there, Orrin? Anything between you two? Is there?

ORRIN: (*Quietly.*) No. No, man, T.D. (*To KATE.*) Well, Kate?
(*KATE says nothing. Pause.*)

SONIA: (*To T.D., loudly.*) If my husband says there's nothing going on between him an' Kate, then there's nothing. Or are you calling my husband a liar, T.D.?
(*A beat.*)

T.D.: Alright. Alright, Sonia. Okay.

TREVOR: (*To ORRIN.*) Helpin' others? Don't make me laugh.

ORRIN: Don't you ever shut up?

TREVOR: You're just doin' dis fo' yuhself. Same old song'n'dance. The more things chain...change, the more they remain the same. You'll make a great pol...itical leader.

(*Pause.*)

SONIA: (*Depressed.*) Does anybody want to open this champagne?

T.D.: Not me.

(*Pause.*)

KATE: (*Deadly.*) Has everybody had their little say now? Because it's my turn.

ORRIN: Jesus, now what?

KATE: T.D. is not the only one who is being sold down the river here.

T.D.: What?

SONIA: (*Unpleasantly.*) Who is selling you down the river, Kate?

KATE: Unless I get something out of all of this, I swear I'll say something I'll regret later!

ORRIN: Kate, Kate.

SONIA: Just what is going on here?

TREVOR: Oh, skunt. Trouble, trouble.

ORRIN: Kate, am, try to remember what Trevor said.

TREVOR: Me?

ORRIN: (*Not interrupted.*) The more things change, the more they remain the same.

(*A beat.*)

KATE: (*Hopefully.*) Really?

SONIA: What are you two saying to each other?

ORRIN: It's not me, dear, I'm referrin' to Kate an' T.D.

SONIA: Kate an' T.D.?

ORRIN: Yes. Didn't T.D. say something about Kate leavin' him? Didn't you, T.D.?

T.D.: Everybody's leaving me.

ORRIN: (*To KATE.*) Well, I think that's unwise, Kate. Very. I think you an' T.D. should stay together. It has its...advantages.

KATE: Oh. Oh, yes. Definitely. (*Then.*) Maybe I was a bit hasty, T.D. Can you ever forgive me, T.D.?

T.D.: Well, I don't know about that.

KATE: Be a sport, T.D.

T.D.: (*Magnanimously.*) Oh, alright. I forgive you.

KATE: (*Sweetly.*) I just hope you never have any cause to regret this, T.D.

SONIA: Look, I don't like the sound of any of this.

T.D.: (*Hurt.*) Aren't you glad that Kate and I have decided to stay together after all?

SONIA: That's not what I meant, T.D.

ORRIN: Dear, I would hope we're all happy for the two of them.

SONIA: (*Snapping at him.*) That's not what I meant! (*Pause, Then a sigh.*) I just hope you know what you're doing, Orrin.

(*A beat. Then she turns to T.D.*)

SONIA: Come on, we're all waiting. Open the champagne, T.D. Please.

T.D.: Alright. Okay. Why not?

(*SONIA with a big smile on her face passes the bottle to T.D.*)

ORRIN: I'll get some glasses.

(*He goes behind bar. He produces some champagne glasses. T.D. uncorks the champagne. ORRIN brings glasses over. Wine is poured. Handed around.*)

SONIA: Make a toast, somebody. (*Then.*) You're being very quiet, Kate.

KATE: (*Toasting ORRIN.*) To the next Councillor of this Ward.

ORRIN: I hope the voters share your confidence.

SONIA: I propose a toast to T.D.

T.D.: Yes, here's to old T.D. who is being betrayed.

ORRIN: Man, T.D.

SONIA: Come on, T.D.

T.D.: (*Placatingly.*) Okay. Okay.

SONIA: Please propose a toast. Please.

T.D.: To George. George Lucas. Wherever he may be.

ORRIN: (*Quietly.*) Yes. To George.

TREVOR: Your turn to make a toast, banner.

ORRIN: Alright, here's one. To West Indian ex-Servicemen everywhere.

T.D.: And to those West Indians who died in the war defending the Mother Country.

TREVOR: The Mother Country?

T.D.: West Indian Servicemen past and present.
(*They drink. TREVOR sighs but he too drinks.*)
Nice. A nice drop of champagne that.

TREVOR: (*Looking for trouble.*) So it's still the 'Mother Country' to you, is it, T.D.?

SONIA: Don't spoil things again, Trevor.

TREVOR: (*To T.D.*) Since the Forties you've lived here, an' you're still an immigrant to dem, yet you still can talk about the 'Mother Country'!

ORRIN: Why don't you sit down, Trevor?

KATE: Yes, do leave T.D. alone, Trevor.

TREVOR: (*Still to T.D. quietly.*) What happened to George, eh?

T.D.: George?

TREVOR: I remember your friend George Lucas. Why did he go back to Trinidad? Because at his work dey never gave him any promotion, dat's why. Bank teller. At dat bank. All the other tellers, women an' men, were in dey twenties. George was in his fifties. Dey passed him up for promotion a dozen times.

ORRIN: Trevor's right. George was a fool.

T.D.: A fool? George? Don't say that.

ORRIN: George, I used to say to him, give up that bloody job at that bank an' come an' work wit me, man. But no.

SONIA: (*Annoyed.*) Why are you sayin' those things about George? (*She points at TREVOR.*) George had a respectable job, he wasn't always drunk like him.

ORRIN: Oh shut up, Sonia. Please.

TREVOR: Thank you.

SONIA: Orrin, kindly do not talk to me like that in front of other people.

ORRIN: I'm sorry. Okay? I'm sorry. (*Pause.*) But he's right. Like T.D., I've been in this country since I was eighteen years old, yet as far as most English people are concerned I'm still an immigrant. That's not right, Sonia. (*Then wry, sad.*) Girl, we should've gone to New York, y'know.

SONIA: You gone back to talkin' about New York.

ORRIN: I like the pace of New York, man.

SONIA: The American Immigration people just wouldn't let us in, remember?

ORRIN: Wasn't just them, Sonia. It was you as well. You didn't want to go. I tried every way to get you to change yuh mind, but no.

SONIA: (*Sucking her teeth, an immovable force.*) What do I want to go to America for?

ORRIN: (*Sad.*) But what about me, Sonia? What about what I wanted?

SONIA: It's too late now anyway.

ORRIN: (*A sigh.*) Yeah. Well. There you go.

T.D.: (*Abruptly.*) You thought he was a fool!

ORRIN: What's this?

T.D.: You thought George was a fool. All these years you've thought George was a fool.

ORRIN: (*No heat.*) George was always too gullible. The poor man believed every word anybody told him. I remember durin' the Rhodesian crisis, Nineteen-sixty something. Seems such a long time ago now, Anyway, one night George an' myself sat up all night over a bottle of Scotch, The man cried. Bitter tears. How could The British Government jus' wash their hands of the whole affair? (*A beat. Sad, not heavy.*)
The man was a child walkin' in his sleep.

T.D.: If you're saying George was a child, then you're saying the same about us. You, Me. All the ones like us. That we too walk in our sleep.

ORRIN: We could still wake up, man. If we want to. Do we? (*Pause. SONIA walks away from them. Sits down.*)

SONIA: When the great debate is over you can come an wake me up.

T.D.: (*To ORRIN.*) She's right, you know. This is Rememberance Sunday. We meet to give thanks an' to be happy.

TREVOR: I hope nobody minds if I've another little drop of champagne!

(*TREVOR helps himself. He is ignored.*)

ORRIN: Anyway, Sonia, you know what's the definition of debate!

SONIA: You tell that joke over an' over again, Orrin. One would think you'd be tired of it by now.

KATE: I haven't heard it.

ORRIN: Debate. That's what catches de fish.

(*KATE laughs momentarily.*)

T.D.: I've got one. I've got one. What is 'copulation?'

KATE: Now don't get carried away, T.D.

ORRIN: Woo! Woo! M'wife goin' to banish you from her livin' room, T.D.

T.D.: Cop-u-lation: sex between consentin' policemen.

ORRIN: T.D., boy, T.D. (*He moves to Luger on wall.*) I still remember that poker game, you know, T.D. When I won this.

TREVOR: Oh skunt, not dat gun again. I surrender, don't shoot.

(*TREVOR is ignored. But ORRIN moves away from the gun.*)

ORRIN: We were billeted in Rugby.

T.D.: I don't care how it sounds. Those were some of the happiest days of my life.

TREVOR: Being stuck out in Rugby of all places?

T.D.: Stop being so ridiculous! I mean the war.

TREVOR: Sorry. Ah sorry bad, T.D.

KATE: When did you first arrive in England, Sonia?

SONIA: In 1952.

ORRIN: Anything of note happened in 1952, T.D?

SONIA: I jus told you. I arrived in this country in fifty two.

ORRIN: I mean, apart from that, dear.

T.D.: Elizabeth the Second ascended the throne that year. Although her actual Coronation wasn't until 1953.

SONIA: I saw it on T.V. The Coronation. She looked so beautiful. Gorgeous. Unforgettable it was. Unforgettable.

TREVOR: I don't believe dis. (*To KATE.*) Do you believe dis?

T.D.: (*To ORRIN.*) Remember '51? The Conservatives got back into power.

ORRIN: Churchill was in an' Attlee was out.

T.D.: Churchill was Prime Minister from '51 to '53.

KATE: I was only about ten in the mid-fifties. I had a cousin who liked Bill Haley, Does anyone remember Bill Haley? (*Nobody cares to remember Bill Haley.*)

SONIA: Brenda was born in '55, Queen Mary Hospital. In the ward where she was born many of the English women were all curious about her. 'Isn't she lov-ly,' they kept saying. 'So well behaved.' In the mid-fifties black babies were still a bit...unfamiliar in England.

TREVOR: T.D., tell me something...do you plan to ever go home again... (*Some mischief here.*) ...when you retire, I mean?

T.D.: (*Putting great expression into the word.*) Home?

ORRIN: Home? Tell him you are home, T.D. Don't you know T.D.'s favourite song 'Maybe it's because I'm a Londoner.'

T.D.: What saddens me most is the way my London has changed these last few years.

TREVOR: Your London?

T.D.: Not just the West End, Have you been around areas like Shepherds Bush lately? A word of warning, Don't.

KATE: (*A private laugh.*) Incredible...!

T.D.: (*Pompously.*) These days you can't even buy any decent fish 'n' chips any more. I certainly do not want to buy my fish 'n' chips from some Italian gentleman.

KATE: What are you saying, T.D?

(*T.D. picks up two of the Glenn Miller records.*)

T.D.: I miss his music as well. I had every record this man ever made. (*To ORRIN sadly.*) Remember all these records I used to have. Once I had a record collection second to none.

TREVOR: A record collection second to none? Glenn Miller?

(*KATE laughs. The others ignore TREVOR.*)

ORRIN: (*To T.D.*) Woo! Woo! In these days you owned more records than a record company, We used to call you 'His Master's Voice,' Eartha Kitt – Billie Eckstine – Mr B! –

Mr B! – Billie Eckstine, An' last but not least – Xavier
Cougat! Woo! Woo! Whatever happened to Xavier Cougat?

T.D.: (*A laugh.*) His Chihuahua must have died.

(*ORRIN suddenly begins to sing some of the lullaby:
'Chihuahua, Chihuahua'.*)

SONIA: Awright, awright, Orrin, no so loud,

TREVOR: I had enough, I'm goin'. You three are too much
fo' me.

(*T.D. is looking through the Glenn Miller records.*)

T.D.: 'In the Mood!' 'In the Mood!' The Master. The Master.

TREVOR: Sonia, I'm goin'. Thanks for the meal.

SONIA: You're welcome, come again, sometime. Next Leap
Year, perhaps. (*She turns away from him.*) Put the records
on, T.D.

TREVOR: T.D., I'm off.

T.D.: (*Moving to record player, carrying records.*) You've been off
for years.

(*TREVOR sighs. He puts out his hand to ORRIN. They shake
hands.*)

TREVOR: Banner, I'll see you, okay.

ORRIN: Try an' make it last, the money I gave you. I won't
be givin' you any more.

(*Pause. TREVOR takes his hand away from ORRIN's.*)

TREVOR: (*To them all.*) Ah'm goin', g'bye. G'bye, Kate.

(*They each give him a little wave or something. TREVOR
starts to leave room. Stops. Faces them.*)

I remember – I remember! You want to hear what I
remember about those same forties an' fifties dat all
of you always go on about?

SONIA: No, thank you. It's bound to be something
unpleasant.

TREVOR: Jus listen f'once, Sonia. Fo' a start it's not about dis
country, it's about the West Indies, Guyana, home.
Schooldays. I remember my school-days. Queens an'
Central High School an' all dat. See me as a boy. A youth.
Fifteen, sixteen. Yuh remember your own school-days?
Eh? (*Sad, not happy.*) Schooldays, boy. Schooldays.

(*A beat.*)

Remember how we used to stand up in assembly...all clean an' smilin' an' Black... an' we used to sing 'Rule Britannia'? Remember? (*He sings very sadly.*)
'Rule Britannia...
Britannia rules the waves,
Britons...never, never, never,
Shall be slaves.'
(*Pause.*) We meant every word we sang. (*Crying it out, grief.*) We believed it all...! (*Pause.*) Now years later here we are in Britain...an' most of them jus wish we hadn't come. (*Pause.*) Enjoy yuh Glenn Miller records.
(*TREVOR goes.*)

SONIA: Put on the music, T.D.
(*T.D. who had stopped what he had been doing to listen to TREVOR, plays the record now. Glenn Miller's 'In The Mood'. T.D. turns to SONIA.*)

T.D.: My dear, may I have this dance?

SONIA: You always were such a gentleman, T.D.
(*SONIA and T.D. begin to dance. ORRIN puts out his hand to KATE.*)

ORRIN: Shall we join them?

KATE: Glenn Miller? Oh, why not?
(*ORRIN and KATE dance. The two couples dance and dance. We watch them for some time. Then a slow curtain.*)

The End.

EL DORADO

Characters

LLOYD

ELIZABETH

MARY

CLAUDE

JESSICA

GREGORY

El Dorado was first performed at the Theatre Royal, Stratford East, on 26 January 1984, with the following cast:

LLOYD, Guy Gregory

ELIZABETH, Carmen Munroe

MARY, Jo Martin

CLAUDE, Allister Bain

JESSICA, Faith Brook

GREGORY, Don Warrington

Place: the West Indies

ACT ONE

Scene 1

The drawing room (downstage) and dining room (upstage) of a large, grand house, or rather a once grand house. The 'Van Den Bergh Building' as it is known locally has seen better days. It would take more than a pot of paint to restore this place to its former glory.

The house dates back to the seventeen hundreds. It is a great wooden structure resting on thick concrete stilts taller than a man. There is no dividing wall between the drawing room and the dining room. But there is a screen which can be drawn across if one so desires.

Drawing room: mainly cane and wicker furniture. One large cane rocking chair (JESSICA's chair). Large palms in pots, a number of them. Side tables a piano against right wall. Vases of flowers. Doorway in right wall. Leads to JESSICA's office.

Dining room: dining table for eight people. Sideboard. A small sofa (up left) against back wall. Two doorways in this room, one doorway (up right) in right wall: to rest of house. Another doorway (down left) in left wall: to hall and front door.

When the curtain rises LLOYD is sitting in the drawing room reading a paperback western, one of Zane Grey's masterpieces. LLOYD is West Indian. A loud man in a loud florid shirt, open almost to the waist. LLOYD burns with secret resentment, his one wish is to dance on the grave of the Van Den Berghs.

Near him, MARY, the maid, black, is doing a spot of dusting. One must get from her a feeling of great activity.

After a moment or two, ELIZABETH, LLOYD's wife, is heard calling from upstairs.

ELIZABETH: (*Off.*) Mary…! Aren't you finished in there as yet?

MARY: Ah'm comin', Miss Elizabet'. Lawd.
  (*ELIZABETH appears, brown skinned rather than black. Her father, a magistrate, was black. JESSICA, her mother, is white. Forty-one years old, ELIZABETH has let her chances*

213

slip by. She still, however, manages a kind of stoic humour.
ELIZABETH is holding a soiled sheet.)

ELIZABETH: Leave that, leave that. Quick. Run up and make Miss Judith's bed for me.

MARY: But ah' ready make up the bed.

ELIZABETH: I'm sorry, Mary, but you'll have to do it again. She's been sick all over her nice, clean sheets. Here. You can wash this out tomorrow.

MARY: Okay, Miss Elizabet' *(MARY takes sheet. Goes.)*

ELIZABETH: *(To LLOYD.)* Will you put away your Zane Grey Novel.

LLOYD: Why?

ELIZABETH: Can't you be of any help? You sit there looking like 'The Lost Chord'. I'm talking to you, Lloyd.

LLOYD: Ah'm being of help. Ah'm keepin' outuh everybody's way.

ELIZABETH: You're not funny!
(She disappears off again. LLOYD turns a page.
ELIZABETH returns. Fresh flowers, scissors she crosses into drawing room. Starts substituting fresh flowers for old ones.)

LLOYD: More flowers? Y'nephew mus' be royalty. How about a twenty gun salute as well?

ELIZABETH: Lloyd, do up your shirt, heaven sakes. You know my mother can't bear to see you like that in her drawing room. Half naked. Like a belly dancer.
(LLOYD makes no move to comply.)

LLOYD: I'm the fresh air dis house needs.

ELIZABETH: Just do up your shirt. Please be reasonable. All right, Mr Fresh Air?
(LLOYD finally does up two buttons.)

LLOYD: Y'sister was as good as gold at firse. Until she saw y'mother. One look at y'mother an' she was sick as a dog. I'd say she was tryin' to tell us something, wouldn't you?

ELIZABETH: *(She ignores him.)* Oh, Lord, look at the time.
(She starts fixing her flowers a bit quicker.)

LLOYD: Stop being so busy! *(Then.)* That damn woman up there turn you against me, completely!

ELIZABETH: Lloyd, try not to refer to my mother as 'that damn woman'. Try, please.

LLOYD: (*Trying a different tack.*) Imagine that my ole man used to have to salute yur ole man. Imagine that.

ELIZABETH: Starting that again, are you?

LLOYD: To think I married you cos ah thought the Van Den Berghs still had a lotuh money. Boy, was I in fo' a surprise. (*Then.*) It's a good thing he's dead, eh. Or the shock would kill 'im dead, yur father. God. Big, big magistrate. Mayor too: When he could spare the time. Kill 'im dead. The shock of it all. Even this house has seen better days. Even this house.

ELIZABETH: 'El Dorado' is over two hundred years old. Still the landmark in this town.

LLOYD: 'El Dorado'! They oughtuh call it 'Dead-orado' This friggin house has bin dyin fo' years.
(*LLOYD laughs happily.*)

ELIZABETH: So loud, ow. And course. That's what I can't stand about you. (*She gathers discarded flowers, scissors, goes into dining room. Deposits flowers and scissors on sideboard.*)

LLOYD: And you're so refined, right? Refined, my ass.
(*ELIZABETH is getting out a tray of silver, a polishing cloth. Starts giving some of the silver a quick wipe.*)

ELIZABETH: Coarse. Coarse and crude. A policeman you call yourself. All you ever do is go around beating up drunks and arresting stray dogs.

LLOYD: I didn't arrest those dogs. I impounded them. How many times I got to tell you that?

ELIZABETH: (*Abrupt cry.*) I have enough on my plate. Stop annoying my soul. The child will soon be here. (*Her face softens.*) M' sweet nephew. Ow, too nice.

LLOYD: I thought 'e was suppose to be twenty-six years ole. To hear you anyone would think 'e was a midget in a pushchair.
(*CLAUDE VAN DEN BERGH, ELIZABETH's brother enters. Makes his way to piano. Younger than his sister, same colour. Wears boring baggy, shabby clothes. His ties are always crooked or they need pulling up or something. Nothing works*)

for CLAUDE, not his ties, not his jokes, nothing. CLAUDE is wearing sunglasses and pretending to be a blind man with a stick.)

CLAUDE: Who am I? Who am I?

(*No-one cares to know.*)

I'm an airline pilot trying to fill his passengers with confidence.

(*No-one laughs.*)

What time is Gregory supposed to be coming?

ELIZABETH: Maybe if you'd gone to the airport, as we'd asked you –

CLAUDE: Forget I asked. (*Whining.*) I can't leave the shop, you know that. Anyway, why me? Why didn't you go?

ELIZABETH: I can't split myself in two, you know. You should've been here when your sister arrived. It wasn't any picnic believe me. Ask him.

LLOYD: Is true. Things woulda bin worse if she hadn't bin here.

CLAUDE: What a house.

ELIZABETH: You haven't remembered those avocado pears have you? Gregory loves avocados.

CLAUDE: Okay, okay, I won't forget again.

LLOYD: Speakin' about dis house… We was jus' talkin about sellin' it, me an' Elizabeth.

ELIZABETH: That's a lie!

(*LLOYD laughs. ELIZABETH smiles, almost in spite of herself. The truth is, she sometimes finds it difficult to stay angry with LLOYD for very long.*)

LLOYD: I tole her about the plans we made the other night – an' she was all in favour!

ELIZABETH: May God forgive you! (*Then.*) What plans? What've you two been cooking up?

CLAUDE: We didn't make any plans, Lloyd. There was a discussion, but no decisions.

LLOYD: Well, it's the same thing, ain' it?

ELIZABETH: Before you sell my mother's house, Lloyd, you'd do best to remember one little fact. My mother doesn't want her home sold.

LLOYD: That's jus' a technicality, woman. (*Then to CLAUDE.*) That American I tole you about, apparently he's really interested.

CLAUDE: But if my mother doesn't want to sell 'El Dorado'…!

LLOYD: Claude, God is a man, not a woman. Thas a good, good reason why your mother is not God. (*Then.*) When is dis family gonna wake up. It's all gone. Bel Air Estate, everything. Finished. Dis house, thas all you got now. It could save this family, all you got to do is sell it. You understan' what I'm tellin' you? Sell 'El Dorado'. (*Pause. A switch.*) Claude, look, I'm not sayin' dis jus' fo' my own good. You know my suggestion makes good sense. You're the son, you've got to be the one to take the lead. The son an' heir. The longer you wait the harder it's gonna be to fetch a good price fo' it.

CLAUDE: I suppose we could at least look into the matter.

LLOYD: Now yuh talkin'…!

ELIZABETH: Claude, she's not going to like this.

CLAUDE: (*A cry.*) We're only going to explore the possibilities…!

LLOYD: We gon' need a solicitor.

CLAUDE: Don't tell me about it. Do whatever has to be done. I'd rather know later than sooner.
(*LLOYD rises.*)

LLOYD: That's what ah like about y'brother. He's so masterful.
(*LLOYD leaves the room. Pause.*)

ELIZABETH: (*To CLAUDE.*) You're a case, you know that? A case. I sent Mary to your shop this morning and she told me it's got worse in there. Ow, Claude. She said you've lost all control over your customers now. She said she had to fight her way through to be served. Whoever heard of a shop where you got to fight the customers to get served. That's not a shop, that's a gym.
(*Pause.*)

CLAUDE: Shall I play you something? Something pastoral, perhaps? Or a bit of Rag Time? Or how about a Fats Waller medley? (*He plays a little.*)

ELIZABETH: Boy, you can't even play the piano anymore. Not like you used to.
(*Pause.*)

CLAUDE: There's this man and he's drowning. And he starts screaming out, 'I can't swim, oh God I can't swim.' Just then a drunk passes by and hears him. And the drunk says, 'So what, I can't play the piano, but you don't hear me shouting about it'
(*Pause. JESSICA is heard, off.*)

JESSICA: (*Off.*) Elizabeth! This office is filthy!
(*CLAUDE rises as if to flee.*)

ELIZABETH: (*Amused.*) Sit down, she's in her office. She's not coming in here.

JESSICA: (*Off.*) The wastepaper basket in here hasn't been emptied either. What do we pay the servants for? To keep the place untidy?
(*Pause.*)

JESSICA: Is my son the grocer out there?

CLAUDE: If you're referring to me, mother I'm here.

JESSICA: (*Off.*) I have a few bills of yours in here in case you're interested.
(*CLAUDE gets up from the piano, sighing. He disappears into the office. MARY enters.*)

MARY: Ah finish upstairs, Miss Elizabet'.

ELIZABETH: Thank you, Mary. Now give me a hand here, please.
(*MARY helps ELIZABETH lay the table.*)

MARY: Will Miss Judit' be down f' dinner, Miss Elizabet'?

ELIZABETH: I doubt it. You'll have to take her food up to her. Before I forget, please tell Cook for me that I'll make the floating island for my nephew. I want to do it myself.

MARY: (*Smiling.*) You and yo' nephew, Miss Elizabet'.

ELIZABETH: I can hardly wait! He's such a darling boy. He's too sweet. You realise it's been seven years, Mary. And now he's a great big doctor. Ow, I'm so happy for him. (*Then.*) Friends used to say we were spoiling him. We've been his mummy and daddy since he was four years old. I've been his mummy and his granny has been his daddy. Ow, too sweet. (*Pause.*) What people don't realise is that he's the last male Van Den Bergh. He carries all our hopes and everything.

MARY: Dat's a lota weight, Miss Elizabeth fo' one boy to carry. Careful.

ELIZABETH: He'll manage. He's more like his granny than even he knows.

(*JESSICA comes out from her office. JESSICA VAN DEN BERGH. White West Indian. English parentage. About seventy. Her accent is neither Home Counties nor West Indian. Suffers from rheumatism in her hands. Something vaguely Victorian about the way she dresses. In some ways her bark is worse than her bite.*)

JESSICA: There you are, Mary. I was looking for you earlier. (*She is making her way to her rocking chair in the drawing room.*) Sometimes I worry about this house. People in here have a tendency to disappear. Especially when I need them.

(*JESSICA settles herself in her rocking chair. From where she is sitting she can see the world passing by on the street outside. ELIZABETH and MARY have finished at the dining table. ELIZABETH signals to MARY that she can go. MARY goes. ELIZABETH joins her mother out in the drawing room.*) It's so hot today. Stuffy.

ELIZABETH: The radio said it was going to be one of the hottest August's on record. Which means for the last five years. (*ELIZABETH is standing by the window.*)

JESSICA: Makes me irritable when its this hot. (*Massaging her knuckles.*) These hands of mine don't help either. They just seem to hurt all the time now. (*Pause.*) He used to say I had such fine hands. (*Pause.*) I can't forgive. He had no right doing this to me. Dying like that. He always was most inconsiderate, your father.

(*Pause.*)

ELIZABETH: Claude forgot those avocados again.

JESSICA: Typical, typical.

(*CLAUDE comes back into the room now. JESSICA faces him.*)

I don't suppose you remembered to hire those gardeners either?

CLAUDE: Either? What sort of sentence is that?

JESSICA: I specifically told you to do something about the grass out there. Have you seen out there lately? It's like a jungle. The whole of Africa could hold a picnic down there.

CLAUDE: (*Whining.*) All right, all right, I'll see to it, I'll see to it.

(*CLAUDE leaves the room. The front door can be heard closing after him.*)

JESSICA: He never tries to be of *any* help. I've had enough upset for one day. All that discord when she arrived. You'd think this house needed exorcism, the amount of fuss she made. (*Pause.*) She didn't even want to see me it's all been such a distressing, sapping, shattering business. (*Pause.*) Judith, I said…she turned away. (*Pause. Abruptly.*) I had to bring all of you up by myself. (*Then.*) Luckily in those days we still owned 'Bel Air Estate'. Thank God for sugar, that's all I have to say. But then of course our wonderful government nationalised it and that was that. Bare-faced theft. I don't care what anybody says. Sheer, bare-faced theft. (*Pause.*) All gone now. This house is all we have left.

ELIZABETH: Mother, now that we have Judith here it's going to mean more work for everyone. And plus Gregory as well. We should get somebody extra in. There's jus' Mary, Cook and myself to run this big, big house.

JESSICA: You're trying to make me feel guilty! You know I can hardly afford Mary and Cook much less anybody else. Nothing is like it used to be anymore.

(*LLOYD appears. Police uniform.*)

ELIZABETH: Ow, man, look at this. Very smart. Who you planning to arrest this time? Or should I say what? How about a jackass or two? You've got a whole police station to choose from.

LLOYD: I tole you before, as soon as I put on this uniform I stop jokin'. I become a policeman. The police doan go in fo' jokes. (*Then.*) I'm off to work now, mother.

(*He gets a lot of pleasure out of addressing JESSICA as 'mother'. Which is the kind of familiarity she can do without.*)

JESSICA: Good, Good.

(*LLOYD goes. Front door is heard as he closes it behind him.*)

Elizabeth, I've asked you this many times…does he have to address me as 'mother'…your policeman friend.

ELIZABETH: He's my husband, he's not my policeman friend.

JESSICA: Don't tell me you two aren't even friends anymore?

ELIZABETH: (*Sucking her teeth, mild boredom.*) Very funny. (*Sound of a car drawing up. Car horn.*)

They've arrived. We'll have to do something about that car. It just eats petrol now. I can see him!

(*She heads for the front door. Sound of car horn, once, twice.*)

JESSICA: Mary…! Where's that girl?!

(*MARY appears.*)

Give Miss Elizabeth a hand – young Master Gregory's just arrived.

(*MARY rushes off to front door.*)

GREGORY: (*Off.*) Hello, aunty, you're looking well.

ELIZABETH: (*Off.*) Oh son, son, give your aunty a big big hug. Thank God, thank God.

MARY: (*Off.*) Welcome back, Masta Gregory.

GREGORY: (*Off.*) Hello, Mary. Nothing's changed around here, I see.

ELIZABETH: (*Off.*) Go in, go in, she's in there.

(*GREGORY appears, carrying a suitcase which he leaves in dining room. Crosses towards his grandmother. GREGORY: mid twenties, reserved, but has enough charm as a counter-balance. A quizzical smile. Has a tendency to cock his head to one side.*)

(*Off.*) Can you manage, Mary?

GREGORY: Hello, gran'mother.

(*He is standing in front of her. One must almost feel the control between them.*)

JESSICA: You look a bit thin. Didn't they feed you in England?

GREGORY: (*Head cocked.*) You'll soon fatten me up, no doubt.

(*ELIZABETH and MARY appear in the dining room. MARY carrying GREGORY's other suitcase. COOK appears (from the right.) All three of them inch forward into drawing room.*)

JESSICA: Seven years. How was it over there, tell your grandmother?

GREGORY: I liked it. On the whole.

(*JESSICA notes the others now.*)

JESSICA: What's everybody staring at? This is not a free show. Go away, go on. I want to be alone with my grandson.

(*Pause. MARY and COOK go off, taking GREGORY's luggage with them. Pause.*)

I suppose you feel you're too old now for me to kiss you.

GREGORY: Don't be silly.

(*He bends down. They embrace.*)

JESSICA: Well, tell us all the news.

(*GREGORY pulls up a chair, sits. ELIZABETH still standing.*)

Aren't you going to sit down?

(*ELIZABETH sits, pleased. JESSICA turns back to GREGORY.*)

Doctor Gregory – congratulations.

GREGORY: Thank you. I must admit I was a bit pleased myself.

ELIZABETH: You always were fortunate, son. Right from a child you knew what you wanted to be when the time came. A doctor. Most people never know what they want to be. Or else others prevent them from being what they want. (*Pause.*) You're lucky chile. (*Pause.*) I know jus' what I'm talking about, my son.

(*Pause.*)

JESSICA: She's in good spirits, isn't she? She'd do very well in vauderville.

GREGORY: Vaudeville? Who's he?

(*All laugh. All happy to be together again.*)

ELIZABETH: Ow, give your ole aunty a kiss! (*She plants a massive kiss on his cheek, practically smothering him.*)

JESSICA: For heaven sakes, Elizabeth, the poor boy hasn't sat down five minutes yet. You can always smother him to death later

ELIZABETH: I'm jus' happy he's back. Ow, thank God.

JESSICA: (*Quietly.*) I would say we're all happy he's back. (*Then.*) So, I'm still waiting…for you to tell us about England.

GREGORY: (*Crooked smile.*) That could take all day.

JESSICA: A sentence or two. I'm not asking for an essay. (*GREGORY laughs.*)

ELIZABETH: Boy, you too wicked. (*Then.*) Why didn't you write us more often, eh? Ow, man. One letter a month jus to make your ole aunty happy. Not too much to ask, is it? I bet even Stalin used to write home more often.

GREGORY: I suppose I'm not a very reliable letter writer. But I used to love receiving your letters. Both yours and gran'mother's.

(*MARY comes in.*)

MARY: Excuse me, Miss Elizabet'. It's Miss Judit'. I jus take up 'er food but she keep throwin' up all de time.
Everytime she take a mout'ful, she bring it all up again.

JESSICA: (*Quiet cry.*) Not again.

GREGORY: What's the matter?

ELIZABETH: (*Rising.*) I'll handle it.

GREGORY: Where is aunt Judith? Is she sick?

ELIZABETH: I'll manage, don't worry, chile. Come on, Mary.

(*ELIZABETH and MARY exit.*)

GREGORY: What's the matter with aunt Judith?
I remember you mentioned something in a letter ages ago, about her being in hospital or something. You were so vague. Anybody would think it was a government secret.

JESSICA: She was in hospital, she isn't anymore.

GREGORY: Tell me what's wrong with aunt Judith?
(*A beat.*)

JESSICA: Not now, son. Not right now. It's not everyday that you come home. Your grandmother is so pleased to see you again, child. (*Pause.*) All right, you'll have to know sooner or later. I don't know if you can remember St. Josephs Hospital anyway we had to send her there. She tried to kill herself. For about the third time. (*Pause.*) She came back this morning after two years.

GREGORY: (*Quietly.*) Two years. Boy.
(*Pause.*)

JESSICA: When she first arrived she was a bit...upset. But she's been quiet as a mouse since. She has always bottled things up, that's her trouble. (*Then.*) For some reason, she seems to have made up her mind to stay up there so what can we do? What can we do?

GREGORY: (*Patting her hand, a doctor first, a grandson second.*) Gran'mother.

JESSICA: We'll get used to it. Soon we'll carry on as if she weren't up there at all. Which is precisely what is so terrible. (*Pause.*) Yes, well. (*Some glimmer of amusement.*) Doesn't sound particularly cheerful, does it. And you've only just got here!

GREGORY: (*Smiling.*) You mean it gets worse.

JESSICA: God forbid.
(*Lights fade to black.*)

Scene 2

Drawing room/dining room. They are gathered around the dining room table. Standing in front of their chairs. Heads bowed. ELIZABETH is about to say a prayer. JESSICA standing at the head of the table. GREGORY and ELIZABETH on either side of her. There is a place (beside ELIZABETH.) laid for LLOYD who has not returned as yet. CLAUDE is at the foot of the table. A moments silence.

ELIZABETH: (*Abruptly, a little over the top in fact.*) Oh, Lord...!
(*GREGORY gives a coughing laugh.*)

Who hears all our prayers, we thank you for bringin
your loved one back to the bosom of his family. He went
away seven years ago not yet a man, now look at him, so
big and strong – ow, man.
(*GREGORY has to cough again.*)
Help him in his endeavours, oh Lord. Make him a good
doctor. Help him too to see how much we love him. We
only want the best for him.
(*GREGORY shuts up.*)
Even though he might find being back here a bit
unexciting after life in vast London, make him see we'll
always be here when he needs us. We're family. (*Pause.*)
He can hurt us more than we could ever hurt him.
(*Pause. GREGORY a little stunned. The others sit down
first. Then GREGORY does as well.*)

GREGORY: What's for first course, Aunty?
(*MARY enters with their soup. Starts serving.*)

ELIZABETH: Well, it was going to be avocado pears but
thanks to some people, it's going to be split peas soup.
Followed by chicken fricassee, cook-up rice, fried yellow
plantains, yams and sweet potatoes. Then there's your
favourite floating island. And if you want, star apples
and mangoes and, oh any fruit you want, an abundance
of fruit.
(*Pause.*)

GREGORY: And what's for second course?

ELIZABETH: Oh you.
(*General laughter, then.*)

CLAUDE: What's wrong with this bowl? It's wet.
(*CLAUDE has been drinking! Is trying to hide that fact.*)

ELIZABETH: Stop being silly, Claude! You know full well
that's your soup.
(*GREGORY laughs.*)

JESSICA: Gregory…

GREGORY: Yes, Gran'mother.

JESSICA: Your appetite's better now, I trust! Tom Thumb
himself would have starved to death on the miserable
amount you used to eat.

GREGORY: I remember you used to pay me a shilling if I ate up all my dinner. If you'd had your way I'd be the richest fat man in the world.

CLAUDE: Gregory.

GREGORY: Yes, uncle?

CLAUDE: Now you're a doctor an' everything, what're your plans?

JESSICA: To go into practice here, of course. What do you think he's going to do – move to Timbuctoo?

GREGORY: Actually, I haven't decided as yet.

JESSICA: Not decided what?

GREGORY: Whether I want to stay here or go back. Live in England, I mean. I've come back to make up my mind.

JESSICA: Live in England – permanently?!

GREGORY: Something like that.

(*Pause.*)

JESSICA: I can't believe it. Go away from us again? Go away for good?

GREGORY: I know a doctor in Brixton. Doctor Bishop. He's Jamaican, he's a lot older than me. I really respect him. He's asked me to join his practice.

JESSICA: Brixton? Do we know anyone in Brixton?

CLAUDE: God forbid, We couldn't have that. Friends in Brixton. What next?

JESSICA: Claude.

CLAUDE: Yes, mother?

JESSICA: Are you drunk by any chance?

CLAUDE: No such luck.

JESSICA: (*To GREGORY.*) What's so special about this Brixton place?

GREGORY: It's got a high immigrant population.

JESSICA: Mainly bus drivers from what I've gathered.

GREGORY: Some. Not all.

ELIZABETH: (*To JESSICA.*) Gregory's just pulling your leg, can't you see that?

GREGORY: I'm not.

JESSICA: Bus drivers! You're not planning to drive a bus I trust?

GREGORY: It's serious. They're crying out for general practitioners in places like Brixton. The pay isn't very good, the working conditions leave a lot to be desired, and last but not least, there's the racial tension. (*His face suddenly breaks into a grin.*) Come to think of it, why would anybody in their right minds want to live in Brixton? (*Then he reaches out, strokes JESSICA's face.*) Look, I really haven't decided anything.

JESSICA: (*To ELIZABETH. An actual attempt at a joke.*). See, you were wrong about him.

ELIZABETH: Me?

(*The three of them laugh briefly, then.*)

Your granny loves you, child! As much as I do, son. And you know how much I love you. So it's only natural that we'd hate to lose you again!

CLAUDE: What goes 'tick-woof'?

JESSICA: Claude, do you have anything of importance to say to us?

CLAUDE: I haven't said anything of importance in years. (*A beat.*)

ELIZABETH: (*To GREGORY.*) Son, what do you feel now you've been back a few hours!

GREGORY: I feel the heat, that's what I feel!

ELIZABETH: Listen to this Englishman.

GREGORY: (*Laughing.*) When I stepped off the plane I felt like somebody had thrown a hot blanket over me! A hot steaming, sweaty blanket.

(*LLOYD enters (from right.) He has come in the back way. Still in his uniform.*)

LLOYD: Ah sorry ah'm late everybody. Ah should still be on duty in fact.

JESSICA: Don't let us keep you. (*Then.*) Sit down, sit down, for heavens sakes.

(*LLOYD sits beside his wife.*)

ELIZABETH: Gregory, this is Lloyd. My husband. He arrests dogs.

(*Short pause. Somehow GREGORY knows better than to laugh.*)

GREGORY: Hello. How're you?

227

LLOYD: Y'aunt is a gambler. She likes to play with 'er life!
(*Pause.*)

ELIZABETH: (*In the general direction of LLOYD, but more to
herself really.*) Boy, I've got no one to blame but myself,
do I? (*Pause.*) We've already had our soup, you want any?

LLOYD: No! I'll just have the meat. Don't worry y'head
over me.

ELIZABETH: (*Almost laughing.*) What's that? Me worry my
head over you. You never stop joking, do you?

CLAUDE: 'We all know marriage is a happy state! But
please God at the church let me turn up...late.'

JESSICA: (*Shouting.*) Claude, I will not stand for this.
(*Pause.*)

CLAUDE: Looks like we're all sitting, if you ask me.
(*GREGORY cannot help himself, he has another minor
coughing fit.*)

JESSICA: Young man, whatever is the matter with you?

GREGORY: Sorry, am, a slight ticking of the throat. I'll
gargle later.

ELIZABETH: (*Pleased.*) Boy, you too story. Satan.

JESSICA: (*She is quite pleased as well.*) He thinks he's
fooling me. But I'm up to his tricks. I'll give you tickle
of the throat!
(*The two women and GREGORY laugh a little! Then.*)

CLAUDE: Gregory...!

GREGORY: Yes, Uncle?

CLAUDE: What goes 'tick woof'?

GREGORY: I give up. What goes 'tick woof?'

CLAUDE: A watch dog! (*He laughs alone.*) A watch dog.
(*Pause.*)

JESSICA: Your pathetic jokes. That's all we ever get from
you. Must you be a buffoon all your life?
(*A moments silence. Then LLOYD laughs! Only LLOYD.
LLOYD thinks it is quite a joke. Then silence again.*)

LLOYD: If you think he's a buffoon here, you oughta see
him when he's in control of his shop. Or radder not in
control.

CLAUDE: (*Remaining seated.*) Mother, can I leave the table?

(*Pause. He and his mother are looking at each other. CLAUDE's eyes become downcast.*)

JESSICA: You haven't finished eating!

CLAUDE: It never lets up, man. On and on. In the shop during the day, here at nights. Unending. Siberia couldn't be worse. I mean, I shouldn't have to beg, after all I'm a grown man. Sometimes I wanna kill some of them in that shop. 'Van, a cupuh rice.' 'Van, pull your finger out'. Kill them. Most of them owe me money, anyway. (*Pause.*) How you think I feel…! Being vomited on daily! (*Pause.*) How do you think I feel? (*Pause. He suddenly begins laughing to himself.*) Aw, what the hell? What goes tick woof? (*Greater laughter.*) A watch dog! (*The laughter turns to tears.*) I should've gone away. London. I should've made a run for it. I might've got away. (*Pause.*) Instead I stay here. Oh God. If you haven't any ambition how do you go about making y'self ambitious? (*He gets up. Leaves the room.*)
(*Pause.*)

JESSICA: (*Abruptly.*) Mary…! (*Some desperation.*) Mary…! (*MARY rushes in.*)

MARY: Yes, main.

JESSICA: Remove all this food – at once – all of it.
(*MARY hurriedly begins clearing the table. JESSICA stands up. Fade to blackout.*)

Scene 3

JESSICA and GREGORY alone in drawing room. JESSICA in her chair. Fan in one hand. A fly whisk in her lap. Ever so often, she uses the fly whisk against mosquitoes. GREGORY standing by one of the windows. We hear thunder.

GREGORY: It's going to rain.

JESSICA: What?

GREGORY: I was thinking…about the difference between English rain and West Indian rain. In England even the rain is polite.

JESSICA: (*Using her fly whisk.*) Blessed mosquitoes. (*Then.*) I heard you speaking to your aunt Judith.

GREGORY: Yes, she remembers me.

JESSICA: I should hope she remembers you – she isn't suffering from amnesia as well.

GREGORY: Poor Aunt Judith. (*Pause.*) It's this house. You can almost feel it. (*Pause.*) I can't escape it either. (*Pause.*) I used to think about this house all the time. In England, you know. (*Pause.*) Not even my best friends would call me particularly imaginative but there's something about this house... I can't shrug it off. (*Pause.*) I remember I'd come back from the pictures about eight, nine o'clock, and I'd find you here, rocking away. With your fly whisk and your fan. Just as you are now. I seem to have done all my growing up sitting out here with you. (*Pause.*) I even remember the gate...that heavy gate out there... I always used to have to struggle with that gate...and then the long driveway. Man, we own so much. Tell you something else I've never forgotten, that library in the next room. While everybody else's grandmother had books about God or the Old Testament, you had books about men with strange, weird names, like Bulldog Drummond and the Saint. And a Belgium detective called Hercule Poirot. Those books. Amazing. By the time I was twelve I knew as much about Agatha Christie as any Englishman on earth. (*Pause.*) Everything about Agatha Christie and nothing, absolutely nothing about Black writers. Amazing.

JESSICA: (*Facing him.*) You feel now that those books weren't good enough for you, is that it?

GREGORY: Gran'mother, I'm not trying to be rude. Look, – I used to know an African writer. He was only in England for about six months. But because he'd written a novel called 'Africa Dreams', which won a prize, the only people he ever met were English.

JESSICA: What's so horrendous about that?

GREGORY: Anyway, one day I took him to a West Indian restaurant. He said to me, 'I'm glad we came here, the way my life's been going lately, I'd begun to worry about losing my identity.' I was so struck by this...

I mean if he was worried about his identity, where does that leave me? What about my identity?

JESSICA: Whatever have they been filling you with in Great Britain?

GREGORY: (*A sigh.*) You're not listening to me.

JESSICA: Were you happy in London or were you not, that's all that matters?

GREGORY: I loved London. But that's not enough. Listen to my voice. I haven't even got my own voice any more.

JESSICA: What are you on about?

GREGORY: I sound like I was invented by the BBC.

JESSICA: What rot.

GREGORY: (*Amused.*) Come the revolution they'll line me up against the wall beside Colonel Blimp and Madam Butterfly.

JESSICA: What revolution?

GREGORY: Grandmother, listen…! They're certain West Indians in England, they've been over there for so long they're worse off than Little Bo Peep's sheep. They've been over in London for years They can't go home again, ever. (*Pause.*) They've had to play so many games in London, many roles…even they don't know who they are anymore. They're grey. Their colour is grey. I don't want to be like them. (*He gets up abruptly, walks to window, agitated.*)

JESSICA: For heaven sakes, child – you'll give me a heart attack just watching you.

GREGORY: I'm furious about something!

JESSICA: What about?

GREGORY: I dunno, I dunno. Gran'mother, there's something I've been meaning to tell you.

JESSICA: Let's hear it.

GREGORY: (*Resolute.*) I have a child.

JESSICA: Never.

(*Pause.*)

GREGORY: I do. A boy.

JESSICA: A child? With your whole future ahead of you.

GREGORY: I didn't want her to have it. I made her take precautions.

JESSICA: (*Not listening.*) How old is this child?

GREGORY: Two. He's about two years old.

JESSICA: Two years old and you're only now telling me? Why bother now? Why not wait until he's fifty?

GREGORY: Why're you so angry?

(*JESSICA has to sit down. Her rocking chair.*)

JESSICA: I didn't bring you up as my own child, my own son, spent all that money on you, to have you do this to me. You had no right doing this without consulting me first.

GREGORY: (*Low.*) Next time I'll get your written permission.

JESSICA: I sent you away at great expense to study, not to have children you can't even afford as yet.

GREGORY: Gran'mother you keep referring to the amount of money you spent sending me away. Well I'm – very grateful and all that – but let's not forget our little pact gran'mother. That as soon as I'm able I have to pay you back. All of it.

JESSICA: You're being unfair, I won't have it. You're making me sound far more mercenary than I really am. Lots of parents finance their children's education, and then expect to be repaid. You've become so impossible now. Maybe it wasn't such a good idea sending you to England. (*Unable to stop herself.*) Anyway – anyway – you owe me far more than you could ever begin to repay. So there.

GREGORY: Good. So it's out in the open now. We don't need to pussy-foot around each other. Not any longer.

JESSICA: I'm sorry. Perhaps I shouldn't have said that. It just...slipped out.

GREGORY: Well, I'm glad it did. I'll pay you back what is owed, then that's it. Finished.

JESSICA: I don't wish to quarrel anymore, son. I said I was sorry.

GREGORY: (*Softening.*) You haven't asked me how it was over there. I mean, really asked me.

JESSICA: I did ask you. If you remember, I inquired the moment you arrived.

(*Pause.*)

GREGORY: There is London and there's Bedsitter London. And the two just never meet. There is nothing you can do non-stop, twenty-four hours a day, in a bed sitter. Not even study. (*Pause.*) I remember it had been advertised as a double room. But that might've been my landlord's idea of a joke, I'm prepared to give him the benefit of the doubt. (*Pause.*) A student from Ceylon had had the room before me. He'd been studying law. I dunno if it was all that English Law that did it, but he cracked up during the third year. They had to put him away. It was while he was in hospital that I took over his room. One night some months later after he'd been discharged and fixed up with a new address and everything – I was awakened by a terrific banging on my door. It was him. Demanding to be let in. He thought he was still living in my room. (*Pause.*) There's nothing you can do non-stop in a bedsitter. Except go quietly mad.
(*Pause.*)

JESSICA: I've no doubt I'd go raving mad. I'm certain I could never learn to live in just one little room all by myself.

GREGORY: (*Quiet amusement.*) Talk about the prodigal son. Some days I used to sit marooned in that room. And I used to think Mary and Cook had it better in this house than I was having it over there. A slight exaggeration perhaps, but not much.
(*Pause.*)

JESSICA: Well – you're back now, that's all that matters. Help me up. Look at those plants. (*She struggles to her feet. Picks up gardening shears. Starts clipping plants.*)

GREGORY: You're not really listening to me. (*Pause.*) 'El Dorado'… What a home. What do I really know about it, its past history? They used to keep slaves under the house here – ages ago, from about the seventeen hundreds. Slaves. Did you know that? Right where we're sitting and standing right now – right under here – slaves. Did you know that, Granmother?

JESSICA: Who told you all of this?

GREGORY: It's a part of Guyanese history now. Seventeen sixty-three – slave rebellion – Cuffy. No-one ever mentions any of this.

JESSICA: I've heard that story in half a dozen different forms. It's all hearsay.

GREGORY: It is not hearsay. Cuffy existed. Cuffy was a slave in this house. He was kept under this house? Didn't grandfather ever try to find out the full facts of the matter?

JESSICA: Your grandfather? What sort of morbid creature do you think he was? Seventeen hundred and sixty-three. He was a magistrate not a historian.
(*Pause.*)

GREGORY: How could Grandfather have just ignored it Slavery poisons forever.

JESSICA: I don't think I particularly care for this topic of conversation.
(*Pause.*)

GREGORY: That's our trouble. Nobody talks about such things in this house. Anything to do with the subject of colour and we leave the room. Under this roof the dirtiest four-letter word is 'race'.

JESSICA: Young man, that sort of topic would only be of interest to a racist or a fool. Neither of whom I would tolerate in this house, I promise you.

GREGORY: I never once in this house ever heard anyone even remark on the fact that you were white and gran'father was black.

JESSICA: It was of no importance.

GREGORY: That's obviously not true, gran'mother come on now. (*Pause.*) It was never mentioned, ever. Surely that is at least a little strange? (*Pause.*) In England there're still a lot of people afraid of sex, here in the West Indies, race is the great taboo word. It still is, even now. It's indelicate. Not the sort of thing middle class West Indians talk about.

JESSICA: Are you quite finished? Anyway, we are not middle class. Thank God. You evidently feel this house needs shaking up. Well, careful, careful. One wouldn't have to have to be Sampson to bring this house to it's knees. (*Pause.*) We never discussed it. The fact that I was white and he wasn't. It simply was never mentioned. You didn't know your grandfather. (*Pause.*) Thirty-five years. Do you realise it has been thirty-five years since your grandfather died. Thirty five years. (*Pause.*) We married when I was twenty three. Before he was forty he was dead. (*Pause.*) I have been alone these thirty five years. (*Pause.*) These days everybody talks about 'White people this, white people that'. As if to be white and Anglo Saxon means they don't feel pain like everybody else. You think I don't feel pain like everybody else. (*Pause.*) Thirty five years. It's like a clap of thunder. (*Pause.*) He was a self-made man, your grandfather. Always kept himself smart, only the best was good enough for him. This house is an example. He was determined to own it. He just wouldn't take 'no' for an answer. In those days 'El Dorado' was the focal point of this town. Still is, no matter what anyone says to the contrary. But then, then it was the house. It was owned by an Englishman, Trevor Hammond, I remember him clearly. It was he who named it 'El Dorado'. The largest house in town. An then lo and behold, your grandfather bought it. From that day on as far as the local people were concerned it became the Van Den Bergh Building. Overnight your grandfather became the most prominent coloured man in this town. (*Pause.*) I married him soon after that. (*Pause.*) It was quite a wedding. As you can imagine. You know how West Indians love weddings. (*Pause.*) The ordinary people loved it. It was an occasion. On bicycles, donkey carts, the lot. They congregated outside the church as if they had come to see an accident. Barrister Van Den Bergh – he wasn't a Magistrate as yet – Barrister Van Den Bergh and his white wife. It was as good as a two day cricket match. I suppose I haven't been that popular since. (*Pause.*) However, the wedding was less successful with certain members of my family. My brother, in particular.

(*Pause.*) His venom…stunned me. (*Pause.*) There are people, some of them one's own relatives walking around hating others with a ferocity that defies all understanding. And for nothing more than the colour of their skin. (*Pause.*) He never even sent a present. Our parents were both dead. It would have meant so much to me if Jonathan had put in a ten minute appearance. (*Pause.*) He shamed me, I never forgave him. (*Pause.*) Your grandfather was an important man – when a man is as important as your grandfather it does not matter what colour he is.

GREGORY: But gran'mother.

JESSICA: Yes, child?

GREGORY: Nothing. (*His eyes dart away momentarily.*) Go on.

JESSICA: Not much more to tell, really.

(*Pause.*)

GREGORY: Tell me about gran'father.

JESSICA: Tell you what? He was a tall man. Unbending, Edwardian almost. He modelled himself on the Edwardians, your grandfather. (*Smiling.*) In a way he was the last of the Edwardians. (*Pause.*) Oh if I could only – just once – make it all return. Turn back the clock. (*Pause.*) Bitter, Bitter. (*Pause.*) I tell you this, I was loved, that man loved me. How many of those fine, expatriate women with their fine expatriate husbands can say as much? (*Pause.*) I was loved. (*Pause.*) When he died, when that man died, oh my heart burst. Your grandmother's heart burst, my child.

(*A beat.*)

Nothing has been the same since. (*She struggles to her feet.*) Thirty five years. It's like a clap of thunder.

(*She goes off. Upstairs. GREGORY is stunned. Pause. GREGORY leaves drawing room. He goes out front door. Stands on front porch. He looks up at the sky. We hear thunder. It is soon going to rain. Suddenly something makes GREGORY look down. CLAUDE appears from under house. A bottle of rum and a glass in hand.*)

GREGORY: Uncle! What're you doing under there?

CLAUDE: Hiding (*Then.*) Has Queen Victoria gone to bed?

GREGORY: Yes, Grandmother has gone to bed.
(*CLAUDE joins GREGORY on porch, he holds his glass out to GREGORY.*)
CLAUDE: Will you have a drink? (*He pulls his hand back.*) No, you're too young. (*GREGORY laughs.*) Quick, quick. There's this little boy, he's about four years old, he's writing and writing on a piece of paper and his mother comes by and she says: 'What you doin', boy?' and the child says 'I'm writin' a letter to Annie.' 'But Boy, you know you can't write' his mother says. And the kid says: 'That's okay, Annie can't read.'
(*CLAUDE dissolves in laughter. GREGORY amused as well. CLAUDE pulls himself together. Pause. He contemplates GREGORY for a few moments, CLAUDE's mood seems to shift ever so slightly.*)
So you're back.
(*A beat.*)
GREGORY: You don't sound too pleased.
CLAUDE: She never offered to send me away, why should I be pleased. (*Then.*) Aah, don't pay no attention to me. I don't really blame you.
GREGORY: All of you in this house think I'm still two years old. Baby Leroy, right?! Well, let's get something straight between us right now: you got some grudge against grandmother, take it out on her, don't come trying it on me. We understand each other, uncle?
(*A beat.*)
CLAUDE: That's a bit strong, isn't it? (*Louder.*) I don't have to put up with that kind of talk from you as well!
(*A beat.*)
Even if I am a bit drunk.
(*Pause.*)
GREGORY: Okay, okay, uncle, maybe I shouldn't talk to you like that. I'm sorry. Okay? (*Pause.*) Christ man, I try to play the role all of you still want me to play, but sometimes it's impossible. England re-made me.
CLAUDE: Left to me you could play any role you want. Even Hamlet.

(*They laugh together, more out of a desire to ease the tension as anything else. Pause.*)

GREGORY: I remember you gave me a pen knife once.

CLAUDE: A pen knife?

GREGORY: A great big one, From your shop. One of those old time combination affairs: complete with a fork and a spoon, and a corkscrew. And a special thing for getting stones out of horses' hooves. In case you should ever run into a horse with a stone in his hoof. It was the kind of knife Lord Baden-Powell might have invented.

CLAUDE: I doubt if they even make knives like that anymore. (*Pause.*) Those were the days. The good old days.

GREGORY: You too?

CLAUDE: (*Not quite focusing.*) Sorry, what?

GREGORY: We always were so English, weren't we...? More English than the English, right?

CLAUDE: What're you talking about?

GREGORY: Jesus. Nothing, forget it.

(*It starts to rain.*)

CLAUDE: You better come in, it's starting to rain.

GREGORY: You go in, uncle. Good night, uncle.

CLAUDE: Boy, you're more crazy than me. Good night.

(*CLAUDE goes indoors. More thunder. The rain falls heavier. GREGORY stands in the rain. MARY appears in the dining room. She starts turning off all the lights in drawing room and dining room. A spot isolates GREGORY. He washes his face with rain caught in his cupped hands.*)

End of Act One.

ACT TWO

Scene 1

Drawing room/dining room. One month later. Five pm. GREGORY sitting in drawing room reading a local newspaper. Does not seem particularly pleased by what he is reading. His irritation is almost comical. He sucks his teeth loudly, turns page. Reads. Sucks his teeth some more. Turns another page. His tennis racket is in a bag at his feet.

GREGORY: Rubbish. (*He squashes the paper up, chucks it on the floor.*)

(*His aunt calls.*)

ELIZABETH: (*Off.*) Gregory.

(*GREGORY picks up the newspaper, hurriedly straightening it out.*)

GREGORY: I'm in the drawing room, aunty.

(*ELIZABETH enters. Seeing him she comes over. She is carrying a small pile of his tennis clothes, all freshly washed and ironed. Plus on top of the pile she has his tennis shoes. However, they are Adidas shoes and she has whitened them, even the stripes, their trademark.*)

ELIZABETH: Son, here are your tennis things.

GREGORY: (*Head buried in newspaper.*) Oh, good. Great. Just put them there, aunty, thank you.

(*ELIZABETH puts his things in his bag. Then.*)

ELIZABETH: My sweet boy. Ow, it's too nice having you here. Give me a kiss, come on.

(*He rises. Offers his cheek, a little diffidently. She kisses both his cheeks.*)

Ow, son. Ow m'Lord.

GREGORY: I've been back nearly a month now, aunty, yet each time you greet me like I've just escaped from Devil's Island.

ELIZABETH: Devil's Island? You too story.

(*GREGORY looks up to heaven for help. Then.*)

GREGORY: Did you want me for anything special, aunty?

ELIZABETH: No, son, all your aunty wanted was a hug 'n'
a kiss from her darling (*She kisses his cheek.*) Ow too
sweet. My favourite nephew.

GREGORY: Aunty, I'm your only nephew.

ELIZABETH: All the more reason why you're my favourite
nephew, son.

GREGORY: (*Throwing up his hands.*) I give up. (*He sits again.
Picks up newspaper again. The paper is still in a sorry state.
He again tries to straighten it out.*)

ELIZABETH: Boy, is that how they teach you to read a
newspaper in England.

GREGORY: You mean gran'mother doesn't prefer her paper
in this state?

ELIZABETH: (*Giving him a mock blow.*) Boy, you too
wicked. (*Then.*) You thirsty? You want your aunty to
make you some nice, cool lemonade.

GREGORY: Thanks but not right now, aunty. (*He suddenly
notices his shoes. He picks them up.*) Aunty, what've you
done to these shoes.

ELIZABETH: What have I done wrong?

GREGORY: You've put white polish on the stripes.

ELIZABETH: That's bad, is it?

GREGORY: (*Lightly.*) That's bad.

ELIZABETH: I'm sorry, son.

GREGORY: It's alright, aunty. It's not the end of the world.
(*He gets up. Kisses her.*) You're my favourite aunt. I love
you aunty.
(*She hugs him. Pause. They separate. Then.*)
Guess what! I've been invited to a gala party. At the
Pegasus Hotel. A carnival party!

ELIZABETH: Sounds wonderful! (*She sits in anticipation.*)

GREGORY: (*Sitting.*) They've even invited a band all the
way from Trinidad.

ELIZABETH: Who're you taking? Who's the lucky girl?

GREGORY: I want to invite. Lorma Walcott.

ELIZABETH: Hmm, mm. Yes, well at least she's pretty.

GREGORY: But I'm going to need your help.

ELIZABETH: (*Pleased.*) Mine?

GREGORY: If I was in England, I'd ask her myself, but here I've got to play by the rules. I want you to phone her mother on my behalf.

ELIZABETH: Of course, son. I'd be only too pleased. Shall I do it – now?! (*And she is already on her feet.*)

GREGORY: No, no, no. It's okay! The party's not until next week. Do it tomorrow.

ELIZABETH: (*A bit disappointed.*) Oh, Okay. (*She sits again.*) But be careful son. Don't let any of those girls get their hooks in you until you are good and ready.

GREGORY: Oh, aunty! It's no wonder in England they think I'm sexist.

ELIZABETH: Sexist? What sort of word is that?

GREGORY: Forget it, forget it. Anyway, no-one's going to get their hooks in me.

ELIZABETH: Tell me more about your son. I know your gran'mother doesn't want to talk about him, but he's your child, your flesh 'n' blood.

GREGORY: Dominic is two years he's…he's very good-looking. What more can I tell you?
(*A beat.*)
Aunty, what's going to happen about Aunt Judith?

ELIZABETH: (*A bit unfocused.*) What, son?

GREGORY: Aunt Judith.

ELIZABETH: Son. I dunno. I really don't know. Only God in his infinite wisdom knows.

GREGORY: That Trinidadian… I remember aunty liked some Trinidadian, didn't she? Everton? Yes Everton, wasn't it?

ELIZABETH: We don't mention his name in this house, chile.

GREGORY: Gran'mother hated him on sight, I remember that clearly. She and Everton took one look at each other and immediately we were back in the Middle Ages. The poor guy didn't stand a chance.

ELIZABETH: It's no wonder Judith doesn't have many happy memories of this house. (*Pause.*) I jus' hope we're doing the right thing bringing her back here. (*Pause.*) Poor girl. And the thing is she's so quiet up there. I don't even hear her up there. Down here things still go on exactly as always. The cooking, the cleaning, the complaining. Exactly as always. There's jus' that closed door up there, that's all.

(*Pause.*)

GREGORY: (*Not directly to ELIZABETH.*) This house it's so…oppressive. Can't you feel it? Long ago they used to keep slaves under this house, right here at 'El Dorado' right under here.

ELIZABETH: Slaves? I don't think about such things, son. That's ole time story. Best forgotten.

(*He gets up. Follows her.*)

GREGORY: Whether we like a thing or not, – we can't keep it locked away behind closed doors for ever!

ELIZABETH: (*Patting his hand.*) Chile, I'm sure you're right. You young people have the right idea. We can't always be ashamed of our past. The good Lord knows all our lives people like us hide from such things. All our lives.

(*Pause.*) Yes, well better go and see how they're getting on in the kitchen. (*Sad breaking down.*) You all right son? You're not unhappy are you This house, chile…things never seem to get any happier.

(*Pause, GREGORY a bit stunned. ELIZABETH kisses his cheek, sadly.*)

Do us proud, son. You're the only one left now. The bearer of all our hopes. (*Pause.*) First my father, then your father…losing the two of them, one after the other, left more of a scar on y'gran'mother than most people realise, chile. Believe me. (*Pause.*) Yes well.

(*CLAUDE enters.*)

CLAUDE: Quick, quick.

ELIZABETH: (*A sigh.*) Oh, Claude.

CLAUDE: A stutterer is being mocked.

ELIZABETH: A stutterer?

CLAUDE: A stutterer. He's being mocked because he stutters, and he says, 'b-b-but everybody has some p-p-peculiarity like that. Take you f-f-for instance. W-w-which hand do you w-w-wipe your ass with?' and the other man says, 'My left hand' and the stutterer says,

'There you go, most people use t-t-toilet paper!' (*He looks pleased with himself.*)

GREGORY: Yes, I must remember that one. Anyway I'm off. (*He picks up his tennis bag.*) Bye, aunty, uncle.

ELIZABETH: Have fun, son.

(*GREGORY goes.*)

CLAUDE: Where's he going?

ELIZABETH: To play tennis, where else?

(*LLOYD enters in police uniform.*)

LLOYD: What a day, what a day. I'm hungry. Where's the food?

ELIZABETH: Aren't you going to give me a kiss, dear?

LLOYD: Don't beg, woman. (*But he still kisses her. Then he turns to CLAUDE.*) I went an' saw the solicitor again today. The American's Lawyer has sent 'im another letter. They want to have a surveyor come here.

CLAUDE: Here? Oh, dear.

LLOYD: (*Contemptuous amusement.*) It's kinduh customary – when yuh sellin' a house. Try sellin' a house wit'out a surveyor, jus' try. You doan even know what day it is, go on admit it.

CLAUDE: I'm well aware of the procedure, I'm not a fool.

LLOYD: Can't take a joke, can 'e?

CLAUDE: Are we in this together or are we not!

LLOYD: I'm the one who's doin' all the gaddamn work, remember?

CLAUDE: You're the one who stands to gain the most, wouldn't you agree?

LLOYD: What the hell yuh talkin' about? You an y'sister will get far more than I'll get.

CLAUDE: You won't do too badly out of it, Lloyd. Anyway isn't my sister's money your money?

(*Pause.*)

LLOYD: Yuh makin' a bad enemy, boy.

ELIZABETH: Lloyd!

LLOYD: (*Not taking his eyes off CLAUDE.*) The worse enemy you could have is a policeman. Doan let anybody tell you diff'rent.

(*Pause.*)

CLAUDE: (*Unsure laugh.*) Now who's the one who can't take a joke?

LLOYD: (*Dismissing CLAUDE with a wave of his hand.*) Aww. Yuh live in a dream world. (*Then.*) Jus' find a way to tell your mother tonight, or yuh can call the whole thing off. That American guy won't wait fo'ever.

ELIZABETH: There's no need to speak to him like that.

LLOYD: Can I help it if you got a friggin' dodo fo' a brother.

CLAUDE: Now look here.

(*Just then JESSICA enters.*)

JESSICA: Claude.

CLAUDE: (*Jumping to attention.*) Yes, mother!

(*LLOYD snickers JESSICA makes her way across to her chair in drawing room. She sits. LLOYD lights a cigarette. JESSICA gives him a look.*)

JESSICA: No Zane Grey tonight, Lloyd? (*Then.*) Where is my bottle of smelling salts? How many times do I have to tell Mary I want it kept on this table? Who's moved my smelling salts?

ELIZABETH: I'll get it, hold your horses.

JESSICA: (*Comparatively mildly.*) Don't you tell me to hold my horses, young lady.

(*ELIZABETH leaves the room. JESSICA turns to CLAUDE.*)

What's happened to your salt fish?

CLAUDE: My what?

JESSICA: Salt fish, salt fish.

CLAUDE: Salt fish?

(*ELIZABETH returns. Hands bottle of smelling salts to JESSICA.*)

JESSICA: Thank you. (*Then to CLAUDE.*) You haven't answered my question. Every time I want to send Mary to your shop for salt fish the answer is always the same. She informs me you haven't any. Why is that?

CLAUDE: Because there's no salt fish to be had. Anywhere. Not just at my shop. There's just none. If I've told you that once, I've told you it a thousand times.

JESSICA: Well, this is the first time I'm hearing about it.

ELIZABETH: (*Wearily.*) It isn't, mother, for heaven sakes. We've all told you. You can't buy any these days, not for love or money.

JESSICA: No salt fish? But it's like rice. Everybody eats salt fish. What about the man in the street?

LLOYD: (*Not too loudly, he's not that brave.*) Since when do you care about the man in the street?

JESSICA: Are you speaking to me, Lloyd?

LLOYD: Oh no, no. Just agreein' wit' you, thas all. Something has gotta be done about the man in the street. (*He can't repress the laugh.*) – Maybe we could fix it so he gets knocked down by a bus!

ELIZABETH: (*Not loudly.*): Lloyd...!

JESSICA: Elizabeth, I don't think we need detain your husband from his Zane Grey any longer.

ELIZABETH: (*Trying to divert attention.*) Tell you what, why don't we play a game of cards?
(*They all turn and look at her.*)
All right, it was only a suggestion. What's wrong with everybody in this house? We used to be happy when we were children. I was thinking about it just the other day. All those card games we used to play. You daddy, me, Kenneth, Claude, Judith. Whisk, Old Maid, Happy Families. (*Pause.*) You'd think it could have gone on forever. We used to be happy, at least sometimes...! (*Pause.*) Ow, Ow, God. What terrible crime did she commit – forgotten up there? My poor sister. What terrible crime? Sometimes I wish she'd died when daddy died. Sometimes I wish I'd died when daddy died.

JESSICA: Rot! Defeatist rot! We are still a family and that is our strength. I will not allow this family to fall apart.

ELIZABETH: (*Sagging.*) Mother, just accept for once in your life. We're not just going through some temporary embarrassment. A change has taken place!

JESSICA: Accept! Don't use that word to me. I don't accept. I have never accepted. There are those who accept and those who don't.

LLOYD: (*To CLAUDE.*) How long yo' plan to wait till yuh tell 'er? Yuh waitin' fo' a sign from the Pope?

CLAUDE: (*Hissing.*) This is not a good time.

JESSICA: A time for what, may I ask?

CLAUDE: Nothing.

LLOYD: Of course it's a good time, Claude. Come on let's see someuh dat masterful spirit of yours.
(*Pause.*)

JESSICA: (*To CLAUDE.*) Well...?

CLAUDE: Yes, well, am, we – that is I, we...am.

LLOYD: Jesus.

CLAUDE: We just think the time has come, y'know... to...well, it's too big for us now, isn't it.

JESSICA: (*Not to anyone particular.*) What is he babbling about?

LLOYD: He's your son, doan ask me.

CLAUDE: We have a buyer, an American, his surveyor wants to look the place over.

JESSICA: (*To ELIZABETH.*) Is he raving?

ELIZABETH: I think you ought to at least listen to what he has to say.

CLAUDE: (*To JESSICA.*) We're drifting towards the rocks now is the time to be prepared.

JESSICA: What?

LLOYD: Rocks – Rocks? The only flamin' rocks is the rocks in yuh head!

ELIZABETH: Lloyd...!

CLAUDE: Mother, at least meet this American. We can t really afford this house any more. Sell now, please.

JESSICA: You can't mean 'El Dorado'! He's suggesting I sell 'El Dorado'? Is that what this is about?

CLAUDE: We have a solicitor – we have a buyer, an American – all we need now is you.

JESSICA: I refuse to believe this. (*Pause.*) My house and you're selling it behind my back...! (*To ELIZABETH.*) You knew about this as well, didn't you? What sort of conspiracy is this? How many times must I say this? Without 'El Dorado' we'd be nothing.

CLAUDE: Please, mother. A smaller house wouldn't kill us. Mother, the days you remember – I know this is painful to you – but the days you remember, they're nothing but a memory now.

JESSICA: Then I'll die here. (*Pause.*) If I can't go back and I can't go forward on my terms, then I will just stop. Come to a full stop. (*Then.*) I'd rather go down with this house than sell it. And that is my final word. (*Then triumphantly.*) Anyway, my grandson is back now. This house is part of his inheritance. His and his alone. (*Pause.*)

ELIZABETH: Thank you, mother.

CLAUDE: (*To JESSICA.*) Yes, thanks a lot.

JESSICA: (*To ELIZABETH.*) I'm not disinheriting you. The house will go to Gregory, but you'll be well taken care of.

LLOYD: That's not good enough for me!

JESSICA: (*Fixing LLOYD with a look.*) As for you, Lloyd…perhaps you'd care to remember this in future. You're only a policeman, not an estate agent.

LLOYD: (*Jumping up.*) I'm sickuh being insulted in this house!

JESSICA: Then why don't you buy a place for yourself – as far away from here as possible.

LLOYD: I got news fo' you. I can afford m'own house now. I finally got enough money put by. Okay? What you thinkuh that?

JESSICA: Good. Then you'll be leaving us any day now. Don't stay on my account.

LLOYD: I read Zane Grey to keep from committin' murder in this house. (*A beat. Then.*)

JESSICA: What did you say? (*But LLOYD has already turned on his heels and is heading out of the room.*) Come back here…! (*LLOYD goes off. Pause. JESSICA rounds on CLAUDE.*) And you never said or did a thing – typical typical.

CLAUDE: What was I supposed to do – call a policeman.

JESSICA: You'd just keep on sitting there even if I was being attacked by a band of maniacs.

CLAUDE: You could hardly expect me to do otherwise.

JESSICA: Typical, typical.

CLAUDE: I know this is the wrong time to say this. But what do you call a homicidal maniac with a gun? (*Pause.*) You call him 'sir'.

ELIZABETH: Oh grow up, Claude.

JESSICA: The number of disappointments I've known in life could fill a list longer than your arm, but your brother never lets me forget he heads that list.
(*Pause. CLAUDE stands up. He leaves the room. Pause.*)
(*Not just dryly, some sadness as well.*) It must be full moon, everyone seems to be walking out on me.
(*Blackout.*)

Scene 2

Drawing room/dining room. About eight o'clock at night. A week later. ELIZABETH is sitting in the drawing room. LLOYD is alone at the dining table finishing his dinner. Actually he has finished eating, he is now drinking a cup of cocoa. LLOYD is not in uniform but is soberly dressed for a change. We see GREGORY in drawing room, reading. At first neither LLOYD or ELIZABETH speak. LLOYD seems to be enjoying his cocoa. Loud drinking sounds.

ELIZABETH: Lloyd...do you have to keep all that noise.
(*She tut-tuts. Looks heavenwards.*) Ow, Heavenly Father, it's like living in Noah's Ark.
(*LLOYD ignores his wife, leans back in his chair and gives a very satisfied belch.*)
Oh God, man! You are a – pig! A pig. The sooner they turn you into bacon the better.
(*LLOYD stretches, yawns.*)

LLOYD: Girl, flattery will get you nowhere.

ELIZABETH: Mary!

MARY: (*Off.*) Yes Miss Elizabeth!

ELIZABETH: My husband is finished eating. Clear up and then you and Cook can go home.

LLOYD: Tell Cook that meat was more-ish.

MARY: (*Cleaning.*) Cook doan like jokes.

LLOYD: (*Amusing to him, but without loud laughter.*) Servants are not expected to like jokes, only to laugh.

MARY: Watch who you callin' a servant. I won't tell you again.

LLOYD: Woman, you think I'm yo' enemy?

MARY: I certainly don't want you fo' no frien'. (*She goes out.*) (*ELIZABETH moves into dining room.*)

LLOYD: (*Calling after her.*) Ah can't stand no lackeys. (*Rounding on ELIZABETH.*) Did you hear dat? Did you hear the way she spoke to me?

ELIZABETH: Now that you've finally finished eating now that you've eaten everything in sight – do you think we could retire in to the drawing room? That is if you can even move.

LLOYD: I'll think about it.
(*Pause.*)

ELIZABETH: Well?

LLOYD: I'm thinkin'. I'm thinkin'!

ELIZABETH: Any night when you're not working all you ever do is stay in your room and read Zane Grey. I might as well be married to a cowboy library for all the good you do me.

LLOYD: Woman, don't you talk to me like that. You want me to slap you?

ELIZABETH: Shh, Lloyd, please. (*She indicates GREGORY in the drawing room with a little motion of her hand.*)

LLOYD: I doan care who hear me!
(*We see GREGORY is hearing all of this.*)
Name me one night when your mother ever makes me feel welcome in dat drawin' room. (*Raising his voice even more.*) You think cos I'm a policeman, I'm here to he walked on!

ELIZABETH: Please, don't shout, Lloyd. Please dear.

LLOYD: Go in dere an' sit with all of you? I'd rather sit with friggin' Daniel in his friggin' lion's den. I'm sick of all of you. Sick! You're m'wife – my wife – it's time for you to take sides. I know I'm loud and I belch – but you think that makes me some animal? How dare you all not respect me.

ELIZABETH: We respect you, Lloyd. Keep your voice
down, please.

LLOYD: (*Almost with a gleeful contempt.*) I'm the one who
don't respect any of you. You're a family of Draculas –
Count Dracula's family. I'd love to be the one to drive a
stake in all yuh hearts, every one of you. Except you aint
worth the price of the friggin stake.

ELIZABETH: May God forgive you.

(*GREGORY gets up. Goes to dining table.*)

GREGORY: (*To LLOYD.*) Don't you speak to my aunt like that.

LLOYD: Look who's here – Golden boy. Count Dracula,
Junior. (*He is amused at his own wit.*)

ELIZABETH: (*To GREGORY.*) Son, it's okay. I'm alright,
I'm fine.

GREGORY: Count Dracula, Junior? That's funny, is it?
I bet you're a riot at The Policeman's Ball.

LLOYD: Listen to this Englishman.

ELIZABETH: Will you two stop it?

GREGORY: (*To LLOYD.*) What's this I hear? You're talking
of selling this house. You own it now, do you? Did it
come with independence?

LLOYD: The best thing anybody could do to dis ole house
is burn the damn thing.

GREGORY: Just remember one thing, Uncle Lloyd. It's my
house to burn, not yours.

LLOYD: (*To ELIZABETH.*) You hear dat? Your mother's not
even dead yet an' he's talkin about 'his house'. Yuh poor,
dear mother.

GREGORY: So you see, one barbarian within the city walls
does not automatically mean a house sale. So go spread
your tent somewhere else, okay?

ELIZABETH: (*Mild reproach.*) Gregory.

LLOYD: (*To GREGORY.*) Like gran'mother, like gran'son.

GREGORY: Exactly, and don't you forget it. To me you're
just a guest in this house.

(*LLOYD jumps up, knocking his chair over.*)

LLOYD: I'll teach you some manners little boy!

ELIZABETH: Lloyd!

GREGORY: (*To LLOYD, unflinching.*) You've got to be joking. You're trained to protect those who own property. Well I own property. You wouldn't lay a finger on me. Not a finger.

LLOYD: I'll... I'll...

GREGORY: You'll what?

(*GREGORY stares LLOYD down. Pause.*)

LLOYD: You shit. An' you talk about helping people? In Brixton! (*Pause.*) The only person you want to help is yourself. What have you come back here for? Your inheritance?

(*Pause. We see that LLOYD has scored against GREGORY, scored quite heavily. Suddenly we hear the sound of a crash coming from upstairs.*)

ELIZABETH: (*Calling out.*) Mother?! Is that you?

JESSICA: (*Off.*) It's Judith!

(*JESSICA is heard knocking on JUDITH's door.*)

Judith, are you alright.

ELIZABETH: (*To LLOYD and GREGORY.*) Are you two satisfied?

(*ELIZABETH goes running upstairs. We hear JESSICA knocking on JUDITH's door.*)

JESSICA: (*Off.*) Judith, let me in!

GREGORY: Oh, God.

LLOYD: It's not my fault.

(*More knocking upstairs.*)

ELIZABETH: (*Off.*) Judith!

GREGORY: Aunty, can I help?!

(*More knocking.*)

JESSICA: (*Off.*) Judith, open this door

ELIZABETH: (*Off.*) Judith, please open the door.

JESSICA: (*Off.*) Judith, I love you.

LLOYD: (*To GREGORY.*) There's your inheritance. Up there in her room. Yuh aunt Judith.

(*The knocking on JUDITH's door continues. Slow blackout.*)

End of Act Two.

ACT THREE

Scene 1

JESSICA and ELIZABETH in drawing room. JESSICA is tending to the plants. Clipping dead leaves, etc. gardening gloves and shears for JESSICA. A watering can nearby. GREGORY appears. Joins them. He has been playing tennis. He is in his tennis clothes. Blazer. Carries a racket.

JESSICA: How did it go, son?

GREGORY: A bit rusty... I didn't play very regularly in London.

JESSICA: Did you win, that's the question?

GREGORY: (*Pleasantly.*) Of course. (*He collapses in to a chair.*)

ELIZABETH: Are you alright?

GREGORY: I'm okay, aunty, a bit tired that's all.

ELIZABETH: Shouldn't you go and change? You'll catch your death of cold.

GREGORY: I'm fine aunty. I had a shower afterwards, I feel fit.

ELIZABETH: You look so much better now than when you first arrived home. You've got all you want right on your own doorstep. People like us live far more comfortably in our own countries than we would anywhere else. No matter what anybody else thinks.

JESSICA: Tell him. Tell him for me.

GREGORY: (*Eyes heavenwards.*) Here we go again.

ELIZABETH: When are you going to open your surgery?

JESSICA: Exactly. Time is getting on.

ELIZABETH: You like your tennis...? Fine. You could go down to the tennis club every afternoon. As for swimming. How many beaches in Britain can compare with Rainbow Beach? And talk about cocktail parties. They've got more cocktail parties now than ever before. With your connections you'll build up a good practice in no time at all.

GREGORY: You make this town seem like a giant holiday camp. A calypso Disneyland. It's not exactly true for everybody is it? Has nothing changed around here in seven years.

JESSICA: (*To ELIZABETH of course.*) What is he talking about? Do you know? Even as a child I could never follow his line of reasoning. He's got worse as he's grown older.

GREGORY: Okay, okay, forget it. I never said a word, okay? (*Getting up.*) Do you have any Bacardi, aunty. I feel for a Bacardi 'n' Coke.

ELIZABETH: (*Rising.*) I'll get it, son, you sit down.

GREGORY: For God's sake... Stop smothering me.

JESSICA: I forbid you to blaspheme in this house!
(*Pause.*)

GREGORY: (*A sigh, under his breath.*) Oh God. (*Then.*) I'm sorry, aunty.
(*Pause.*)

ELIZABETH: I like doing things for you, my son. Allow me my little pleasure. Don't mind your old aunty.

GREGORY: Nothing's changed. In this house I'm always six years old!

ELIZABETH: (*Gentle scolding.*) Stop that, silly. We know you're a grown up young man now.

GREGORY: (*Quietly, doggedly.*) I have to go. I want to go back to England. I've no need or wish to be spoilt anymore.

ELIZABETH: (*She holds GREGORY's arm.*) Gregory!

JESSICA: Let him go. If he wants to go, let him go. He can pack his bags, I won't stop him.

ELIZABETH: (*To him, loud cry.*) We only want to love you. Why do you have to make us feel like it's some crime or something!

GREGORY: Every time I open my mouth I feel guilty – I dunno what to say.

JESSICA: Let him go I said. He knows just what we've done for him, if that is not enough to hold him let him get on with it.

GREGORY: I have to make my own decisions now, gran'mother. You should allow me that much. After all I'm twenty six years old.

JESSICA: It's your attitude, that's what I don't like about you now.

GREGORY: What you want is for everyone to go in fear of you.

JESSICA: I don't want anyone to be afraid of me. The idea! Bloody cheek.

GREGORY: You take it for granted that everybody will do only what you want! The great, big mother country.

JESSICA: I won't have you talking to me like this!

GREGORY: See, that's exactly what I mean.

JESSICA: Go!!!!! Why don't you go.

GREGORY: That's why Aunt Judith is up there now. Hidden away. She's all the proof anyone needs.

ELIZABETH: Gregory!

JESSICA: (*That he should dare.*) What!

GREGORY: I'm sorry but it has to be said.

JESSICA: He's blaming me! He's blaming me! How dare you!

GREGORY: Aunt Judith was always afraid of you. Even more afraid than Uncle Claude!

JESSICA: (*Trying to ward the words off as if they were blows.*) No, no that's not true. No!

ELIZABETH: Stop it. Will you two stop it! God, man!

GREGORY: What about that Trinidadian she liked?

JESSICA: Trinidadian? What Trinidadian?

ELIZABETH: Gregory!

GREGORY: Everton or whatever his name was. He used to work at the Post Office, a clerk or something.

ELIZABETH: Gregory!

GREGORY: You broke them up the way you take a stick and snap it across your knee! Crack.

JESSICA: His name is never mentioned in this house! Never never!

GREGORY: Who says!

JESSICA: I say!

GREGORY: Which proves my case, doesn't it!

JESSICA: I should've had him whipped! The man sold stamps for a living! Stamps! Selling two air letter forms was his idea of big business! (*Pause.*) And a man like that was the cause of her misery! (*Then.*) That man hurt her! I can't believe it even – now!

GREGORY: (*Quietly, shaking his head over it.*) Oh God, Gran'mother… It's just…incredible. (*Plaintive.*) When are we going to open a few windows in this house?

JESSICA: Windows? What windows?

GREGORY: The truth is it was you, not him! We all know that and yet no-one ever challenges you! You dear God, not him…

JESSICA: You don't know what you're saying.

GREGORY: You hurt her by locking the front door in his face…

JESSICA: I'm not listening, I'm not listening!

GREGORY: You, personally… They'd arranged to go to some party, or film, or something and when he turned up to collect her you went to that front door out there and locked it! Locked and bolted it. And you sent Aunt Judith upstairs to her room, screaming… Banished to her room… Like she was a naughty five year old.. While down here he knocked, and knocked, and knocked…

ELIZABETH: It's true! I can bear witness… I can remember the poor young man crying and we did nothing… Claude and I did nothing! Neither of us dared! Ow, man. (*Pause.*) That was the last any of us ever saw of him!

JESSICA: I've no wish to hear your views on the matter! Look who you ended up marrying. Far worse. A man who seems to have only one ambition in life: To be Deputy Sheriff of Dodge City.

ELIZABETH: Yet you never objected to me marrying him not half as much as you'd objected to Judith wanting to marry Everton…

JESSICA: I'd have thought I made it abundantly clear of my opinion of Lloyd – from the word go. As far as I could see they only made him a policeman so they could keep an eye on him!

ELIZABETH: Ow, God… That is so – unfair… Whatever clse Lloyd may be, he is not dishonest.

JESSICA: All right, all right, maybe I am overestimating him… Some people are too stupid to be crooked… But if that's a recommendation, God help him…

ELIZABETH: I know why you objected to Everton more than to Lloyd... You loved her more so you protected her more... You always have!

JESSICA: Now you're saying I never loved you. Believe what you want... I can't stop you...

ELIZABETH: She was your favourite, that's all I'm saying. (*Then.*) I've always had to live with that knowledge.

JESSICA: Oh don't be so soft.

ELIZABETH: (*Boiling up but not boiling over.*) Oh, It's quite true... But maybe I should be thanking my lucky stars instead of complaining... At least I'm down here, while she's up there... Cut off... Concealed... Isolated (*Then.*) People don't die of your love, they go mad of it...
(*ELIZABETH has got through, she has drawn blood.*)

JESSICA: You can say that to me? You can say thing like that to me?

ELIZABETH: And what of me? My feelings? I'm not a pin cushion, mother... (*Pause.*) The daily grinding down. I put up with it. How do you like being on the receiving end for a change?

JESSICA: You'll have us all wet with tears in a minute...

ELIZABETH: I refuse to carry on this...infighting...
(*Pause.*) I still have some dignity even though you don't seem to want to allow me any...
(*Pause. ELIZABETH starts to leave the room.*)

JESSICA: (*Surprisingly desperate.*) That's it, that's it run away... You think you're punishing me all of you, but you're not... What do any of you know about the price I pay...
(*ELIZABETH goes. Pause. Rounding on GREGORY.*)
As for you – you've turned out in fine fashion... Attack, attack, attack, that's all I've had from you since you've come back. I blame England! God only knows what they put in your head over there... Do you vote 'communist' as well?

GREGORY: What're you talking about? (*Plaintive.*) Stop now, f'godsakes. Open a few windows in this house... Please...

JESSICA: You must be mad, boy... I'm surrounded by lunatics...

GREGORY: What did I come back for...

JESSICA: I had such hopes where you were concerned. Such hopes... 'El Dorado.' Whatever I still have in the bank... Everything... It's not as much as it used to be, but it is adequate... What more do you want? (*Pause.*) Son, being a Van Den Bergh still counts for something in this town...

GREGORY: (*Wrung from him.*) But at whose expense? I came back to find my roots... I found only dead and dying roots. If I don't leave now, I never will... I'll end up like Cuffy, chained to this house.

JESSICA: Oh, go on with you! Stop talking in riddles, and start questioning your own motives...

GREGORY: Meaning?

JESSICA: You don't have to go to England to help others... So if you're still so determined it must be because of other things...

GREGORY: Such as?

JESSICA: The mother of your child, perhaps? Is she the reason?

GREGORY: No.

JESSICA: Well perhaps it is not her in particular but English girls in general... You feel that's the one thing lacking in the West Indies, a surfeit of English young ladies...

GREGORY: You think that's my weak spot, right?

JESSICA: Isn't it? Not that there's anything wrong with that of course...

GREGORY: (*Quietly.*) God... You're insidious... Oh Gran'mother you really and truly are...

JESSICA: You can talk freely to your grandmother. There's just the two of us here... Many professional West Indians are attracted to Caucasian women. In fact, it's one way to tell a successful coloured man... Big car, smart clothes and a Caucasian woman looking adoringly at him... His three prime status symbols... And why not? I'm not criticising it, I'm just stating what's obvious even to a blind person...

GREGORY: I don't have to deny or admit anything to you... Not anymore (*Then.*) I'm sorry, I'm not Uncle Claude.

JESSICA: I'll draw my own conclusions in that case...

GREGORY: I'll tell you something you should think about... All that brainwashing you've been coming out with about white women and black women, it's that kind of thinking that contributed to here being up there right now. Aunt Judith.

JESSICA: What? You keep returning to Judith... Just what are you trying to accuse me of, young man?

GREGORY: (*Sadly.*) I'm a doctor, gran'mother, not a priest or a policeman. (*Pause.*) But it's true... It damaged her head.. Aunt Judith had no outlet for her blackness... I remember all that white face powder she used to hide behind... And the bleach and the straightening of the hair... Terrifying. Along that road lies madness... There were terrible things done in this house... Crimes...

JESSICA: Crimes?

GREGORY: Yes! We were for ever trying to kill our black roots – that's a crime in my eyes... Our white side was everything... But black, black was for – losers... We were brought up to think that way...

JESSICA: I never brought you up to think like that! Never!

GREGORY: Granmother you better not excite yourself too much...

JESSICA: (*Shouting.*) I never brought any of you up that way.

GREGORY: Gran'mother, control yourself...

JESSICA: Don't tell me to control myself! Anyway, crimes? Crimes? If having the hair straightened was a crime, half the West Indians we know would be serving life sentences right at this minute...

GREGORY: I'm not talking about whether somebody straightens their hair or not.. I'm talking about the negative way some West Indians think. Used to think... Still do in many cases... Black is to be confined. (*Pause.*) And the most guilty of all are the middle class West

Indians... Middle class non whites everywhere... We're
for ever being torn in two... No culture of our own,
nothing. (*Loudly.*) Conspiring with the CIA... That's
about all we're good for... I still remember sometimes
the Tarzan films I used to see as a boy... Tarzan
swinging through the trees... Tarzan triumphant over
every native in sight... Tarzan, Lord of the Jungle...
(*Pause.*) How they used to fear and respect him, all those
witch doctors, and pigmies, and leopard-men... How
they used to scream when great good Tarzan would
unleash his elephants on them... And we paid our money
to see that...! There was never any doubt whose side we
were on... We used to pay to see Tarzan defeat our own
kind... And we'd come out of that cinema feeling
refreshed.

JESSICA: You're not African!

GREGORY: I'm not white either, Gran'mother. (*Pause.*) Nor
is Aunt Judith for that matter.
(*A beat.*)
She was never allowed any outlet for her blackness...

JESSICA: I've heard enough about Judith from you... Now
shut up... Why have you come back? Just to plague me?
Why don't you go... Go back to England – see how
happy they are to have you there!

GREGORY: Gran'mother...

JESSICA: We don't want you here anymore – isn't that
plain enough for you!

GREGORY: (*Icy.*) Control y'self, gran'mother...

JESSICA: Go, go, go – GO!
(*ELIZABETH comes rushing in. Approaches.*)

ELIZABETH: Jesus God, have you two gone crazy! You've
woken her up there you'll have to contend with her as
well in a minute...
(*JESSICA is not listening. She seems to be having trouble
breathing. For a while neither GREGORY nor ELIZABETH
notice her.*)

GREGORY: I'll leave tomorrow... I've had enough of this
house...

ELIZABETH: Upsetting her like that... Didn't I warn you about upsetting her...

GREGORY: Why doesn't anyone in this house ever put the blame right where it belongs...! (*A cry.*) Why are we always so forgiving...?

JESSICA: Elizabeth...

ELIZABETH: Oh, Jesus...

JESSICA: My smelling...my salts... (*She is fighting for breath.*)

GREGORY: Christ, Where's her bottle of smelling salts!?

ELIZABETH: She keeps it over – no, she had it earlier... It's on her..

(*JESSICA is barely conscious. GREGORY searches her body for the bottle of smelling salts. It has fallen on the floor.*)

ELIZABETH: Here it is...!

(*GREGORY snatches it from her. Takes top off. Holds bottle to JESSICA's nose. JESSICA starts. She tries to sit up.*)

GREGORY: Don't move, be still. (*He massages her hands.*) It's all right, it's all right... (*To ELIZABETH.*) Auntie, my bag's upstairs, would you get it for me... My medical bag...

(*ELIZABETH leaves the room.*)

You're going to be allright, gran'mother, I promise. (*Pause. Slow blackout.*)

Scene 2

Drawing room/dining room. Three days later. Drawing room and dining room empty. JESSICA enters being helped by ELIZABETH.

ELIZABETH: Both Dr. Lee and Gregory said the same thing: Don't exert yourself.

JESSICA: Exert myself? I'm only going to sit down.

(*ELIZABETH helps her into her rocking chair.*)

Anyway, I was sitting in this chair when he arrived, and I plan to be sitting in it when he goes.

ELIZABETH: I thought that was it.

JESSICA: You think too much. (*Pause.*) Is he all packed and ready?

ELIZABETH: I believe so.

(*JESSICA fans herself.*)

JESSICA: This blessed heat.

ELIZABETH: Bound to be jus' as hot tomorrow.

JESSICA: You always were a ray of sunshine, weren't you?

ELIZABETH: Maybe if I didn't have to work so hard in this house, I'd be more cheerful.

JESSICA: That's it, blame me. I was in bed for two days but don't let that stop you. Anyway, what are you complaining about, I've hired a nurse now for Judith, haven't I? She may be a bit fat but Judith seems to like her. Thank God.

ELIZABETH: A bit fat? She's a whole football team rolled into one. She's not a nurse, she's a weightlifter. Anyway, Mother, it's not her weight that worries me. It's the fact that she's about a hundred years old.

JESSICA: I prefer you when you're not cheerful.

ELIZABETH: Who says I'm cheerful? I deny I'm cheerful.

JESSICA: All right, all right, you've convinced me. (*Then.*) What is he still doing up there? Gregory.

ELIZABETH: He's saying goodbye to Judith. (*Then.*) Mother, I want to talk to you.

JESSICA: What about?

ELIZABETH: My husband.

JESSICA: That's not talking to me, that's provoking me.

ELIZABETH: (*Heavenwards, not loudly.*) My God. (*Then.*) He's not as stupid as you think he is you know. Anyway won't you at least consider it? His suggestion. About sellin' this house.

JESSICA: (*A plaintive, terrible cry.*) This house is what separates us from the barbarians out there...!

ELIZABETH: (*Some trepidation.*) Awright, awright, mother, calm down...don't get upset, no need to get so upset.

JESSICA: We'd be nothing without this house. I'd rather die in it than sell it.

ELIZABETH: F'Godsakes, mother, don't be so stubborn, please! It'll soon be too late! Please, please.

JESSICA: I just happen to care about this house, how does that make me stubborn?

ELIZABETH: But you don't care about me, do you? You don't stop to think that maybe I'm sick 'n' tired of being an unpaid servant in this household.

JESSICA: What on earth are you saying?!

ELIZABETH: How you think all the work in this house gets done – by remote control?

JESSICA: A servant!

ELIZABETH: You think Cook and Mary are enough for this big, big house?

JESSICA: A servant! Don't say that. (*Trying to pull herself together.*) Anyway, anyway I don't want to talk about it.

ELIZABETH: I'm more a servant than Mary! That's been my role fo' years, mother. Years. Servant. Without PAY.

JESSICA: I've heard enough...! (*Pause.*) I'd rather not discuss it any further.

ELIZABETH: We've never known what it feels like to discuss anything with you. Your will. That's how it's always been.

JESSICA: What do you mean, 'we'?

ELIZABETH: What does that matter? It's true, that's what matters.

JESSICA: I asked you a question, young lady!

ELIZABETH: I'm forty-one years old, when do I stop being a young lady to you?
(*Pause.*)

JESSICA: I'm still waiting.

ELIZABETH: (*On her feet.*) There's nothing to wait for you know that... We are never going to boil over. Not me, not Claude, none of us. You're too good a lid, mother. We're the saucepan and you're the lid.

JESSICA: Thank you very much.

ELIZABETH: There are things I could say. Things I keep bottled up here. (*Her bosom.*) Here. Things. It breaks my heart. (*Then.*) I wish I had the tongue of Angels. (*Pause.*) Mother, I am forty-one years old. Fo' Godsakes, all I have ever done is take care of you, take care of this house. I've never had the time for a life of my own. For a change I'd like to live a life free of sacrifice. I've sacrificed enough. (*Pause.*) I ache to take for a change

instead of always, always having to be the one who gives.
I want people to call me selfish. I want to hear them say
it. I want to enjoy.
(*Pause.*)

JESSICA: (*With sympathy.*) For heavensakes, try to control
yourself or something. (*She produces a handkerchief offers it
to ELIZABETH.*) Here. You don't want him to see you
crying, do you. (*Then.*) It's not true that I don't love you.

ELIZABETH: Oh, mother.

(*ELIZABETH bends down. Mother and daughter embrace.
Pause. ELIZABETH straightens up again then she takes the
handkerchief. Wipes her nose. GREGORY is heard on the
stairs.*)

GREGORY: (*Off.*) Aunty. Aunt Elizabeth.

ELIZABETH: I'm in here child.

(*GREGORY appears. Carrying one of his suitcases, which he
leaves in the dining room. He comes to join JESSICA and
ELIZABETH.*)

GREGORY: (*To JESSICA.*) Hello, should you be up?

JESSICA: Why? Is it way past my bedtime?

GREGORY: Okay, okay, you know best.

LLOYD: (*Off.*) Elizabeth…

ELIZABETH: Jus' a minute.

LLOYD: (*Off.*) I ain' got all day.

JESSICA: Does he really have to shout so?

ELIZABETH: (*To GREGORY.*) What was it you wanted, son?

GREGORY: Just looking to say goodby, aunty.

ELIZABETH: But you're not going yet, chile. Hendricks
isn't even here yet.

GREGORY: (*Mischievously.*) I thought I'd give you enough
time to get in all your hugs and kisses. I might as well
be hugged to death now as later.

(*ELIZABETH gives him a mock blow. Or tries to. He jumps
away, laughing.*)

ELIZABETH: Come 'ere, Satan. (*Kisses him loudly.*) Child,
m'boy. So sweet. Take care, you hear me. Take care. And
write more often. You hardly ever write. (*She is crying.*)

GREGORY: I'm sorry aunty, but sometimes I'm so busy,
you know. I'm sorry.

ELIZABETH: It's okay, chile, I know you still love us, I know that, my child. And we'll always love you, you know that, don't you? We hurt each other and yet we love each other, all of us.

LLOYD: (*Off.*) Elizabeth!

ELIZABETH: I'm coming!

LLOYD: Stop coming an' come.

ELIZABETH: I better go and see what he wants. (*Doesn't move.*) Give us a shout when Henricks arrives. Okay? (*Then.*) Ow, son I'm going to miss you bad! Your ole aunty is going to miss you bad, bad.

GREGORY: I'm going to miss you too, aunty.

ELIZABETH: Go with God, child.

(*She leaves the room. Pause.*)

JESSICA: She'd give her life for you.

GREGORY: Stop it, gran'mother. Please.

(*Pause. JESSICA staring straight ahead of her.*)

JESSICA: You're quite certain are you, that this is what you want to do? (*Pause.*) I trust you've taken into account the present racial climate in Great Britain. Even Great Britain. (*Pause.*) If you were English you could always pass by on the other side, but that's one luxury you will never be able to afford. (*She faces him. Pause.*) My son, my son. (*Pause.*)

GREGORY: (*Looking at JESSICA but almost to himself.*) That's precisely why I'm going. I have something to contribute. I don't want to sit on the fence anymore. (*Pause.*)

JESSICA: (*Straight ahead again.*) What about us? It's selfish of me, I know. I'm old, the old have a right to be selfish. What about us? What about me?

GREGORY: (*A cry.*) You'd never let go of me if I didn't go now! (*Then.*) I have to go for my sake. This house, you, all of it, there's just too much holding me here. I want to be my own man. (*Pause.*) I haven't told you much about Dr. Bishop. He's one of your old-time family doctors. People queue up to bring him their troubles… They look up to him. That's the sort of doctor I would like to be.

JESSICA: That all sounds very commendable very noble. But what about your son? You don't seem to care very much for him.

GREGORY: You don't know what I feel about anything…!

JESSICA: You hardly even mention the child. Whatever you think of me, are you any better?

GREGORY: I bottle up my feelings, but that doesn't mean I don't care!

JESSICA: Most of the time I doubt if you even remember he exists. Do you?

(*GREGORY rises.*)

GREGORY: Maybe, like you, gran'mother, I can't help being a mass of contradictions.

JESSICA: So you're going…? You'd think at my age I'd be immune to this sort of thing. I must have lost enough by now. I never seemed to have known a day, a moment when I wasn't being hurt, feeling hurt. But I am expected to endure. It is expected of me. I was made to pay for marrying a man who wasn't even half white. Listen, I know my son, what it means to be discriminated against. I had let the side down. There was no forgiveness after that. Old George Robinson's daughter had let the side down.

(*A beat.*)

I too have lain awake nights…thanks to my own race. (*Pause.*) It seems to me I have been asked to endure too much. I have sat here evening after evening…unloved. I seem to have sat here all my life waiting for love. If it hadn't been for those few precious years with your grandfather, I don't know what I'd have done. (*Then.*) It was worthwhile while it lasted. So perhaps I have not always lost, after all. It's not an awful lot though, is it? Ten years out of sixty eight. Because that's all it was, ten years. Not exactly a lifetime, but some people never have even that much.

(*Pause. Sound of car horn.*)

GREGORY: He's here. Hendricks. Goodbye, Gran'mnother. (*He kisses her on the cheek.*) Thank you, it was good being

back, no matter what I say. (*Another kiss on cheek.*) I'll
write, okay? Bye bye. (*He starts to walk away. Suddenly he
stops. He returns to her side. He hugs her tightly.*) Oh,
Gran'mother.

(*They hug each other. Pause. They release each other, she holds
on a bit longer than he does. He goes quickly in to dining
room. His suitcase.*).

Aunty! Hendricks is here!

ELIZABETH: (*Off.*) Hold on, hold on, child. (*She appears,
hugs him.*) Stay, stay. Please stay.

GREGORY: You know I have to go, aunty. Thank you for
everything.

ELIZABETH: You more than welcome, son. More than
welcome.

GREGORY: (*Calling as he goes.*) Bye, bye, gran'mother. I'll
write. Promise.

JESSICA: You'll never write.

(*GREGORY goes. ELIZABETH goes off with him. Pause.
We hear car starting up – off.*)

ELIZABETH: (*Off.*) G'bye son!

(*Just for a moment, JESSICA's face crumbles. CLAUDE
comes rushing in. He has come in the back way. JESSICA
quickly pulls herself together.*)

CLAUDE: Where's Gregory? I want to tell him goodbye!

JESSICA: You'd be two days late for your own funeral.

CLAUDE: (*An aside.*) We all make mistakes. That's what the
porcupine said to the hairbrush.

(*LLOYD enters. Joins JESSICA and CLAUDE in drawing
room. He stands by one of the windows.*)

LLOYD: (*Not looking directly at JESSICA but he's addressing
her.*) So be gone. Oh, God. Golden Boy gone. Englan'.
Englan', boy. I wonder who is goin' to get the house
now? The favourite gran son...gone away. I'm sad, I'm
so sad.

CLAUDE: For Godsakes, Lloyd!

LLOYD: What? Have I said something wrong?

JESSICA: (*Abruptly.*) Elizabeth!

CLAUDE: (*Heavenwards.*) I know I should've stayed in the
shop.

(*ELIZABETH appears.*)

ELIZABETH: Yes, mother.

JESSICA: (*Indicating LLOYD.*) I want this man out of my house.

ELIZABETH: What?

JESSICA: This man here. I'm sure he'd prefer to live somewhere else.

LLOYD: (*To ELIZABETH.*) Tell her now about my house.

CLAUDE: Anybody want a drink? I'd love a drink.

(*CLAUDE is ignored.*)

LLOYD: (*To ELIZABETH.*) Tell her.

ELIZABETH: Mother… Lloyd has found a house. He could buy it tomorrow if he so wishes.

JESSICA: It's on the other side of town I hope.

ELIZABETH: Do you understand what I'm saying, mother? If he goes I'll have to choose between you and him. I mean, you realize that ? He's my husband.

JESSICA: Must you keep reminding me of that? You're not helping matters, believe me.

ELIZABETH: (*Loss, grieving.*) There'll be no turning back. This time once ah gone, ah gone; gone for good. You understand what I'm saying, mother. (*Pause.*) I'll never set foot in this house again. Okay?

JESSICA: (*Plaintive.*) This is blackmail.

LLOYD: No. We're jus givin you a taste of your own medicine. Where would you be without us? Who would take care of you? Who needs who? You need us.

ELIZABETH: It's up to you, mother. Do I go or stay?

LLOYD: (*To JESSICA: indicating CLAUDE.*) You'll only have him to rely on. Dats worse dan being alone.

CLAUDE: Take that back. I demand an apology. Or better yet, a drink.

(*CLAUDE is ignored.*)

ELIZABETH: Well, mother?

JESSICA: Alright, alright – you can stay – you know you can stay.

LLOYD: Both of us, mother?

(*Pause.*)

JESSICA: Yes, yes. Both of you.
  (*A beat.*)
  It hardly matters anymore. With him gone. (*Then.*) Do what you want, you two.
LLOYD: What, even send for the surveyor?
JESSICA: If you must.
LLOYD: (*To ELIZABETH, not able to believe his ears.*) What did she say?
ELIZABETH: Are you serious?!
JESSICA: I wont shoot him, if that's what you mean. Mind you, I'm not promising anything either. Now I think I've been sitting long enough. (*She struggles to her feet.*) I'd like to go for a little walk in my garden.
ELIZABETH: Mother, you know what the doctor said.
JESSICA: I'm older than my doctor.
  (*She takes a few steps. She is unsteady. ELIZABETH takes her arm.*)
  I can manage thank you.
  (*A beat. ELIZABETH releases her. JESSICA takes a few more steps. Stops. Faces ELIZABETH.*)
  Maybe I could do with a little help.
  (*ELIZABETH smiles, pleased. She takes JESSICA's arm. Mother and daughter leave the room. Go out front door.*)
LLOYD: (*To CLAUDE. Triumphantly.*) Did you hear what she said?
CLAUDE: I'll believe it when I see it. You don't know my mother. (*Then.*) I really could do with a drink!
  (*CLAUDE exits in direction of kitchen – off. LLOYD alone on stage. He looks around to make sure everybody else has gone. He then goes and sits in JESSICA's rocking chair. The lights start to fade. The last image we see is LLOYD in JESSICA's chair.*)

The End.